D1366811

SEED THOUGHTS

A Daily Devotional

By

RON HINDT

ISBN 978-0-9778928-2-2
Library of Congress Control Number 20079606881

Book cover designed by: Adam Sylvester

Published by
LTL Publishing
3700 FM 528
Friendswood, TX 77546
1.800.898.9673

For book orders contact Ron Hindt
info@calvaryh.org
1.800.898.9673

Printed in the U.S.A. by
UBS Publishing
2577 Research Drive
Corona, CA 92882
951.273.7900

Dedication

To Kym, whom God gave the strength and tenacity to look adversity dead in the eye and say, "Bring it on, Chica!"

Special Thanks

To those who helped start this journey so long ago: Mark Hansen, Kathy Hansen, Suzanne Bethurum, Betty Steinkuehler, Debi Castillo, Kyla Nichols, Linda Colby, Mary Ellen Quigley, Dawn Briggs, Mark Briggs, Liz Bigouette, and anyone whom I have missed, please know that I am truly grateful for all that you have done.

Above all, thank you to our Lord and Savior Jesus Christ who plants the original "seed thought" in all of us.

Grant us today to be heavenly minded.

True Peace

Today, people across the world are celebrating another year's beginning and making one or more New Year's resolutions.

Some will attempt to stop smoking; some will attempt to stop drinking; some will attempt to manage their money better; some will attempt to make their marriage better; some will attempt to reconcile long-lasting differences in their family; countless other changes will commence on this day in the quest for true happiness and peace.

But the fact of the matter is this: Without the Prince of Peace in your life, there can be no true happiness and no lasting peace. If you have never asked Jesus Christ into your life, make Him your aim this day.

Make Him your aim this year. Seek to know the only way, truth, and life. I guarantee you will not be disappointed. Isaiah 26:3 says, "You will keep him in perfect peace, Whose mind is stayed on You, Because he trusts in You." This year, may you come to trust in the only true source of peace—Jesus Christ, the Righteous!

Drop Thy still dews of quietness,
Till all our strivings cease;
Take from our souls the strain and stress;
And let our ordered lives confess
The beauty of Thy peace.

John G. Whittier

January 2

Committed to the Word

The New Year has begun, and with it comes all of the many resolutions we make with good intentions.

As we look back on the past year, I think we can all find areas in our lives that need improvement or change. But none can compare to the need for a deeper, more intimate knowledge of Jesus Christ.

Every day we are given the ability to learn and grow in Christ. More than that, Scripture tells us that God desires to be found by us. Jeremiah 29:13 says, "And you will seek Me and find Me, when you search for Me with all your heart." It should stir our hearts to know that we worship a God who longs to reveal Himself to those who will diligently seek Him (Hebrews 11:16). Psalm 34:18 says, "The LORD is near to those who have a broken heart, and saves such as have a contrite spirit."

We would all agree there is a vast difference between knowing about God and knowing Him as the Scriptures reveal Him. Knowledge refers to facts that can be learned by investigation. Every Christian knows God through salvation, but beyond that initial knowledge is a greater intimate knowledge of God that should be the pursuit of every believer! The knowledge of God is to love truth, and to love truth is to love His Word!

As the New Year begins, I pray our commitment to loving and learning more about our God increases and strengthens each day. May God's Word supply all the strength, instruction, and comfort you need to be equipped for every good work. The apostle Paul said in Acts 20:32, "So now, brethren, I commend you to God and to the word of His grace, which is able to build you up and give you an inheritance among all those who are sanctified." As we commit ourselves this year to God's Word, He will be faithful to build us up!

Nobody ever outgrows Scripture:
the Book widens and deepens with our years.

C. H. Spurgeon

Heavenly Minded

Have you ever heard the expression "He's so heavenly minded that he's no earthly good"? Well, the Bible says in Colossians 3:2, "Set your mind on things above, not on things on the earth." In other words, we should be heavenly minded, and yet how often do we see the body of Christ earthly minded?

This is a problem. We are preoccupied with the things of this world: money, prestige, fame, popularity, fashion, and so forth. As long as these are the things we love the most, we will be earthly and ineffective for ministry, unable to reach the world for Christ as God would have us do. When you are tangled up in the world, you cannot have the proper heavenly perspective of God; therefore, you won't have the same heart, mind, and compassion of God.

Grant us today to be heavenly minded.

> *Oh, how greatly has the man advanced*
> *who has learned not to be his own,*
> *not to be governed by his own reason,*
> *but surrender his mind to God!*

John Calvin

Let Us Arise and Build

One of the most important spiritual principles you can learn as a Christian, which was evident in Nehemiah's day and continues to be evident today, is this: when God's people say, "Let us arise and build," the enemy says, "Let us arise and oppose!" Listen, when you make a stand for Christ, and you set out to serve Him with a humble, tenacious heart, you're going to come up against opposition. Why? Because you're a threat to the devil's plan. He wants to breed apathy and influence in the church. So when you come along with zeal to further God's purposes, the devil is going to throw everything he can at you to stop you.

And let me say this: the devil is not concerned with lukewarm, half-hearted Christians. Why? Because they are no threat to him. But as soon as you get a Christian or a church that is on fire for God, as soon as you get people who are sold out to God no matter what, watch out because there is going to be a battle!

Romans 8:37 tells us that we are more than conquerors, and 1 John 4:4 tells us that God in us is greater than the god of this world. In light of those truths, let's get on fire for God and get on the frontlines!

Nothing promotes activity of the devil more than the Christian's proximity to God.

Anonymous

Secret Saints

In John 12:42–43 we read, "Nevertheless even among the rulers many believed in Him, but because of the Pharisees they did not confess Him, lest they should be put out of the synagogue; for they loved the praise of men more than the praise of God."

What tragic words! We read that these people believed in Jesus, and yet they were ashamed to confess Him. In all actuality, what we have here are not regenerate people but people who thought they believed. In the end they were not believers at all. How do we know these people weren't saved? There are three reasons.

Number one: It tells us they did not confess Him. Jesus said in Matthew 10:32–33: "Therefore whoever confesses Me before men, him I will also confess before My Father who is in heaven. But whoever denies Me before men, him I will also deny before My Father who is in heaven." The Bible says in Romans 10:9, "That if you confess with your mouth the Lord Jesus and believe in your heart that God has raised Him from the dead, you will be saved." These people wouldn't confess.

Number two: They were afraid. They didn't confess Christ, "lest they should be put out of the synagogue." They were fearful, and yet isn't it true that when we are first saved, we are the most bold? The woman of Samaria couldn't wait to tell the very people who had formerly ostracized her about her new faith.

Number three: They loved the praise of men more than the praise of God. That's not Christian! Christians are not looking for praises of men; we're looking for the affirmations of God.

The point is this: There is no such thing as a secret disciple of Christ! You either are, or you are not. God has not called us to be undercover Christians, but luminous reflectors of His glory in this dark and dying world!

> *Secret discipleship is a contradiction in terms, for either the secrecy kills the discipleship, or the discipleship kills the secrecy.*

William Barclay

No Such Thing as Luck

In Acts 23, as Paul is imprisoned for his faith, forty religious rebels take an oath to kill him and plan to ambush him as he's led from his prison cell to trial. However, we read in verse 16, "So when Paul's sister's son heard of their ambush, he went and entered the barracks and told Paul." As the story unfolds, the guards are warned and Paul's life is spared.

The interesting thing is this: we have no mention of Paul's relatives in the Bible, and then, all of a sudden, Paul has a sister and a nephew. Not only that, but his nephew happens to be at the right place at the right time to hear the plot to kill his uncle, and Paul is saved.

Luck? Coincidence? Happenstance? No! This is what we call the providence of God. The fact is there is no such thing as luck or coincidence in the life of the believer. God's sovereignty orders all things according to His perfect will. Psalm 37:23 tells us, "The steps of a good man are ordered by the Lord, And He delights in his way."

As we place our trust in the Lord, we can know with all certainty that everything that happens in our lives today is not coincidence or happenstance, but the providence of God ordering our steps.

While providence supports,
Let saints securely dwell;
The hand, which bears all nature up,
Shall guide his children well.

Philip Doddridge

The Bounties of Prayer

Have you ever stopped to think about the great privilege we have in prayer? Do you realize the great resource we have in Christ?

In speaking on prayer, Charles Haddon Spurgeon once wrote:

> We do not come as it were in prayer; only to God's benevolent fund where He dispenses His favors to the poor; nor do we come to the back door of the house of mercy to receive the broken scraps; though that is more than we deserve. But when we pray, we are standing in the palace; on the glittering floor of the great King's own reception room. In prayer we stand where angels bow with veiled faces. And shall we come there with stunned request and narrow and contracted faith? No, it does not become a king to be giving away pennies and nickels; He distributes large pieces of gold.

People, Christ is our resource! And when we earnestly entreat Him according to His will, He grants our prayers. Be it wisdom for guidance, discernment toward individuals, or day-to-day physical provision, Christ is our resource!

Let me ask you, have you come to the King's court today?

Ask, and it will be given to you; seek, and you will find; knock, and it will be opened to you. For everyone who asks receives, and he who seeks finds, and to him who knocks it will be opened.

Matthew 7:7–8

Good News

Matthew 9:35 says, "Then Jesus went about all the cities and villages, teaching in their synagogues, preaching the gospel of the kingdom."

The Greek word for gospel is euangelion; it means "good tidings or good news." This is where we get our word evangelize. It was used in classical Greek to describe a city that was at war with another city and whose people were waiting for news of the outcome. They didn't have telegraphs or telephones, so they would wait in anticipation for news by way of a messenger. They would see the messenger coming from the battlefield. If he had grief on his face, then it was a sure sign of defeat. But if he had a wreath on his spear and a laurel on his head, then he would shout: "We have won! We have won!" The word used to describe this latter scene was euangelion, which came to be known as the good news of victory!

Isn't it fitting that this is the word the Bible chooses to describe the gospel of Jesus Christ? Truly, we have reason to shout: "Euangelion! Euangelion!" Why? Because Christ has defeated sin and death and has won the victory!

What is offered to men in the gospel? It is not the possibility of salvation, not simply the opportunity of salvation. What is offered is salvation.

John Murray

Upholding All Things

Hebrews 1:3 tells us that Jesus Christ is "upholding all things by the word of His power." In other words, our Lord at this very moment is actively involved in keeping this world from falling apart. Colossians 1:17 says that "He is before all things, and in Him all things consist." The word consist also speaks of holding something together.

You see, if Christ were not holding this world together, this world would fall apart. Neutrons and protons would repel one another. The only reason they don't, but attract instead, is because Christ is keeping them together. If the earth's rotation were to slow down just a little bit, we would fly into space. If we moved just a little closer to the sun, we would be scorched. If we drifted just a little bit away, we would all freeze to death. The earth is tilted at twenty-three degrees; if it changed just slightly, vapors from the oceans would build up and cause massive continents of ice. If the moon didn't keep its exact distance, our oceans would overflow onto our continents. Who keeps it all in balance? Who holds it all together? Jesus Christ!

And if Christ can hold our world, our solar system, our galaxy, and all of the other vast galaxies together, then He can hold my life together as well. Oh, thank the Lord today for a Savior who can hold every bit of your life together as you give it to Him.

It is not your hold of Christ that saves,
but His hold of you!

C. H. Spurgeon

No Butter, Please

First Peter 2:2 says, "As newborn babes, desire the pure milk of the word, that you may grow thereby."

Today I want to remind you of the importance of doctrinal clarity and the importance of being taught the pure milk of the Word. You see, when the pure milk of God's Word is not taught, all you have is butter. Many of the TV evangelists we see today are butter makers. They take just a little of God's Word, and they churn it and churn it until they whip up some kind of conglomeration. They really know how to whip it up, but when all is said and done, it amounts to nothing more than butter that easily melts under the heat of true Christian living.

But when you get a man of God who gives God's people the pure milk of the Word, then those people grow, and there is real substance. Make no mistake about it—the difference between defeated Christian living and victorious Christian living is the teaching and reception of God's pure Word! As Christians we should be saying, "No butter please; just the pure milk of the Word!"

I have made a covenant with God that He sends me neither visions, dreams, nor even angels. I am well satisfied with the gift of the Holy Scriptures, which give me abundant instruction and all I need to know both for this life and for that which is to come.

Martin Luther

Intercessory Prayer

Intercessory prayer is a powerful tool in the hands of a righteous person (James 5:16). Paul modeled this kind of selfless prayer, and he followed a legacy of others who did the same.

Nothing can compare, however, with the example of intercession given to us by our beloved Lord in John 17 and the intercession of the Holy Spirit we read about in Romans 8:26. With these inspiring examples before us, Christians ought to be moved to a life of intercession. When the Spirit of God is controlling your life and you are living in obedience to God's Word, you will delight in praying for others!

Paul said in Philippians 1:4 that it was his joy to pray for others. Making requests for others through prayer is a principle of true joy. You can tell if you are experiencing Spirit-produced joy when you delight in interceding on someone else's behalf! Biblical joy will always find its expression in the delight of intercessory prayer.

There is a beautiful example of intercessory prayer given by a nurse who understood its importance. Because her work was done with her hands, she used them as an instrument of prayer. Each finger stood for someone. The thumb was nearest to her, and it reminded her to pray for those who were nearest and closest to her. The index finger was used for pointing, as those who teach us, so her second finger stood for all her teachers. The third finger was the tallest, and it stood for leaders in every sphere of life. The fourth finger was the weakest, and it stood for those who were weak, in trouble, or in pain. The little finger, being the smallest and the most unimportant, she used in reference to herself. What a beautiful scheme of prayer! This is what intercession is, putting others first and ourselves last.

God grant that we be intercessors today!

Time spent in prayer is never wasted.

François Fénelon

Forgiveness

As we read our Bibles over and over again, we are constantly brought face-to-face with one of God's greatest attributes: His forgiveness. When we come to God with a penitent heart, the Lord grants us His forgiveness. Psalm 103:12 says, "As far as the east is from the west, So far has He removed our transgressions from us."

The Bible tells us five wonderful things about God's forgiveness. First, it is gracious. Ephesians 1:7 tells us that God grants forgiveness in accordance with the riches of His grace. Second, God's forgiveness is bountiful. Romans 5:20 says, "But where sin abounded, grace abounded much more." In other words, God's forgiveness is not miserly, but abundant. Third, God is eager to forgive. God is eagerly waiting for you to confess your sins so He can smother you with His loving arms. Fourth, God's forgiveness is certain. Numbers 23:19 tells us that God cannot lie. And fifth, God's forgiveness is unequaled. Romans 5:8 says, "But God demonstrates His own love toward us, in that while we were still sinners, Christ died for us." Let's thank God for His unfathomable forgiveness!

> *It would tire the hands of an angel*
> *to write down all the pardons God bestows upon true,*
> *penitent believers.*
>
> *William Bates*

Bewitched

We read in Galatians 3:1: "O foolish Galatians! Who has bewitched you that you should not obey the truth?" The Galatians believers had been duped by false teachers into believing that faith in Jesus Christ was not enough. Though they were saved by faith alone, they had been bewitched to trust in their works.

There are a lot of believers like that today who get bewitched by various false truths. Some fall into the trap of ritual and liturgy. Instead of reading the Word of God and praying as their source of spiritual growth and stability, they believe that by going through certain forms of religious activity, they are somehow brought further along with God.

There are others who trust in emotionalism. Their Christian walk is something like a roller-coaster ride. They are constantly looking for a new "experience," which they believe is the key to "deeper life." Then there are others who attribute their "deeper" walk with the Lord to what they do and don't do. The fact, though, is this: The moment we leave the simple truth that we are saved by grace and maintained by grace, it is then that we gravitate to trust in other forms of religiosity as the means of a deeper walk with the Lord. This is the point at which we become just like the Galatian believers—bewitched by false truth. The fact of the matter is we are saved by faith, maintained by faith, and grow close to the Lord as we grow in His grace (2 Peter 3:18).

Grace is what all need what none can merit,
and what God alone can give.

George Barlow

17

Bearing with One Another

As Christians it is often easier for us to receive the forgiveness of God and to enjoy its benefits than to extend the forgiveness to others within the body of Christ.

Very often we say that we will bury the hatchet, and yet we leave the handle exposed so that we can take it out on another occasion and fling it again. We need to have what one pastor called for, saying: "Every man should have a fair-sized cemetery in which to bury the faults of his friends." Those are good words! You see, it is not easy for us to live in perfect harmony with one another. In fact, it's hard work because none of us are perfect.

I think we would all agree with the people who say: "To live above with saints we love, oh, that will be glory. But to live below with saints we know, well, that's another story." Ephesians 4:2 says, "With longsuffering, bearing with one another in love." May we, through the power of the Holy Spirit, display the love of Christ toward those in our midst.

You never so touch the ocean of God's love as when you forgive and love your enemies.

Corrie ten Boom

An Encourager, Not a Discourager

In Acts 11, Peter had just come from the great outpouring of the Spirit upon the Gentiles. He was excited to share the good news with the Jewish believers in Jerusalem. However, upon arriving, we read in verse 2, "And when Peter came up to Jerusalem, those of the circumcision contended with him." These were the Judaizers, the legalists. They believed you had to become a Jew first; then you could become a Christian. So, rather than being an encouragement, they were a discouragement.

The story goes that one time the devil had an auction, and many people came. As they were perusing the various items up for bid, one man picked up a little tool and said to the devil, "I'd like to bid on this, but it's not marked."

The devil then said to him, "You can bid on any item you want but that one."

Puzzled by the devil's remark, the man responded, "Why?"

And the devil said: "Because that is my best tool. I call it discouragement, and it works almost all of the time."

Praise the Lord that Peter, through the strength of God, was able to look past the discouragement of these legalistic believers. Ask yourself, Have my legalistic attitudes toward certain issues (that are not necessarily black and white in God's Word) caused me to be a hindrance or a help toward others in the body of Christ?

God help us to be encouragers instead of discouragers.

Encouragement is oxygen to the soul.

George M. Adams

Are You Dead or Alive?

When Jesus spoke to the church in Sardis, He said in Revelation 3:1, "You have a name that you are alive, but you are dead." In other words, you look fine on the outside, but in reality, you're dead. Tragic, dismal words—the antithesis of what a church should be.

But why were they dead? Simply put, they relied on their past victories. When I was a young boy, my grandmother took me on a trip to an old mining town in Colorado called Silverton. I remember the trip very vividly, because we took an old coal-fed locomotive all the way to the town. You had to keep the windows of the train rolled up to keep the soot and the smoke from getting into the passenger car. The locomotive was fed with coal the whole way. However, when the town was still a distance away, the engineer stopped feeding the furnace with coal. There was enough energy in the furnace to move the train to Silverton, though the engineer was not putting any more energy into it.

This is what Jesus was telling this dead church or, for the matter, any dead church or cold believer. You see, the moment you start relying on your past victories, there will, in a sense, be some external activity for a while. And you may even seem to be in a perfectly good spiritual condition to those around you. Yet because no current energy is being put into your relationship with Jesus Christ, you will soon sputter out. You will be a Christian in name only, but in reality, your walk will be dead.

May God help us to keep our walk with Him current and thus enjoy the benefits of a living faith.

*Let your religion be less of theory
and more of a love affair.*

G. K. Chesterton

January 17

Everything Matters

As Christians, we are to be faithful stewards and servants of God. First Corinthians 4:2 says, "Moreover it is required in stewards that one be found faithful."

Regrettably, in my years of ministry, I have witnessed far too many unfaithful servants of Christ. Somewhere down the line, the church has bought into the idea that the little things don't really matter; just make sure the big things get done.

Let me tell you that everything matters in service to the King. Amy Carmichael, that great missionary to India, once said: "Many of you are preparing for service; this is my word for you: Don't say 'it doesn't matter' about anything, except your own feelings, for everything matters. Everything is important, even the tiniest thing. If you do everything, whether great or small, for the sake of your Savior and Lord, then you will be ready for whatever work He has chosen for you to do later."

Faithfulness in little things is a big thing.

Chrysostom

21

Pray for All Men

Paul said in 1 Timothy 2:1–2, "Therefore I exhort first of all that supplications, prayers, intercessions, and giving of thanks be made for all men, for kings and all who are in authority."

Have you ever stopped to think what would happen if the church prayed for those in authority instead of criticizing them? What if we prayed for our councilmen, our judges, our mayors, our governors, our senators, our vice president and our president? Understand that the Bible doesn't command us to pray for the removal of our leaders. The Bible exhorts us to pray for them, to pray that they might have wisdom, and more importantly, to pray that they might receive salvation. If the church spent as much time on their knees praying for those in authority as they do lobbying them, I believe it would have a profound effect.

All too often believers forget that "the weapons of our warfare are not carnal but mighty in God" (2 Corinthians 10:4). We need to recognize that God has placed them there to influence our society (Romans 13). However, we can influence them through our prayers. The apostle Paul exhorts us to pray for all men. That tells us that we are to pray for the salvation of all men whether or not they abuse their authority. In other words, no one is outside of a Christian's prayer life, because no one is outside of God's love.

God tells us that He desires all men to come to salvation (1 Timothy 2:4). As Walter Lock said, "God's will to save is as wide as His will to create." In light of that, may it ever and always be our earnest desire and practice to pray for all men, especially those who are in positions of authority.

There is nothing that makes us love a man so much as praying for him.

William Law

In His Time

In Acts 12, we read about the prayer meeting at John Mark's house or Peter's release from prison. Though they were praying for Peter's release, they really didn't believe that God would answer their prayer. When Peter arrived at the door, the girl who answered the door left him outside while she told everyone in the prayer meeting that he had arrived. Their response is found in Acts 12:15: "'You are beside yourself!' . . . 'It is his angel.'" Finally, they answered the door and let Peter in.

Often we are the same way. We'll pray for God to work, but deep down inside we really don't believe that He will. I think we can all agree with the man who said to Jesus in Mark 9:24, "Lord, I believe; help my unbelief!"

May we learn in our walks with the Lord to trust in Him and to know that He has a perfect time and a perfect will in all that we ask of Him. The beautiful thing is that although the faith of the people in this prayer meeting was faint, God still answered their prayer.

How encouraging it is to know that although God wants me to increase in my faith, His answers to my prayers aren't contingent on my faith! They are solely according to His timing and His sovereign purposes.

Prayer is a mighty instrument, not for getting man's will done in heaven, but for getting God's will done in Earth.

Robert Law

Blessed Discontent

Do you crave God's Word? Do you long to read it every day? Or are you content to read it whenever you get around to it, which is probably not very often?

Listen, spiritual growth rises out of discontent of spiritual maturity. Oh, blessed discontent! You see, the devil's lie is this: "You're fine: you're not in serious danger; you do not need to get fanatical and read your Bible every day." But let me tell you–once you are content with your spiritual state, you will not grow!

That's why the apostle Paul said in Philippians 3:13–14, "Brethren, I do not count myself to have appreciated; but one thing I do, forgetting those things which are behind and reaching forward to those things which are ahead, I press toward the goal for the prize of the upward call of God in Christ Jesus." Don't buy into the notion that you have spiritually arrived, but lay hold of God's Word until His Words lays hold of you. Let me tell you, it's a lifelong adventure!

> *Just as the sinner's despair of any help from himself is the first prerequisite of a sound conversion, so the loss of all confidence in himself is the first essential in the believer's growth in grace.*

A.W. Pink

Search the Scriptures Daily

When the apostle Paul preached in the city of Berea, he commended them in Acts 17:11 because they "searched the Scriptures daily."

Let me ask you: Do you search the Scriptures daily? Do you have a desire to know God's Word better, not to have mental or intellectual knowledge, but to have a personal relationship with the Lord?

God wants us to read His Word and search the Scriptures daily, but not so as to put another notch on our belts and say, "Well, I've read through the Bible once again." God doesn't want us to read His Word so we can argue theological platitudes with the best of men. God wants us to read His Word so that we can develop a more intimate relationship with Him and, in so doing, worship Him in an even greater way. You see, it's not how many times you've gone through the Bible, but that the Bible has gone through you. It's not how many verses you have underlined in your Bible, but that those verses have underlined you. God wants us to search the Scriptures daily so we can develop a spiritual relationship.

May each of us read His Word in order to grow in our relationship with our gracious Lord.

> *Bible study is the metal that makes a Christian. This is the strong meat on which holy men are nourished. This is that which makes the bone and the sinew of men who keep God's way in defiance of every adversary.*

C. H. Spurgeon

The Anorexic Christian

Jeremiah 15:16 says, "Your words were found, and I ate them, And Your word was to me the joy and rejoicing of my heart."

Did you know that when we don't nourish ourselves on God's Word daily that we become spiritual anorexics? Anorexia nervosa is a disorder caused by a lack of eating. There are four symptoms. One is long periods without eating, with periodic binges and vomiting. This is the Christian who reads the Bible sporadically. The second symptom is excessive exercise. The Christian who doesn't read the Bible tries to make up for it with activity. The third symptom is depression. The Christian who doesn't read the Bible will find himself or herself depressed. The fourth symptom is denial and social isolation. Christians who don't read the Bible will deny that they have a problem, and when someone tries to bring the Word of God to bear on their life, they get upset, leave the church, and isolate themselves.

Do you know what the cure for anorexia nervosa is? Eat! Listen, if you're an anorexic Christian, you need to read the Word of God!

Philosophy and religion may reform,
but only the Bible can transform.

Brian H. Edwards

Let Jesus Build the Church

Jesus said in Matthew 16:18, "I will build My church." Think about it. If Jesus is building His church, then He has the blueprints; He has the plan.

I read of a contractor in Michigan who was building a house, and the construction of the first floor went smoothly. But when they started on the second floor; they had nothing but trouble. None of the materials from the lumberyard would fit properly. Then they discovered the reason. They were working with two different sets of blueprints! Once they got rid of the old set, everything went well and they built a lovely house.

Too often, Christians hinder the building of the church because they are following the wrong plans. They are following their plans instead of Jesus' plan. Jesus said, "I will build My church." Listen, He can do a much better job than we can. Let's get out of the way and follow His direction as He guides us in our individual ministries within His church.

What the world needs is neither a Christless churchianity nor a churchless Christianity, but Christ the Head living afresh in His body, the church.

Vance Havner

Searching the Scriptures

Jesus said to the religious leaders of His day, "You search the Scriptures, for in them you think you have eternal life; and these are they which testify of Me" (John 5:39).

The problem with the religious leaders was that they studied God's Word to acquire knowledge. They presumed that eternal life was found in one's study of the Word. Because they had an intellectual knowledge of what they considered truth, they felt they had arrived. As a result, they became smug and complacent in their rites and rituals, sacrifices and Sabbaths, and traditions and teachings, so that they actually became strangers to the truth of God and thus never saw the truth about Christ in the Scriptures.

Why do you read God's Word? Are you doing so simply to acquire knowledge for knowledge's sake? Or are you reading God's Word in order to fall more in love with Him?

J. C. Laney said, "Eternal life is not found in the Word as an end in itself (the paper, ink, letters, and sentences), but through the word as it points to Christ." Let me put it another way: the Bible is not an end in itself; the Bible is a means to an end, which is faith in Jesus Christ!

To search through the Scriptures and miss Christ is the greatest tragedy that can ever befall an individual. The religious leaders of Jesus' day missed the truth, and tragically, there are still people today who read the Bible yet miss the message of Christ.

Charles Haddon Spurgeon once said: "Beware of the study of doctrine, precept, or experiences apart from the Lord Jesus, who is the soul of all. Doctrine without Christ will be nothing better than His tomb." In other words, it's one thing to have the Scriptures in our hands and in our heads; it's quite another to have it in our hearts. David said in Psalm 119:11: "Your word I have hidden in my heart, That I might not sin against You."

May we hide God's Word in our hearts, not for knowledge's sake, but for love's sake.

> *Read it to get the facts,*
> *study it to get the meaning,*
> *meditate on it to get the benefit.*

> *David Shepherd*

A Pebble

Have you ever dropped a pebble into a calm pool of water and watched what happens? We all have. It sends out ripples to the very edge of the body of water.

In effect, that's what Jesus has told us to do with the gospel. In Acts 1:8, He said, "You shall witnesses to Me in Jerusalem, and in all Judea and Samaria, and to the end of the earth." That command was given to the disciples, but it's the same for us.

We're to take the gospel to our Jerusalem—in other words, to our community, to our neighbors, to our family, and to our friends. We are to take the gospel to our Judea, our state. We're to take the gospel to our Samaria, the United States of America, and then to the ends of the earth. All of us should be involved in being witness for Jesus Christ to the ends of the earth.

Now, God may not send you to the ends of the earth, but you can certainly pray for or support someone who is going to the ends of the earth. The fact is all of us are witnesses. Our lives are the pebble that has been dropped in the water and is sending ripples throughout the world. The question is this: What is the message going forth from those ripples?

> *If you were arrested for being a Christian, would there be enough evidence to convict you?*
>
> *Anonymous*

The Good Life?

Solomon was the wealthiest man who ever lived. The Bible tells us that he had everything. He had women, gardens, musicians, pools, horses, stables, and bodyguards. He tried stimulants, sex, and all the pleasures of his world. The Bible also tells us that he was the wisest man on earth. He had it all. In fact, when the queen of Sheba visited Solomon, 2 Chronicles 9:4 tells us that she was overwhelmed. Solomon lived the good life!

You would think that Solomon would have been the happiest man alive, and yet when he had tried it all, he said in Ecclesiastes 2:17, "Therefore I hated life." We think to ourselves, "Lord, let me have such a problem"; yet when it would be all said and done, we would come to the same conclusion.

You see, the things of this world will never satisfy; they will always leave us empty, wanting more. That's why Jesus said in John 4:14, "Whoever drinks of the water that I shall give him will never thirst." That is truly the good life!

> *Man is most truly himself not when he struts about in pride of ability and possession, but when he sees himself as a creature of God and submits to the will of his Creator, which is his true happiness.*
>
> *Warren A. Quanbeck*

Mother's Translation

The Bible exhorts us in 1 Timothy 2:2 "that we may lead a quiet and peaceable life in all godliness and reverence."

I'm sure we have all heard it said that our actions speak louder than our words. As Christians, one of the greatest witnesses we can give the world is a life that quietly lives out biblical truth in everyday life.

Four ministers were discussing the merits of various translations of the Bible. One liked the King James Version because of its beautiful English. Another liked the New American Standard because it was more literal. Another liked Moffitt's translation because it had up-to-date vocabulary. The fourth minister was silent. When asked to express his opinion, he replied, "I like Mother's translation best." The other three looked bewildered and wondered what he was driving at. "Yes," he replied, "Mother translated the Bible into everyday life, and it was the most convincing translation I ever saw."

God help us to live the Bible out in our daily lives!

If you want your neighbor to know
what Christ will do for him,
let your neighbor see
what Christ has done for you.

Henry Ward Beecher

A Gray Area?

Romans 6:12 says, "Therefore do not let sin reign in your mortal body, that you should obey it in its lust." We all know that, and yet we all struggle with sin.

The other day I went to the movie theater with my family. We arrived late, so we had to enter into the theater when it was dark. I noticed that when we first walked in, it was hard to see. We were bumping into seats and trying to feel our way down the aisle. Yet remarkably, our eyes adapted quickly to the darkness, and we soon were able to see across the whole theater with ease.

Unfortunately, that's how sin is. It creeps into our lives. At first we see it as an awful darkness, and then we gradually get used to it and only call it a little gray area. That's why Romans 6:12 says to not let it reign at all! Don't let it get a foothold!

Christian—keep a short account with God! Deal with your sin as soon as you sin! Don't let that darkness be called a gray area!

Never suffer sin to remain upon you; let it not grow old in you; wipe it off while it is fresh, else it will stain; let it not get ingrained; let it not eat its way in, and rust in you.

John Henry Newman

Redeeming Time

The Bible exhorts us in Ephesians 5:16 to be "redeeming the time, because the days are evil."

Time is an issue to God. The question is, what do we do with our time? The average life span is about seventy-three years. It's a drop in the bucket as compared to eternity. So what are you doing with the short time that you have?

Our generation has become a fast-paced generation—fast food, fast cars, fast computers, and fast cash. Technology has enabled us to get things done quicker and more efficiently. Do you fill up your extra time with nonsense? Do you fill it up spending more time on yourself? Where does God fit into the picture? Do you spend your time profitably in God's service, or wastefully vegging out in front of a television set?

May the Lord help us today to realize, as James did, that our life is but a vapor; it's here for a while, and then it vanishes away. God help us to redeem the short time we have here on earth for His glory!

Time is not commodity that can be stored for future use. It must be invested hour by hour, or else it is gone forever.

Thomas Edison

Too Busy

In Luke 14, Jesus gave a parable concerning entrance into His kingdom. A certain man invited many people to his great supper. The problem was that many made excuses and, in essence, told him that they were too busy to come. Sadly, that's the way many people still treat the kingdom of God! They say they're too busy now, but one day in the future, they'll make time for God!

As the poet said:

Too busy to read the Bible, too busy to wait and pray.

Too busy to speak out kindly to someone by the way.

Too busy to care and struggle, to think of the life to come.

Too busy building mansions, to plan for the heavenly home.

Too busy to help a brother who faces the winter blast.

Too busy to share his burden when self in the balance is cast.

Too busy for all that is holy on earth beneath the sky.

To busy to serve the Master but not too busy to die!

Listen, we will all die one day, and we don't know when. So don't put Christ off another day!

Faith in tomorrow instead of Christ is Satan's nurse for man's perdition.

George B. Cheever

Delivered from the Cesspool

Peter makes reference in 1 Peter 4:4 to the way the world now perceives us as Christians. He says, "In regard to these, they think it strange that you do not run with them in the same flood of dissipation."

The phrase "flood of dissipation" speaks of waste flowing into a cesspool. Dissipation speaks of evil indulgence, a euphoric passion for evil. It's the picture of a large crowd of people, running in a euphoric stampede to evil, like wastewater goes into the sewer. Peter is saying this: Your old friends in the world think you're strange because you don't want to live your life in the same cesspool of existence that you used to live. You don't want to get drunk with them anymore. You don't like to indulge in the same sins that you used to indulge. As a result, they think you're strange, and now you will be under the scorn and ridicule of their jokes. But let's give thanks to God today, because He has delivered us from the kingdom of darkness and placed us into the kingdom of light!

Salvation is moving from living death to deathless life.

Jack Odell

The Eternal Perspective

God calls us to follow Him even in the difficult times of life. He asks us to trust Him when we don't understand our circumstances or know any of the details! These tests often can be very painful. Yet it is in these precious times of trial and difficulty that God tests our faith to produce endurance and spiritual maturity in us.

If this life of faith is a challenge for us today, imagine what Abraham must have felt when God called him to leave everything he knew and loved and move to a foreign land (Genesis 12:1–3). And yet he did so.

Though Abraham had no Bible, no church, and no Christian fellowship to encourage him in this venture of faith, he had the promise of an omnipotent, loving God—and that was all he needed! Abraham separated himself from the pleasures of his world to follow God in a race of faith and endurance. He kept moving forward with a courageous persistence, trusting in the promises of God. And through it all, Abraham kept an eternal perspective, focusing on a heavenly city whose architect and builder was God.

Reflect on it: Are you becoming weary in well-doing (Galatians 6:9)? Perhaps the race of faith has moved into rough terrain and is making you feel faint. Take heart—God does not give us more than we are able to bear (1 Corinthians 10:13). He knows exactly what we're dealing with. He has promised never to leave or forsake us (Hebrews 13:5–6). He has hedged us in, before and behind (Psalm 139:5), and will continue to move us forward in victory because we are in Him (Colossians 2:10).

May we be encouraged today as we, like Abraham, focus our hearts on our eternal home "whose builder and maker is God" (Hebrews 11:10).

> *Live near to God, and all things will appear little to you in comparison with eternal realities.*
>
> *Robert Murray M'Cheyne*

Each One Has a Gift

Did you know that each one of us has been given a gift with which to bless the body of Christ? That's right! 1 Peter 4:10 says, "As each one has received a gift, minister it to one another."

The gifts of the Holy Spirit are listed in 1 Corinthians 12 and again in Romans 12. But in a sense, these are only partial lists because God takes each one of our lives and combines our spirit with His Spirit in such a way that each one of us is a unique spiritual snowflake, or a spiritual fingerprint. None of us is exactly the same. That is why Peter says each one. Each of us has been uniquely gifted with a divine enablement to bless the body of Christ.

Are you ministering your giftedness to the body of Christ? Don't say, "But I do not have a gift." The Bible says you do!

John Calvin wrote, "There is none so poor in the church of Christ who may not impart to us something of value." If you do not know your spiritual giftedness, make a commitment today to seek that giftedness earnestly. God can then use you even more to minister to the body of Christ.

To place ourselves in range of God's choicest of gifts, we have to walk with God, work with God, lean on God, cling to God, come to have the sense and feel of God, refer all things to God.

Cornelius Plantinga

February 3

The Cure for Lukewarmness

Have you ever worked outside on a hot day and then gone to the hose to quench your thirst, only to get a mouthful of lukewarm water? What was your first reaction? If you are like most people, you spit it out. Why? Because it had no thirst-quenching value.

In Revelation 3:15–16, Jesus said to a group of believers: "I know your works, that you are neither cold nor hot. I could wish you were cold or hot. So then, because you are lukewarm, and neither cold nor hot, I will vomit you out of My mouth." What a tragic statement. Yet when we as Christians try to straddle both sides of the fence by walking in the world and attempting to walk with Christ, we become lukewarm, tepid, and halfhearted in our service to the Lord. In short, not very refreshing to Him at all.

What is the cure for being lukewarm? In Revelation 3:20, Jesus said to that same group of believers: "Behold, I stand at the door and knock. If anyone hears My voice and opens the door, I will come in to him and dine with him, and he with Me." The cure for being lukewarm is a readmission of Christ in our life. All Jesus wants us to do is repent and get on fire for Him again. The opening of that door is repentance of self-reliance and, in turn, complete abandonment of the world and surrender to Christ.

When we are in a state of being spiritually lukewarm, we need to invite the Lord back into our life. He is just outside the door waiting to come in and fellowship with us, and His desire is that each of us has a relationship that is on fire for Him.

Many Christians have enough religion to make them decent but not enough to make them dynamic.

Kenneth Grider

We Are His Sheep

God often refers to His children as sheep. Psalm 95:7 says, "For He is our God, And we are the people of His pasture, And the sheep of His hand."

Sheep have several unique characteristics. First, they cannot protect themselves. They are defenseless animals. Second, they easily wader from the shepherd's path, so they must be watched over constantly. Third, they must be led to food and water. Unlike most animals, they have not natural sense of what is good or bad for them. Fourth, they must be constantly cleaned. Their skin is naturally greasy, which causes the wood to pick up everything in their environment, such as burrs, seeds, dirt, and bugs. Without constant tending, sheep make a mess of themselves. Fifth, because of the natural tendency to pick up all kinds of parasites and diseases, the shepherd must look over each of his sheep daily to make sure that none is infested.

When we mull it over, it seems as though God created sheep specifically to be a spiritual example for His people. How grateful we should be for His daily watchful care. Let's give thanks today for our Great Shepherd!

How good is the God we adore,
Our faithful, unchangeable friend!
His love is as great as His power,
And knows neither measure nor end!

Joseph Hart

Maintaining the Basics

I was involved in various sports in high school. Yet no matter the sport, the coach always had the players practice the basics of that particular sport. It is the same way in college sports and even professional sports. If it's football, they practice blocking, tackling, throwing, and hitting. If it's baseball, they practice throwing, catching, and hitting. If it's basketball, they practice dribbling, blocking, shooting, and passing.

Why the emphasis on practicing the basics? That is where most mistakes are made. The football game is lost because a man misses a tackle. The baseball game is lost because a man misses a fly ball. The basketball game is lost because a man misses a basket.

It is the same in the Christian life. When we fail to maintain the basics in our walk with the Lord, we find the rest of our life offtrack and not satisfying. What are the basics in our walk with the Lord? They are reading God's Word, prayer, and consistent fellowship; God help us to maintain these three!

> *A good Christian is not like Hezekiah's sun that went backwards, nor Joshua's sun that stood still, but is always advancing in holiness, and increasing with the increase of God.*
>
> *Thomas Watson*

A Sure Foundation

There was a very short man who wanted to drive a nail into his wall to hang a picture. He stood on a chair, but it was not high enough. His wife placed a box on the chair, but he was still short of his goal. So he put a stool on top of the box. Balancing himself precariously, the do-it-yourself picture hanger began to tap timidly with his hammer.

"Why don't you hit it hard?" asked his wife. "You'll never drive the nail in that way!"

The man looked down from his perch and replied, "How can a man hit anything on such a shaky foundation as this?"

The same holds true for us as Christians. We will never make an impact on the world unless our foundational walk with the Lord is secure. In 1 Corinthians 3:11 Paul teaches us, "For no other foundation can anyone lay than that which is laid, which is Jesus Christ."

As Christians, though our faith is placed in Christ, we often allow other things to get between the Lord and us. In doing so, our spiritual walks can look more like a balancing act than a solid foundation. When we stand on unstable things, we need to set them aside and stand on Christ alone.

My hope is built on nothing less
Than Jesus' blood and righteousness;
I dare not trust the sweetest frame,
But wholly lean on Jesus' name.
On Christ, the solid Rock, I stand;
All other ground is sinking sand.

Edward Mote

How Can You Know For Sure?

During the early part of construction of the Golden Gate Bridge in San Francisco, no safety devices were used. As a result, twenty-three men fell to their death. During the last part of the project, however, a large net was employed at the cost of hundred thousand dollars. At least ten men fell into the net and were saved. An interesting sidelight about the net was this: the overall work rate increased 25 percent because the men were assured of their safety.

We need to ask ourselves: Am I assured of my salvation? Am I assured of my eternal safety?

First John gives us four ways we can know without doubt:

If we confess that Jesus is God. (1 John 4:15)

If the Holy Spirit abides in us. (1 John 3:24)

If we yearn to keep God's Word. (1 John 2:5)

If we love one another. (1 John 2:10)

John tells us we can be assured of our salvation by meeting these four requirements. John also says in 1 John 5:13, "These things I have written to you who believe in the name of the Son of God, that you may know that you have eternal life."

We don't need to question our eternal destination—we can know!

Assurance enables a child of God to feel that the great business of life is a settled business, the great debt a paid debt, the great disease a healed disease, and the great work a finished work.

J. C. Ryle

Read the Word

I am always amazed at the lengths Christians will go to in order to defeat sin—yet won't read their Bibles. The truth is, we will never have victory over sin until we have victory over the laziness that keeps us from God's Word. God's Word can and will enable us to have victory over sin if we just read and apply it.

David wrote in Psalm 119:11, "Your word I have hidden in my heart, That I might not sin against You." Ephesians 6:17 tells us God's Word is the sword of the Spirit. Hebrews 4:12 tells us it is a double-edged sword that is living and powerful. So why do we try to defeat sin on our own when God has given us His Word?

May the Lord grant us victory over anything that is keeping us from His Word, whether it is apathy, indifference, or laziness. Sin will keep us from reading the Bible, but reading and applying the Bible will keep us from sin!

> *Make it the first morning business of your life to understand some part of the Bible clearly, and make it your daily business to obey it in all that you do understand.*
>
> *John Ruskin*

A-C-T-S

Prayer is the Christian's spiritual oxygen. Just as our atmosphere naturally allows our bodies to breathe, so spiritual life in Christ is dependent upon communication with God. What should our prayers consist of? A good way to remember what should be included in our prayers is to use the acronym ACTS.

"A" is for adoration. Spend time just worshiping the Lord for who He is. Jesus said to hallow God's name. (Matthew 6:9)

"C" is for confessing our sin. Come before God with a clean heart. Jesus said to ask for forgiveness. (Matthew 6:12)

"T" is for thanksgiving. Spending time giving thanks to God for all the wonderful things He has done in your life. Jesus thanked the Father for believers. (Matthew 11:25)

"S" is for supplication. This means we should spend time interceding for others. This is the hardest form of prayer, and yet this is most often where the blessings come from. Jesus interceded for us in John 17:20. What a joy it is to intercede for someone else and then be able to celebrate with those you have prayed for when the answer comes.

So when you pray, use ACTS: Adoration, Confession, Thanksgiving, and Supplication.

To pray is to expose the shores of the mind to the incoming tide of God.

Ralph W. Sockman

The Necessity of Trials

When moths emerge from their cocoons, it is quite a struggle. The story is told of a person who saw this struggle and opened the sheath of the cocoon in an effort to help the moth, not realizing the necessity of the struggle. When the moth emerged, its wings were all crimped and shriveled. The moth, which in a few moments would have stretched those wings to fly, was now left to live its brief life crawling on the ground.

It is necessary for the moth to struggle out of its cocoon in order to develop the muscle system of its body by pushing body fluids out to the wings to expand them. When this person tried to cut short the moth's struggle, he actually crippled the moth and doomed its existence.

We read in James 1:2–4: "My brethren count it all joy when you fall into various trials, knowing that the testing of your faith produces patience. But let patience have its perfect work, that you may be perfect and complete, lacking nothing."

Our struggles are much like the cocoon of this moth. God uses the adversities and the trials in our lives to develop our spiritual muscle system. Instead of praying for God to cut our trails short, let's pray for a greater strengthening as a result of them.

> *I am sure I have derived more real benefit and permanent strength and growth in grace, and every precious thing, from the furnace of affliction, than I have ever derived from prosperity.*
>
> *C. H. Spurgeon*

February 11

Go to Christ in Temptation

Since the fall of man, everyone has struggled with temptation. It is a consistent part of life that cannot be escaped.

Saint Benedict of Nursia sought exemption from temptation by wearing a rough hair skirt and living for three years in a desolate cave, where his meager food was lowered to him by a rope. Once he threw himself naked into a clump of thorns and briars until his body was covered with bleeding wounds—all because he had thoughts of a dear lady. However, after it was all said and done, he found no escape from temptation.

Paul's first epistle to the Corinthians tells us that temptation is common to all of us (10:13). Charles Haddon Spurgeon once said, "Holy Scripture is full of narratives of temptations. Expect, therefore, Christian, that your life will be as abundantly garnished with them as a rose with thorns." He's right!

The truth is, no one will escape the everyday turmoil of temptation. The question then becomes: To whom do you turn in temptation? The only answer, the only victory, and the only relief come through Christ.

Unless there is within us that which is above us, we shall soon yield to that which is about us.

P. T. Forsyth

February 12

Jesus Is the Light

Without light in our physical world, we would be doomed to everyday darkness. But much worse: without Jesus Christ as our Savior, we would be doomed to eternal darkness and separation from God.

One of the most beautiful metaphors in the Bible used to describe the nature and character of Jesus is light. John 1:4 says, "In Him was life, and the life was the light of men." John 3:19 says, "Light has come into the world." Jesus Himself said in John 9:5, "I am the light of the world," and in John 12:46, "I have come as a light into the world, that whoever believes in Me should not abide in darkness."

Have you come to the light of Jesus Christ? Jesus wants to permeate every part of your life. Are there areas in your life that you keep tucked away in a dark corner or packed away in a dark closet? Jesus wants every part of your life. He has come as a light to break through your darkness!

In darkness there is no choice. It is light that enables us to see the differences between things; and it is Christ who gives us light.

C. T. Whitmell

A Heartthrob for the Lost

The Bible tells us in 2 Peter 3:9 that "the Lord is . . . not willing that any should perish but that all should come to repentance." God has great concern for the lost! In Matthew 23:37 we read of Jesus weeping for the salvation of Jerusalem. Evangelism for the lost has always been the cry and concern of our Lord. Both the Old and the New Testaments are filled with men and women who cried out to God. From Moses to Paul, mighty men of God were extremely zealous for the salvation of their countrymen. But this passion is found not only in the Bible. Throughout the ages, the church has been full of people who have had evangelism as their heartthrob.

John Knox declared, "Give me Scotland, or I die!" John Wesley stated, "The world is my parish!" Women like Amy Carmichael and Corrie ten Boom gave every ounce of their lives to see the gospel planted and nurtured. The fact is God would have us all consumed with the same zeal to see the life of God come into the soul of men, women, and children.

Let our daily prayer be to see people within our sphere of influence come to the wonderful saving knowledge of Jesus Christ!

If sinners will be damned, at least let them leap to Hell over our bodies.

C. H. Spurgeon

Stop Criticizing, Start Praying

As a pastor, I am often amazed by the many people who want to criticize other Christians for the methods they use to bring people to Christ. It always reminds me of what one person said to the famed evangelist D. L. Moody.

One day a lady in church criticized him for his methods of evangelism. Moody's reply was: "I agree with you. I don't like the way I do it either. Tell me, how do you do it?" The lady replied, "I don't." Moody then replied," "Then I like my way of doing it better than your way of doing it."

If the gospel message is preached, if repentance to salvation is preached, and if the whole counsel of God is preached and presented, then let's stop criticizing those who are on the frontlines doing it. Let's get in there and start supporting them with our prayers. The apostle Paul sought the prayers of the church in regard to evangelizing (Colossians 4:3). We should also pray for those who are out there seeking to win the lost.

Many of us cannot reach the mission fields with our feet, but we can reach them on our knees.

T. J. Bach

Love's Command

Jesus said to His disciples in John 13:34, "A new commandment I give to you, that you love one another; as I have loved you, that you also love one another." The command to love wasn't a new one. The Pentateuch said in Leviticus 19:18, "You shall love your neighbor as yourself." So the command to love wasn't new; however, the measure of love was.

Jesus says, "I want you to love others as I have loved you." And how much did Jesus love His disciples? John 13:1 says, "Having loved His own who were in the world, He loved them to the end." The word end means "to the uttermost." Listen, Jesus loved His disciples—and us—so much that He died for us. Jesus wants us to love others as He loved us. The distinguishing mark of true believers is that they display Christ-like love, or what the Bible calls agape love, which means "unconditional or sacrificial love."

The world says, "I'll love you if you'll love me in return. Give only when you know you're going to get. Love if it will benefit you." However, Jesus never thought of Himself. His one desire in life was to be obedient to the Father, to the point of the cross, so that others might benefit. If Christ so loved, then we also ought to love in like manner.

Ask yourself: How am I living up to this command? Do I love others as Christ loves me? Would I say that on a scale of one to ten my love is a flaming ten . . . or a smoldering two?

May our earnest desire be to love others as Christ loved us!

If my heart is right with God, every human being is my neighbor.

Oswald Chambers

Prayer Precedes Power

Prior to the outpouring of the Holy Spirit in Acts 2, the early believers were preoccupied with one important thing: prayer! Throughout the course of their three-year training period with Jesus, they had come to realize that prayer always precedes the power of God.

Over and over, Jesus modeled the importance of prayer. In Mark 1:35, He got up early in the morning to pray. In Luke 5:16, He withdrew to a solitary place to pray. In Luke 6:12, He spent the whole night in prayer before selecting His disciples. He prayed before feeding the five thousand. He prayed with the seventy witnesses. In Luke 9:28, He prayed with His disciples on the top of the mountain.

Then in Luke 11:1, the disciples evidenced their understanding of the importance of prayer by asking, "Lord, teach us to pray." You see, they made the connection that before Jesus made an important decision, He prayed. Before He launched on a journey, He prayed. Before any real ministry took place, He prayed. Jesus was ever and always teaching His disciples that prayer always precedes the power of God.

In light of that, it is no surprise that prior to the day of Pentecost we find the disciples in the upper room praying. It was only after a ten day prayer meeting that the power of the Holy Spirit was eventually poured out.

May we learn that important lesson as well: prayer always precedes the power of God. Lasting or effective ministry always begins with prayer!

Prayer is the slender sinew that moves the muscle of Omnipotence.

J. Edwin Hartill

Mending the Sinner

What should we do if we see our brother or sister overcome by a sin? Paul tells us clearly in Galatians 6:1, "Brethren, if a man is overtaken in any trespass, you who are spiritual restore such a one in a spirit of gentleness, considering yourself lest you also be tempted."

That word restore is the Greek word katartizo, which means "to put back to one's former condition." It is actually a medical term that speaks of a fractured bone that has been reset. What Paul is saying is this: when we see our fellow believers in sin, we ought to love them enough to help their fractured walk. How do we do that? What kind of attitude should we have? Paul tells us to do so in the spirit of gentleness, considering ourselves lest we be tempted.

"Gentleness is translated here from the Greek word proates, which means "firm, yet gentle."

Have you ever had a broken bone reset by a doctor? Does the doctor come right up and just yank that bone back into place without any consideration of how you feel? No! With all that he can, he considers your pain, he considers your discomfort, and then he resets the bone. Though it will be painful, he does it just as delicately as the situation permits.

That is how we need to go to our fellow believer who is overtaken in sin. Let us confront him, but let us do it in a firm, yet gentle way, in order to restore him.

> *How much we appreciate it when the doctor uses tenderness*
> *as he sets a broken bone. And how much more should we use*
> *"tender loving care" when we seek to restore a broken life.*
>
> *Warren Wiersbe*

When the Opposition Gets Tough

Throughout the book of Acts, the Word of God was always met with opposition when taken into new territories. In Acts 8, when the gospel first went to Samaria, Philip met up with Simon the sorcerer. In Acts 13, when the gospel first went to the island of Cyprus, Paul came face-to-face with Elymas the sorcerer. In Acts 16, when the gospel first went to Europe, Paul and his party were confronted with a demon-possessed girl.

The Bible tells us that the devil is the god of this world. Thus, when we step out in faith to take back what is rightfully God's, it is important to understand that we are treading on Satan's usurped territory and he doesn't like it. Whenever God's people say, "Let us arise and share the gospel!" Satan and his demons say, "Let us arise and oppose the gospel!" The moment we make a decision to serve the Lord tenaciously wherever He has planted us, we are going to come up against opposition. The opposition says things like "Don't be so fanatical. Take it easy. Give it a rest." However, as Christians, we must realize that when opposition gets tough, we get tougher.

Christians, don't cave in to Satan's opposition. Rather, dig into God's precious Word and cultivate the righteous tenacity to "stick to it" through personal devotion and prayer.

It is impossible to be a true soldier of Jesus Christ and not fight.

J. Gresham Machen

The Way Up Is the Way Down

So often, we want God to use us in a grand way. And yet, unless there is humility, God cannot use us at all. Humility is the key to usefulness in God's kingdom. Nothing will keep us back from usefulness in God's kingdom more than pride. On the other hand, nothing will liberate us more for God's usefulness than humility.

James 4:10 says, "Humble yourselves in the sight of the Lord, and He will lift you up." If we want to be lifted up and used by God, then we must first be brought low. The way up is the way down. As Martin Luther once said, "Until a man is nothing, God can make nothing of him."

How do we remain humble in order to remain useful? We take our eyes off ourselves and place them on God. We consider others as better than ourselves (Philippians 2:3–4). We continually pray for God to make us a humble vessel for His use.

*Humility is to the Christian what ballast is to the ship;
it keeps him in his proper position and regulates all his
thoughts and feelings.*

Archibald Alexander

A Lopsided Walk

During the time of Christ, four main groups existed within the religious society: the Pharisees, the Sadducees, the Essenes, and the Zealots.

The Pharisees were the traditional legalists; their happiness was in the past tradition. The Sadducees were the liberals, who liked to modify the Scriptures; their happiness was in the present. The Essenes were the ascetics; their happiness was in separation. The Zealots were the political nationalists; their happiness was in revolution. You could summarize these four groups as follows: the Pharisees said, "Go back," the Sadducees said, "Go forward," the Essenes said, "Go away," and the Zealots said, "Go against!"

When you think about it, these categories still exist in the church today. The traditionalist wants to stay in the past and says, "This is the way we've always done it." The liberal wants to modify the Scriptures. The separatist says, "Holiness is in escaping life." And the militant says, "We need to fight for everything instead of trusting God!"

God help us not to have tunnel vision and live a lopsided Christian walk. May we have a godly perspective that flows from a balanced teaching of God's Word and a righteous desire to serve God instead of our own agenda.

Balance in our Christian walk is
as important as a tuning fork
is to a concert pianist.
It keeps us in tune with God.

Ron Hindt

The Shield and Helmet

As we study the armor of God, we read in Ephesians 6:16, "Above all, taking the shield of faith with which you will be able to quench all the fiery darts of the wicked one." The shield referred to here was not the small shield used in hand-to-hand combat, but the large shield that the Romans used when taking a walled city. These shields were approximately three by six feet—large enough for a Roman soldier to hide behind when an enemy was shooting fiery arrows.

Paul is saying that instead of trying to withstand the enemy with a dinky shield like a trash can lid, we need to withstand him with a faith that covers our whole body. Instead of little faith, we need to have great faith. The greater our faith and trust in Christ, the greater our defense against the lies of the enemy. His lies will be deflected because our firm trust is in Christ.

The next piece of armor is found in verse 17: "the helmet of salvation." The battle for the believer begins in the mind. The devil wants our thoughts. How do we fight that? How do we win the war in our heads? By putting on the helmet of salvation. In other words, we keep our minds focused on the things that make up our salvation. Paul puts it this way in Philippians 4:8: "Finally, brethren, whatever things are true, whatever things are noble, whatever things are just, whatever things are pure, whatever things are lovely, whatever things are of good report, if there is any virtue and if there is anything praiseworthy—meditate on these things."

May our faith cover our lives, and may our minds be set on Christ!

There is no holiness without warfare.

J. C. Ryle

I'm Not So Bad

In the spring of 1931, one of the most notorious criminals of that day was captured. Known as "Two-Gun" Crowley, he had brutally murdered a mass of people, including a policeman. It is said that when he was finally captured in his girlfriend's apartment after a gun battle, the police found a blood-stained note on him that read, "Under my coat is a weary heart, but a kind one, one that would do nobody any harm." That speaks of the power of self-deception! Even though he was one of the worst murderers ever, he was trying to exonerate himself!

In a sense, haven't we all done that at one time or another? "Hey, I'm not so bad. I've never murdered anyone. Sure I've made some mistakes, but I'm not that bad a person." The apostle John wrote, "If we say that we have not sin, we deceive ourselves, and the truth is not in us" (1 John 1:8). We are all sinners! Joy and deliverance from self-deceit comes only when we go to the Lord daily and recognize and confess ours sins to Him. As a result we receive the forgiveness of God!

We need to spend time in honest prayer asking God to search the deep recesses of our hearts. We need to ask that He reveal things we may never have seen before—things that stunt our spiritual growth. In doing so, we can repent of it and grow closer to Him.

Search me, O God, and know my heart;
Try me, and know my anxieties;
And see if there is any wicked way in me,
And lead me in the way everlasting.

Psalm 139:23–24

Leaves Only

On one occasion Jesus was hungry; and seeing a fig tree on the side of the road, He went to it to eat of its fruit. However, as He inspected it, He found only leaves. As a result, the fig tree was cursed.

That fig tree was symbolic of the nation of Israel. Israel should have brought forth much fruit. The nation which should have received their Messiah was, in fact, fruitless. They were spiritually barren. They bore only the leaves of external, ritualistic religiosity. What a tragedy! The very nation that was to be the epicenter of godliness was, in fact, fruitless.

Does our walk with the Lord consist of more than leaves? The Lord is looking for more than church-going, prayer meetings, and Bible readings. If there is no inward life, those things can be of no more than leaves. The Lord looks for inward faith. He looks for the indwelling of the Holy Spirit, who very naturally produces fruit.

Let us examine our lives today to see if we are producing more than leaves. As the saying goes, "Fruit is the evidence of the root." May our root, our faith, be bound in Christ, who through the Holy Spirit bears fruit in our lives.

Our Lord never thought of a relationship to Him that does not issue in fruitfulness for Him.

Vance Havner

Mountain-Moving Faith

On one occasion the disciples were frustrated because they couldn't cast a demon out of a boy; so they asked Jesus why they couldn't do it. Jesus said in Matthew 17:20, "Because of your unbelief; for assuredly, I say to you if you have faith as a mustard seed, you will say to this mountain, 'Move from here to there,' and it will move; and nothing will be impossible for you."

Jesus told them they couldn't cast the demon out because they didn't persist. A mustard seed starts off very small but grows into a large tree. Jesus was teaching that to have the power that overcomes mountainous problems, such as casting out the demon, we need to have the kind of faith that continues to grow like the mustard seed. We need the kind of faith that trusts in God and persists.

Jesus wanted to move His disciples, as He does all believers, from the point of being the "O ye of little faith" congregation to the "mustard seed, mountain-moving faith delegation"! May it be so with us as well! May we mature from being the kind of people who faint in our faith, to people who persist in our faith!

Faith makes invisible things visible, absent things present, and things that are very far off to be very near to the soul.

Thomas Brooks

Raise the Standard!

It has been said that when sex is warped, cheapened, and exploited, the whole social fabric of a society deteriorates. A prophetic word for today! We live in a world of unbridled indulgence in sexual passion. Sexual perversion is everywhere: on television, in magazines, in newspapers, in movies, and in school classrooms.

The media uses sex to sell its products, and it is promoted with such flippant commonness that it has desensitized most people. Television programming today is often "R-rated." As a result of the portrayal of adultery and sexual promiscuity as the norm, adultery, sexual perversion, and divorce are at an all-time high. In fact, today marriage is regarded as a throwaway commodity.

Christians today who speak up for sexual fidelity and marriage are considered moral dinosaurs by the world.

What do we do as Christians? Do we give in to the morals of situational ethics? Do we lower the standard? Absolutely not! As Christians we raise the standard!

Oh, heavenly Father, we lift up to You those families and marriages that are under attack. Lord, we ask that Your Spirit becomes active all across our nation, so that there will be repentance and spiritual healing in this great country. Amen.

If My people who are called by My name will humble themselves, and pray and seek My face and turn from their wicked ways, then I will hear from heaven, and will forgive their sin and heal their land.

2 Chronicles 7:14

The Cost of Serving

We learn firsthand from the apostle Paul what serving the Lord all is about. He wrote in Acts 20:19 that he was "serving the Lord with all humility, with many tears and trials." If we want to serve the Lord, we need to realize up front that it's going to involve three things: (1) humiliation, (2) tears, and (3) temptation.

Serving the Lord will involve humility. The word servant comes from the root word meaning "slave." A slave had no choice. A slave had no agenda. He simply served his master. If you want to know if you are a servant, ask yourself: How do I react when someone treats me like a servant?

There will be many tears when serving the Lord. Serving others can cause tough heartaches because of the realities of sin and the waywardness of men's hearts.

Temptations will abound while serving the Lord. The word temptations is better translated sufferings. Paul suffered often at the hands of those to whom he preached. The cost of serving the Lord is full of suffering at the hands of those being ministered to because Satan is a viable foe who hates God's people.

Is serving our Lord worth the humiliation, tears, and sufferings? Absolutely! Paul put it this way in 2 Corinthians 12:15: "And I will very gladly spend and be spent for your souls."

God help us to be spent for others as we rise to the call of service!

Service is the overflow of superabounding devotion.

Oswald Chambers

February 27

Existential Relativism

We live in a society of "existential relativism." There are no absolutes; it's only your opinion or the way you were brought up. In fact, our government functions in that manner. One year something may be illegal, and the next year the law regarding it may be overturned. It's all relative to what the people vote on. No absolutes!

The root of this problem is based on the rejection of authority. People don't like rules, laws, and regulations. It's called "antinomianism," the rejection of law. We are fast becoming an antinomian society! "Don't tell me what to do and don't tell me how to live. Just let me run my own life according to my own rules."

The truth is there are absolutes! Jesus said in Mark 13:31, "Heaven and earth will pass away, but My words will be no means pass away." Jesus' words are eternal guidelines for life! The Bible is the absolute authority for our lives! Those who do not follow it have no footing, no guidance. However, those who adhere to God's Word have a lamp to their feet and a light to their path (Psalm 119:105).

May we shun existential relativism and embrace the solid reality of God's Word!

All who forsake the Word fall into idolatry.

John Calvin

External Religion Is Deadly

External religion is deadly! It lives like the Pharisees lived.

The Pharisees were high on ceremonial rituals and how they appeared on the outside, yet they did not consider what was on the inside. Because of that, they believed it was okay to hate someone in your heart, as long as you didn't murder that person. They lusted after women; but because they didn't commit adultery, they believed it was okay. In other words, you could sin in your heart all you wanted as long as you didn't carry out those thoughts externally.

However, Jesus said in Matthew 23:27 that these men were "like whitewashed tombs which indeed appear beautiful outwardly, but inside are full of dead men's bones."

Jesus is concerned about our hearts. He is concerned with what is happening on the inside. Why? For out of the heart come the issues of life (Proverbs 4:23). External religion can keep a person from being born again. It happened to the religious leaders and it can happen today.

May we constantly keep our hearts pliable and shun the outward trappings of religiosity, which can insulate us from God.

The whole world has been booby-trapped by the devil, and the deadliest trap of all is the religious one.

A. W. Tozer

Jesus Understands

Contemplate this: When Jesus walked the earth, He never once performed a miracle for His own benefit or comfort. All of His miracles were on behalf of others. Even though He was the Bread of Life and could have created bread, He experienced hunger. Even though He was the living water and could have brought forth water from a rock, he experienced thirst. He got tired and slept. He groaned, sighed, and wept. He exposed Himself to the same limitation of humanity that we face. Why? Hebrews 4:15 tells us, "For we do not have a High Priest who cannot sympathize with our weaknesses, but was in all points tempted as we are, yet without sin."

Jesus humbled Himself in humanity to empathize with us, to understand everything we go through. When we experience tremendous pain—He did also. If we are misunderstood or misjudged—so was He. If we are deserted and abandoned by our closest friends—so was He. Everything we go through, Jesus went through. He lived everything to a deeper degree of intensity than we will ever have to go through.

Be encouraged! Jesus understands whatever it is we are going through! He is our sympathizing Savior!

We are never nearer Christ than when we find ourselves—
lost in a holy amazement at his
unspeakable love.

John Owen

Stephen: An Example

In the book of Acts, Stephen stands out as a man of great character. His character was a result of being filled with four things: faith, the Holy Spirit, grace, and power (Acts 6:5, 8).

First, he was full of faith. He had an endless trust in Christ. In fact, his faith was so strong that when it came time to choose between buckling under or standing strong in the face of persecution, he rose to the occasion and bet his life on God.

Second, he was full of the Holy Spirit. The Holy Spirit controlled him. He was dead to himself and living in obedience to what God wanted him to do. He trusted God and he obeyed God.

Third, he was full of grace. Grace is always the result of faith. "For by grace you have been saved through faith" (Ephesians 2:8). When we place our faith in God, he places His grace upon us, and we in turn extend that grace to others. Stephen was a man of grace.

Fourth, he was full of power. If faith brings grace, then know for certain the Holy Spirit brings power. The Greek word for power is dunamis, for which we get the English word dynamite. When we walk in the Spirit, God enables us to walk in power.

So by example, we have four things to pray for in our own lives: faith, obedience to the Holy Spirit, and the resulting grace and power. As we seek to pray for these things in our lives, may it be said of us that we are full of faith, the Holy Spirit, grace, and power.

Power in the Christian life depends upon our communication with the source of power.

L. Nelson Bell

Living Sacrifices

The apostle Paul wrote in Romans 12:1, "I beseech you therefore, brethren, by the mercies of God, that you present your bodies a living sacrifice, holy, acceptable to God, which is your reasonable service." As believers, we are called to live sacrificially. The key to being a living sacrifice is a willingness to give up everything!

It has been said that the only problem with a living sacrifice is that it tends to crawl off the altar! Sacrificial living demands spiritual discipline, the lack of which often keeps us from doing what we know we ought to do. The motivation for sacrificial living is found in, as Paul says, "the mercies of God." In the first eleven chapters of Romans, Paul explains the mercies of God. For example, the mercy of God is the love of God shed abroad in the heart of a believer (Romans 5:5), His grace (Romans 1, 3, 4, 5), His Holy Spirit (Romans 8:2, 4, 9, 11), and His peace (Romans1:7). It is faith and comfort (Romans 1:12), power (Romans 1:16), hope (Romans 5:2), patience (Romans 9), and kindness (Romans 2:4). God's mercy is in His security, forgiveness, reconciliation, righteousness, honor, inheritance, and intercession. All of these and more are our motivation for sacrificial living.

But what does Paul mean when he says a "living sacrifice"? A living sacrifice is one that lasts in perpetuity! In the Old Testament, when an animal was sacrificed, it was a one-time event. What God wants is not something you bring only once, but something that is perpetually offered to Him and never dies. A living sacrifice is the surrender of self in total submission to Jesus Christ.

Jesus said in Luke 9:23, "If anyone desires to come after Me, let him deny himself and take up his cross daily, and follow Me."

May we each be a living sacrifice throughout this day and then perpetually throughout our Christian walk until the Lord comes.

Let God have your life;
He can do more with it than you can.

D. L. Moody

Salty Christians

In Matthew 5:13, Jesus said, "You are the salt of the earth." What did He mean by that? Salt is used for a lot of things.

Salt was used as a preservative by rubbing it into meat. As Christians, we are supposed to rub ourselves into the world; the world is not supposed to rub off on us.

Salt creates thirst. Our daily lives should create a spiritual thirst in the lives of those around us.

Salt was put on wounds, and when it was applied, it stung. When we live a godly life, we are a sting to the world. We live by absolutes according to God's Word, in a world that is governed by situational ethics. However, the same salt that stings also heals.

Salt represented purity. As Christians, we are to live a pure life in an impure society.

Salt was a valued commodity. Roman soldiers were often paid in salt. We get the expression "He's not worth his salt" from that very fact.

Let us be worthy of our salt—today and every day. Let us be salty Christians in this world!

> *We are the salt of the earth, not the sugar, and our ministry is truly to cleanse and not just to change the taste.*
>
> *Vance Havner*

Scars of Love

As John was allowed to see our glorified Lord, he recorded what he saw in Revelation 5:6: "And I looked, and behold, in the midst of the throne and of the four living creatures, and in the midst of the elders, stood a Lamb as though it has been slain." The Bible tells us that Jesus Christ is that Lamb. Often people wonder about what they'll see when they get to heaven. They question whether it will be hard to look at the scars that Jesus had to bear for us. Will it be repulsive and painful?

I once heard the story of a little girl who was repulsed when she saw her mother's badly disfigured hands. They had been terribly burned and scarred in a fire. The little girl said: "Mommy, your hands are so ugly and hard to look at. What happened to them?"

The mother replied: "Well, sweetheart, many years ago when you were a little baby, there was a fire in our home and the fire spread to your room. The only way to get you to safety was to reach my hand into the fire and pull you out."

The little girl paused for a moment, took her mother's hands in hers, and said, "Mommy, your hands are the most beautiful hands I know of."

When we get to heaven and look at the wounds that our Savior bore for us on the cross, we will not recoil; we will rejoice! Why? Because those scars defeated Satan and sealed our destiny in heaven for eternity. We will praise the Lord throughout eternity, realizing that it wasn't nails that held Him to the cross, but His love for you and me.

This one event of the cross of Christ is a final revelation both of the character and consequence of human sin and of the wonder and sacrifice of divine love.

Alan Stibbs

The Way, the Truth, and the Life

Jesus said in John 14:6: "I am the way, the truth, and the life. No one comes to the Father except through Me." These three great statements define who Jesus is.

First, He is the Way. The way where? The way to God. Before Christ came, no one could go directly to God. When people died, they went to the center of the earth, either to hell or to paradise—also called Abraham's bosom (Luke 16:19–31). However, when Jesus rose from the dead, He led captivity captive (Ephesians 4:8) and took those in paradise into heaven. And so when we die, we go directly to be with the Lord (2 Corinthians 5:8). Jesus Christ alone is the way to God.

Second, He is he Truth. What does that mean? It means He is the full revelation and embodiment of the redemptive purpose of God. In other words, God's redemptive truth has its ultimate realization in Him. He is the sum, substance, and source of redemptive truth. In John 18:38, Pilate asked, "What is truth?" Jesus says here, "I am Truth!"

Third, Jesus is the Life. John 1:4 says, "In Him was life, and the life was the light of men." Because Jesus is the life and has made provision for eternal life through his death and resurrection, without Christ we are without life.

The only way to the Father is by coming to the Way, the Truth, and the Life. It has been said that "without the Way, there is no going; without the Truth, there is no knowing; and without the Life, there is no living." Jesus Christ alone is the way to God, the truth that sets us free, and the life that gives us eternal hope.

To save a single soul is beyond the combined legislation of the world's governments, the combined power of the world's armies, the combined wealth of the world's banks and the combined skill of the world's creators.

John Blanchard

Overcoming Opposition

During the days of Nehemiah, when the enemies of the Jews tried to keep them from building the walls of Jerusalem, the people of God rose to the occasion.

First, we read in Nehemiah 4:6 that "the people had a mind to work." In other words, they did not cave in to the enemy's mockery and persecution. They set their hands to do the work, and they did not quit! If the devil can get us to quit, then he has won the battle. Our job as a servant of God is to simply do what the Lord has called us to do and ignore the threats of the world.

Second, the people of God had a heart to pray. In Nehemiah 4:9, we read, "Nevertheless [in other words, in spite of their threats] we made our prayer to our God." If we want to overcome opposition, we are going to have to become people of prayer. Satan is not half as worried about our physical service as he is about our spiritual service rendered in prayer. The victory is won on our knees!

Third, the people of God had an eye to watch. On Nehemiah 4:9, we read again, "We set a watch against them day and night." Yes, it is important to work. Yes, it is important to pray. But we must also keep on our guard. We are called to walk circumspectly, wisely, and not as fools.

Nehemiah's secret to overcoming opposition was threefold: (1) the people had a mind to work, (2) they had a heart to pray, and (3) they had an eye to watch.

May the Holy Spirit give us victory as we seek to apply these principles in our daily lives. May we strive to use these guidelines to overcome the opposition of the devil.

Satan, the hinderer, may build a barrier about us, but he can never roof us in, so that we cannot look up.

Hudson Taylor

In Case of Emergency

The Houston area where I live floods quite a bit, especially during hurricane season. Those who live in such flood zones usually keep a water pump and a generator handy (or know where to borrow one). Other important tools and reserve food items are stored as well. Yet they hope that there will never be an emergency that requires these to be used.

Unfortunately, a lot of Christians treat prayer in the same way. They never use it unless there is an emergency. However, prayer is not just a 911 number to reach the Lord in case of an emergency. Prayer is talking to God. Prayer is to be a daily dialogue between us and the Lord. It is communicating with our heavenly Father.

Think of how heartbreaking it would be as a parent if your children only came to you when they hurt themselves. You would be devastated. The Bible declares that we are God's children, and He has set up the unique vehicle of prayer for communicating with Him at any time. Hebrews 4:16 encourages us to "come boldly to the throne of grace," and the idea is to do it habitually and consistently. Why? Because we consistently need His grace.

Remember: Prayer is not only for emergencies. Prayer is not only for special moments. Prayer is to be our daily communication with our heavenly Father.

Prayer honors God, acknowledges His being, exalts His power, adores His providence and secures His aid.

E. M. Bounds

First God, Then Me

There are those within the body of Christ who come to God in prayer and attempt to make God their genie, demanding that He give them whatever they want—just because they ask for it. This understanding of the power of words causes frustration in some believers. The truth is, no matter how much faith you have, you are not going to get your request if it isn't in God's will.

The Bible says in James 4:3, "You ask and do not receive, because you ask amiss, that you may spend it on your pleasures." In other words, you are a greedy, discontent Christian. You see, God promises in Philippians 4:19 to "supply all your need according to His riches in glory by Christ Jesus," not all your greed.

Those who believe and teach that we should forcefully come before God's throne demanding our whims, as if we were the masters of our own destinies, have never understood the Lord's Prayer. Jesus gave us a pattern for our prayer life in Luke 11:2–4, in what is commonly called the Lord's Prayer. Jesus taught us that before you ever get to "give us, forgive us, and lead us," our prayer should begin with "Hallowed be Your name. Your kingdom come. Your will be done."

We need to understand that prayer is never to be "me first"; it is to be God first! Once God is first, then we don't need to worry about our plans, our ideas, our needs, because as we seek first His kingdom and His righteousness, He promises to provide everything we need (Matthew 6:33).

May we put God first in prayer and in our lives today. May our love and gratitude be reflected in our communications with Him.

Prayer is not a convenient device for imposing our will upon God, or bending his will to ours, but the prescribed way of subordinating our will to his.

John R. W. Stott

No Account

I heard once of a wealthy Englishman who was satisfied with nothing but the best. This attitude even extended to his cars. His pride and joy was a Rolls-Royce he had owned for years that had given him great service. One day while driving down the road, his car hit a pothole and broke the rear axle. The owner had the car shipped back to the plant in England and was overwhelmed by the surprisingly quick repair and return of the car. Knowing that his warranty had previously expired, he was expecting a bill. However, he never received one. When he called the company about the bill for his car's repair, their response was "Sir, we have thoroughly searched our files, and we find no record of any Rolls-Royce ever breaking an axle."

The excellence of that company would never permit a flaw in workmanship or performance to be known. It is the same with our sin. Through faith in Jesus Christ, our flaws are forgiven and God keeps no record of them.

We read in Colossians 2:13–14: "And you, being dead in your trespasses and the uncircumcision of your flesh, He has made alive together with Him, having forgiven you all trespasses, having wiped out the handwriting of requirements that was against us, which was contrary to us. And He has taken it out of the way, having nailed it to the cross."

O God, teach us to know that Your forgiveness is eternal and that Your love is a never-ending constant. Help us to see ourselves and others as Jesus sees us!

God does not wish us to remember
what he is willing to forget.

G.A. Buttrick

Coming Individually

In Matthew 7:13, Jesus said, "Enter by the narrow gate, for wide is the gate and broad is the way that leads to destruction."

To enter the kingdom of heaven, we must go through a narrow gate. In fact, Jesus said it is so narrow that it's difficult to pass through (verse 14). Picture a subway turnstile that allows only one person in at a time. We come into the kingdom in the same way—individually. We don't get in because our parents got in. We don't get in because we're married to a saved spouse. We don't get saved in pairs or trios. Each individual must make a personal decision to make Jesus Christ the Savior Lord of his or her life. We won't be able to slip into heaven with a group of friends, hoping that the Lord doesn't see us! We must enter through a narrow gate, which allows only one individual to pass through at a time.

Have you entered through that gate? Or are you resting your hopes on the entrance of others? We must each make a personal decision. Jesus said in John 10:9: "I am the door. If anyone enters by Me, he will be saved."

Open the door; enter through His gate; walk His path, and you will never be disappointed!

There are too many grandchildren of Christ in the world, whose parents were Christians but they aren't. Nowhere in the Bible does God claim grandchildren—just children, born again by faith in Christ.

Bob Pierce

March 12

Concerning Spiritual Gifts

In 1 Corinthians 12:1, Paul wrote, "Now concerning spiritual gifts, brethren, I do not want you to be ignorant." However, isn't it amazing that after all these years, many within the body of Christ are still ignorant concerning the gifts of the Holy Spirit? In fact, it has become an issue of great controversy and division within the church.

On the one hand, there are those who totally discount the gifts for today. Their lives are so organized that they crowd the work of the Holy Spirit right out of their lives. On the other hand, there are those who abuse the gifts, validating anything that produces a tingle as spiritual—as long as it is done in the name of Jesus. That is experiential Christianity!

The truth is that there must be a balance, and that is exactly why Paul wrote 1 Corinthians 12 and 14. You see, we don't want to live such a rigid life that we toss out the gifts altogether. But neither do we want to abuse them and see them operate in a way that is not biblical.

As Christians, it is important that we begin to understand where our spiritual giftedness is in the body of Christ and then begin operating in the Spirit's power according to God's Word.

The Spirit-filled life is not a special, deluxe edition of Christianity. It is part and parcel of the total plan of God for His people.

A. W. Tozer

What Are the Spiritual Gifts?

When we talk about the gifts of the Holy Spirit, what are we talking about? What are spiritual gifts? Simply put, spiritual gifts are divine enablements for service in the body of Christ. They are gifts empowered by the Holy Spirit to express on earth what Christ did when He was on earth. The church continues to live out Christ's life on earth through the power of His Spirit working through His people.

You may be thinking to yourself: "Well, maybe so, but I don't have a gift. I don't have a divine enablement." Yes, you do! The Bible makes it very clear that everyone born into God's family is given a giftedness that is unique to them for the edification of the body of Christ.

First Peter 4:10 says, "As each one has received a gift, minister it to one another." First Corinthians 12:11 says, "The same Spirit works all these things, distributing to each one individually as He wills."

My friend, if you are saved, you have been divinely endowed by the Holy Spirit. May the Lord direct you in your giftedness to bless God's people, bring God glory, and in the process, be blessed yourself!

> *For multitudes of professed Christians today the Holy Spirit is not a necessity. They have learned to cheer their hearts and warm their hands at other fires.*
>
> *A. W. Tozer*

Authority

The word authority carries a lot of meaning. A person who exercises authority has great influence and power. In our society, we realize that we cannot function properly without authority. A line of authority occurs within the family. Positions of authority exist in the work place. Seats of authority are also in our society and government. Policemen are given authority to keep law and order. In every dimension of life, we find authority.

When we talk about a person who has authority, we are talking about a person who has rule, privilege, control, influence, importance, command, and power. The one who has more authority than anyone else is Jesus Christ! Jesus said in Mathew 28:18, "All authority has been given to Me in heaven and on earth." In light of that, Jesus wants to be the final authority in our homes, jobs, conversations, and churches. In order for that to happen, we must make a conscious effort every day to bow our hearts before Him and pledge our devotion. As we relinquish our authority, our plans, and our agenda to Him every day, we invite Him to take the lead. When He does, we find freedom and joy. Surrender your authority today to the one who has all authority!

There is nothing holier, or better, or safer, than to content ourselves with the authority of Christ alone.

John Calvin

Majoring in Minors

So often, Christians disagree over minor differences. I heard of two congregations that were only two blocks apart in a small community. Both of them were struggling financially, so they decided that they would be more effective if they combined their congregations into one strong church instead of two struggling entities. Sadly though, they could not pull it off. They were unable to decide how to recite the Lord's Prayer. One group wanted "Forgive us our trespasses," while the other group wanted "Forgive us our debts." As a result, they went back to their former situations: one church to its trespasses; the other to its debts.

How sad it was when Christians major on minors and, as a result, break sweet fellowship with the brethren.

There are things that are essential doctrines over which we must agree in order to have fellowship. For example, there must be the recognition of the virgin birth, the deity of Jesus, the vicarious work of Jesus on the cross for our sins, and the resurrection of Jesus—just to name a few. But when Christians major on minors, then the body of Christ is divided, and we lose some of our collective effectiveness.

First Peter 3:8 says, "Finally, all of you be of one mind, having compassion for one another; love as brothers, be tenderhearted, be courteous." May we be in agreement over the essential doctrines of Christian faith and avoid majoring in minors.

God calls us not to solitary sainthood but to fellowship in a company of committed men.

David Schuller

Religion of Divine Accomplishment

In Matthew 7:13–14, Jesus talked about two roads—a narrow road and a broad road. The narrow road leads to His kingdom, and the broad road leads to eternal destruction.

The broad road is the religion of human achievement. It says you can do whatever you want, go through life with any religion you want, or go through life without any religion at all. It says you are the captain of your own destiny and can do whatever seems right in your own eyes—just be a good person according to your own standard. The problem is that the Bible says, "There is a way that seems right to a man, But its end is the way of death" (Proverbs 16:25).

The narrow road is the relationship based upon divine accomplishment. In other words, you can't do anything. It is all based on what Christ has already done. You can't work your way to God because you will fall short every time. The beautiful thing is that when you give up all that you are, you receive all that He is! In John 10:9, Jesus said: "I am the door. If anyone enters by Me, he will be saved."

Let us thank God today for our relationship based upon the divine accomplishment of Jesus Christ!

A man cannot be thoroughly humbled, until he comes to know that his salvation is utterly beyond his own powers, counsel, endeavors, will and works, and absolutely depending on the will, counsel, and pleasure, and work of another.

Martin Luther

Obedience Saves Lives

In Galatians 5:7, Paul wrote: "You ran well. Who hindered you from obeying the truth?" Obedience is the key to spiritual life!

There was a man in the Royal Navy who recounted an experience concerning obedience while at sea. He explained that he was on a ship that was towing a much heavier vessel in a rough sea. The vessel was attached to his ship by a large cable. Suddenly, in the midst of the wind and spray, there came a single, insistent command from the captain of the ship. "Down!" he shouted. Immediately the crew flung themselves down. Just at the moment, the cable being used to tow the vessel snapped. Broken pieces of it whipped about like a maddened steel snake. If any man had been struck by it, he would have been killed instantly. But the crew automatically obeyed the command of its captain, and no one was injured. Had anyone stopped to argue or ask any questions, that crewman would have been dead.

Obedience saves lives! When God ask us to be obedient to His Word, He does so because He wants us to be protected and blessed. Obedience is the key to spiritual life.

May God never have to come to us and say, "You ran well" (past tense), but rather, "You are running well" (present tense). May we, as the writer of Hebrews states, "run with endurance the race that is set before us" (Hebrews 12:1).

Faith is the starting-post of obedience.

Thomas Chalmers

You Are Not Going Under

In Mark 4:35, Jesus told His disciples to launch out in their boats. He said, "Let us cross over to the other side." During the course of their trip, though, a tremendous storm rolled in and they were fearful of their lives. To make matters worse, Jesus was asleep in the hull of the boat. Verse 38 tells us the disciples awoke Jesus and asked, "Do You not care that we are perishing?" Jesus looked at them and replied, "O you of little faith" (Matthew 8:26). Then He instantly calmed the storm, and a short time later they arrived safely on the other side.

Isn't that how we are when trials hit us? We plead, Lord, don't you care that I'm perishing? Don't you know what's happening to me? I'm drowning out here! I'll never make it to the other side. We need to regularly ask ourselves: Does God fall asleep on the job at times? Does He forget what is happening to us? The answer is, no!

The fact is, had the disciples listened to the Lord, there would have been no need to fear. Jesus had told them, "Let us cross over to the other side." Rest assured that when Jesus says, "Let's go over," there is no way you are going under! Be encouraged today. If Christ is on your boat, you are not going under; you are going over!

> *Assurance does not grow like a hot-house plant, pampered in an even temperature and sheltered from every puff of wind! It is an outdoor species, meant to flourish in the ever-changing weather conditions of the world.*
>
> *J. C. P. Cockerton*

Recognize, Resist, Rejoice

First John 5:19 states: "We know that we are of God, and the whole world lies under the sway of the wicked one." The wicked one is Satan; and to fight against our common foe, we need to do three things: recognize, resist, and rejoice.

First, we need to recognize that Satan is real and that the battle against him is real. Don't think he doesn't exist because you don't see a physical person in a red suit with horns and a pitchfork. The Bible tells us that he disguises himself as an angel of the light in order to deceive men (2 Corinthians 11:14).

Second, we need to resist. James 4:7 tells us: "Therefore submit to God. Resist the devil and he will flee from you." When we submit ourselves to the authority of God's Word, we can resist the devil by putting on the armor of God as described in Ephesians 6.

Third, we need to rejoice. Rejoice that when Christ is in you, you already have the victory! First John 4:4 says, "He who is in you is greater than he who is in the world."

Consequently, we need to be aware of the fact that we have an enemy. When he attacks, we need to resist him proactively. The good news, however, is this: every time we do so in Christ's strength, we will win!

Satan cannot give the Christian anything,
for he has everything;
nor can he take away anything,
because he has nothing.

Vance Havner

No More Death

We are living in a dying world. We live with the reality that one day we will all die. That statistic is staggering: one out of one dies. From the time we are born, we grow up only to be deteriorating. We live with the stark reality of death. In fact, the earth is marked with graves as a reminder that death looms on the horizon for every living person.

Why must everyone die? It is because of the curse of sin. The fall of man brought sin into the world. Since then we have been spiraling downward into pain, sickness, and ultimately death.

The good news is in this: Because Jesus died on the cross for our sins, He reversed the curse. Those who place their faith in Him will live in a new world—they will live in God's kingdom. Revelation 21:4 promises: "And God will wipe away every tear from their eyes; there shall be no more death, nor sorrow, nor crying. There shall be no more pain, for the former things have passed away."

Christian, be encouraged today, for that is our foundation of hope!

Take the deepest enhancement that you have ever known, the loftiest ecstasy that you have ever felt. Take that moment when you felt most totally alive. Then intensify that instant a millionfold, and perhaps you will be getting within range of imagining what heaven is like.

Roy Clements

Jesus Is Available

One of the most beautiful things about our Lord, as seen in the Gospels, is that He was always approachable and available to those around Him. Throughout the Gospels we read accounts of great multitudes following Him. And seeing them, as we read in Matthew 9:36, "[Jesus] was moved with compassion for them, because they were weary and scattered, like sheep having no shepherd."

Jesus was always accessible to children, tax collectors, and prostitutes. He was even accessible to his critics, the scribes and Pharisees. He was accessible to the rich, as well as the poor. No one was a nuisance to Jesus. Jesus wasn't like some guru set apart and cut off from the people. He wasn't locked up in an ivory tower. People didn't have to go through His bodyguards to get to Him. He was always accessible and available. The King of the universe, the omnipotent Holy God, the Alpha and Omega, walked within His creation to have personal encounters with His people.

Jesus wants to have a personal encounter with you today. He is approachable, He is accessible, and He is available. Don't pass up that glorious opportunity! Even today, right now, take the time to enjoy His fellowship and His companionship.

Have your heart right with Christ, and He will visit you often, and so turn weekdays into Sundays, meals into sacraments, homes into temples, and earth into heaven.

C. H. Spurgeon

Teaching and Preaching

Matthew 9:35 says, "Then Jesus went about all the cities and villages, teaching in their synagogues, preaching the gospel." We need to learn an important message from this passage.

First, we read that Jesus taught in the synagogues. The common form of teaching in the synagogue at the time was expositional teaching. Passages of Scripture were read verse by verse, and then the teacher would explain its meaning. In this way, the people grew to understand God's Word.

Second, we read that Jesus preached. The word preach is the Greek word kerusso meaning "to herald or make a public announcement." Do you see the distinction? Jesus was in the synagogue teaching, and He was in the streets preaching. It should be no different in our churches today. Yes, the gospel needs to be preached from our pulpits, but the majority of the people in the church are already saved. We need expositional teaching for the congregation to mature. The natural results of teaching the Word of God in the assembly of saints will be the maturing of the sheep and those healthy sheep will, in turn, go to the streets and be the evangelists who preach the gospel.

The dual tasks of teaching the Word and proclaiming the gospel are still the primary ministry of the church today. Our first calling is to teach men the truth of God's Word and to lead then to a saving knowledge of Jesus Christ.

John MacArthur

True Disciples

What is the first thing that comes to mind when you think of the twelve disciples? Men of renown? Men of superior ability? Men so great in character that Jesus Himself chose them to be the instruments to birth the church? Well, not quite. In fact, one of the greatest encouragements we gain from the gospel accounts of the disciples is that none of them had it all together. Yet Jesus was able to take the raw material of these men and make them apostles.

What kind of men did Jesus select? Some were fisherman, one was a tax collector, and one was a civil disputer; others were nondescript. They were quite a motley crew. At first glance, you may think the Lord had the wrong group of men. Yet Jesus took these twelve men and poured three years of His life into them so that by the time He was ready to depart, they had graduated and were ready to take the gospel to the world.

In these disciples, Jesus didn't have much to work with, but then again, He doesn't have much to work within us either. The lives of those early disciples give us hope.

It has been said that Jesus doesn't call the qualified; He qualifies the called. In other words, He is simply looking for obedient and eager servants. Jesus is not looking for a life that is fully together. What He is looking for are servants who are willing to learn and to submit to His lordship. May we be those servants today!

*God uses men who are week and feeble enough
to lean on Him.*

Hudson Taylor

Leaning on the Lord's Power

It is encouraging to look at the twelve apostles and evaluate their lives. Why? As we do, it becomes apparent that in their humanness, they had no spiritual abilities in and of themselves. It was only in Christ that they were divinely enabled to turn the world upside down. They lacked spiritual understanding. Most of the time, the things that Jesus taught them went right over their heads. Furthermore, they lacked humility. They were constantly arguing among themselves over who would be the greatest in the kingdom. They lacked faith. Jesus repeatedly rebuked them, saying, "O ye of little faith." Additionally, they lacked commitment. Judas turned his back on Jesus (being an apostate), Peter denied Him, and the rest of the disciples scattered when the first sign of real persecution came. Finally, they lacked power for service. It was only after Jesus empowered them for service that they had any effectiveness (Acts 1:8).

There is a lesson to be learned: the only way we will ever be effective is through the power of the Lord. Our flesh will only produce a weak, feeble, and corruptible harvest. But when we walk in the Spirit, when we walk in Christ's enablement, then we will produce a harvest—some thirty-, some sixty-, some a hundredfold.

Today, let us commit to lean upon the Lord's power and not our own!

Trust in the Lord with all your heart,
And lean not on your own understanding;
In all your ways acknowledge Him,
And He shall direct your paths.

Proverbs 3:5–6

A New Creation

In 2 Corinthians 5:17, the apostle Paul says, "Therefore, if anyone is in Christ, he is a new creation; old things have passed away; behold, all things have become new."

Someone once said that a great writer can take a worthless piece of paper, write a poem on it, and instantly make it extremely valuable. A famous artist can take a piece of canvas worth fifty cents and, by painting a picture on it, make it priceless. A wealthy man can sign his name to a worthless piece of paper and make it worth a million dollars. However, in an infinitely greater way, Jesus Christ can take a worthless, corrupted, and repulsive life and transform it into a beautiful and valuable child of God.

The Bible says that our righteousness is as filthy rags. It tells us that we have done what we want, the way we want, and as a result, we are at opposite ends with God. In other words, in our sinful state we are worthless. We hold no eternal value. Yet because Jesus died on the cross for our sins to pay the penalty of sin, through faith He transmits His righteousness toward us, making us new creations. When we place our faith in Him, we become justified and made right before God. Thus, in the eyes of God, we are priceless and holy. What an awesome truth!

A friend tells me that even after forty years of being born again, she still gets goose bumps and teary eyed when she meditates on the sacrifice of love Christ made for her—and she repeats: "For me, Pastor! It is incredible, and I gratefully praise Him for it."

Today, let us praise God for that glorious transformation!

Christ hides our unrighteousness with His righteousness; He covers our disobedience with His obedience; He shadows our death with His death, that the wrath of God cannot find us.

Henry Smith

The Ordinary to Do the Extraordinary

God is in the business of using common people to accomplish uncommon tasks. So often we fall into the trap of telling ourselves that God can't work through us because we are not a pastor or an evangelist. The truth is God is in the business of doing extraordinary things through people who will simply make themselves available.

In fact, God loves the opportunity to work through the minority when there is an opposing majority. For example, look at the prophet Elijah: he single-handedly defeated 450 prophets of Baal (1 Kings 18). Consider Samson: he killed 1,000 Philistines with the jawbone on an ass (Judges 15). Then there was Shamgar: he defeated 600 men with an ox goad (Judges 3). Remember Deborah? She was the key to the defeat of the entire Philistine army (Judges 4). And Gideon: he defeated the mass of Midianites with only 300 men armed only with swords, trumpets, torches, and water pitchers (Judges 7). And, last but not least, Jonathan: with only his armor bearer at his side, he slew the Philistine army and sent them retreating (1 Samuel 14).

The lessons are clear: God is in the business of doing the extraordinary through ordinary men and women who yield themselves to Him. Let us be willing to be such a person today!

Faith sees the invisible, believes the unbelievable, and receives the impossible.

Corrie ten Boom

Just Christians

John Wesley had a dream one night that he was at the gates of hell. He knocked on the gates and said, "Hello in there; are there any Roman Catholics in there?"

The answer came back, "Yes, there are many."

He stopped and then asked, "Are there any in there from the Church of England?"

The answer that came back was "Yes, there are lots of them here."

He asked, "Are there any Presbyterians in there?"

Again, the reply was "Yes, a mass of them."

Getting frightful and sweaty, he asked, "Are there any Wesleyans in there."

To which the reply was "Yes, there are lots of them."

He was shocked and thought how horrible it was. Disappointed and dismayed at the last reply, he turned his steps upward and found himself at the gates of heaven. There he repeated the same questions. "Are there any Roman Catholics in there?"

The answer that came back was "No!"

"Is there anybody in there from the Church of England?"

"No!" was the response.

"Are there any Presbyterians in there?"

Again, the reply was "No!"

Now, he was afraid to even ask the next question, but he did: "Are there any Wesleyans in there?"

And again, he heard "No!"

Perplexed, Wesley then asked, "Well then, who is in there?"

The reply that came back: "Christians, and that is all!"

You see, God knows nothing of denominationalism. Yet, so often we allow our petty issues to divide us. May we love those today who love Christ. For those who love Christ and act on His Word are our brothers and sisters.

Unity is of the essence in the body of Christ.

R. B. Kniper

Five Loaves & Two Small Fishes

We often feel we have nothing to bring to the Lord. We have no real resource. We feel that we have nothing substantial to give in service to Christ. In reality, that is true! Before a Holy God, we are trivial. What little we are, and have, is rather insignificant. And yet that is exactly what God is looking for. He is looking for humble people who realize that they have no resource in themselves, yet what little they have, they are willing to bring to Him.

In John 6, the account is given of a young lad who had only five barley loaves and two fish. But he gave what he had to Jesus, and those few loaves and fishes were multiplied to feed five thousand. May we give all that we have to the Lord.

I have not much to offer to Christ, my Lord and king.

No wealth, no might, now wisdom, no noble gift to bring.

Five loaves and two small fishes? But what alas are they?

Among the throngs of hungry, who crowd life's troubled way?

Five loaves and two small fishes?
Not much, dear heart 'tis true,
But yield them to the Master, and see what He can do.
Placed in His hands of mercy, thy little will be much,
'Tis not thy gift that matters, but His almighty touch!

Anonymous

Do You Qualify?

We live in a qualification-conscious society. We have to qualify for everything: to get a job, to be on a team, to be in a club, to get in to a school, to get a loan, to get a credit card, to get a car, and to purchase a house.

If we were to think in these terms of qualifying in order to be used of God, none of us would qualify. We are all imperfect! But the truth is that God is in the business of using the unqualified. God is in the business of using the imperfect. In fact, it is the only situation I know where the lack of qualification makes you—qualified.

For example, God used Noah, a man who got drunk and conducted himself lewdly. Abraham, the father of the faithful, lied twice about his wife and committed adultery. Isaac followed in his father's footsteps. Jacob was a deceiver. Moses misrepresented God. Aaron led the Israelites into idolatry. David was an adulterer. The apostle Paul was a murderer. And on and on goes the list of God's unqualified servants.

If perfection were the prerequisite, then none of these people would have qualified, and neither would we. The lesson is that Jesus is willing to use us where we are, if we are willing to take who we are and surrender it all to Him.

Today let us yield our entire existence to Jesus Christ as Lord, and He will use each one according to His perfect plan.

Those whom God will employ are first struck with a sense of their unworthiness to be employed.

Matthew Henry

Christ's Hands

A church in Strasbourg was bombed during World War II. When the people of the church returned after the bombing, they found that the entire roof of the church had fallen in. But there, in the middle of the church where a very beautiful statue of Christ with outstretched hands had been, to their surprise, they found the statue still standing. However, one of the beams had fallen across both hands and had sheared them off.

The townspeople hurried to a sculptor who lived in the town and asked, "Would you be kind enough to replace the hands on our statue?" He responded that he was willing to do it for nothing. But after a meeting of the townspeople, they announced to the artist that they had reconsidered and were rejecting his offer. The reason was that they felt the statue without the hands would be the greatest illustration that God does His work through His people, and the only hands He has are their hands. So, the statue remains today without hands.

Christians, remember that we are Christ's hands in this life. May they not be idle hands, but rather hands in gracious service giving back to God a portion of what He has given to us.

Make our life a mission—not an intermission.

Arnold Glasgow

Jesus Is Knocking

In Revelation 3:20, Jesus says: "Behold, I stand at the door and knock. If anyone hears My voice and opens the door, I will come in to him and dine with him, and he with Me." Here we have a beautiful picture of Jesus standing outside the door of a man's heart, knocking on it, that He may come in for eternal fellowship. He is ever and always knocking on men's hearts to get them to respond in repentance and receive His kingdom.

The beautiful thing is that Jesus uses all kinds of methods to knock on men's hearts. He knocks through a sermon, a book, a tract, a Scripture, or through a godly life. He knocks through marital problems or a death in the family. He knocks through the loss of a job or through pain, suffering, and loneliness. He may even be knocking through this reading. Jesus is continuously knocking to get people to respond to His love.

If you have never opened your heart to Jesus Christ, I encourage you to do it right now. Open your heart to Christ, and you will have joy for eternity! The Bible says in Acts 3:19, "Repent therefore and be converted, that your sins may be blotted out, so that times of refreshing may come from the presence of the Lord."

True conversion is the heart turning from Satan's control to God's, from sin to holiness,
from the world to Christ.

A.W. Pink

God's Will

In the Lord's Prayer, Jesus instructed the disciples to pray, "Thy kingdom come, Thy will be done . . ."

I am always amazed at the many people who are afraid of God's will. They seem to be frightened by it. They think that if they pray for God's will, they won't get their will—and they are right! But who wants something that is not God's intended best? God's will is a perfect will. That is why Jesus' life and ministry (from the beginning to the end) was in complete harmony with the Father's will.

Numerous examples in the Gospels cite Jesus doing His Father's will. In Luke 2:49, when Mary and Joseph found Jesus in the temple at the age of 12, Jesus said, "Did you not know that I must be about My Father's business?" Then, in John 4:34, He said, "My food is to do the will of Him who sent Me." And again, in John 8:29, He said, "The Father has not left Me alone, for I always do those things that please Him."

Let us ask ourselves: Is it our desire to be about our heavenly Father's business? Is it our desire always to do those things that please Him? Be assured, this is God's will for each of our lives today!

There are no disappointments to those whose wills are buried in the will of God.

Frederick W. Faber

April 2

External Morality

In Matthew 5:20, Jesus said, "For I say to you, that unless your righteousness exceeds the righteousness of the scribes and Pharisees, you will by no means enter the kingdom of heaven." In light of the fact that everyone saw these men as the epitome of godliness, we need to ask what Jesus meant.

The answer lies in the reality that the Pharisees were classic moralists. They had a high code of conduct. They had a high standard for daily living and were ethical and concerned about religion. But it was all external. You see, morality by itself is more dangerous than immorality. Why? Because external morality pats itself on the back and says, "I'm a good person. I don't need a change of heart." However, you can be the greatest philanthropist, the greatest moralist, and the greatest example of a person who has cleaned up his or her life on the outside, and you can still be empty on the inside. Such was the situation of the scribes and Pharisees.

There are many people like that today. You may know one or two of them. They live exemplary lives. They are seen as models of morality, but without Jesus Christ, they are unable to enter the kingdom of God. You see, morality falsely declares safety, when in reality; there is no assurance of access to the kingdom at all. This is why our righteousness must exceed external morality. True righteousness, Christ's righteousness, comes by grace alone, through faith alone in Jesus Christ.

God is not interested in religion that is external.
He desires a relationship that is internal.

Anonymous

Victory over Sin and Death

The greatest event of all time, without a doubt, was the resurrection of our Lord. If Jesus had come to earth only to die on the cross and remain in the grave, we would still be in our sins, and we would have no hope. But because Jesus rose from the grave, we have the hope of eternal life and the power to have victory over sin.

In Romans 6:9–10, the apostle Paul says: "Knowing that Christ, having been raised from the dead, dies no more. Death no longer has dominion over Him. For the death that He died, He died to sin once for all; but the life that He lives, He lives to God." Then Paul says to us in verse 11, "Likewise you also, reckon yourselves to be dead indeed to sin, but alive to God in Christ Jesus our Lord."

When Christ rose from the dead and ascended into heaven, He fulfilled His promise of sending the Comforter, the Holy Spirit. When we give our lives to Christ, God comes to live in us. He takes up residency in our hearts. Then, as we yield ourselves to the Holy Spirit, we have victory over sin. Because Jesus rose from the dead, we have the hope of eternal life, victory over the penalty of sin. We also have the promise of daily victory over sin as we yield ourselves to the Spirit of God. May we walk in the reality of that truth today!

The way we can thank Jesus most in this life for His act of redemption is no longer to tolerate sin.

Basilea Schlink

Blessed, Broken, and Given

As Christians, we desire to be used mightily for the Lord. We talk of being blessed and used greatly. But as A. W. Tozer once said, "God cannot use a man greatly, until He has wounded him deeply." In other words, there is no shortcut to holiness. We talk of being used in the Lord's service in a great way, but we avoid talking about being broken and dying to self.

When Jesus fed the five thousand, He blessed the bread; then He broke the bread; then He gave it out. Even though God wants us to have blessed lives, we still need to understand that blessedness comes only through brokenness. Only as we come to God with a broken and contrite spirit, and only after He has molded and shaped our lives through the crucible of trials, are we really able to experience the blessed life. Once God blesses us and breaks us and knows that we will not steal His glory, He disperses us to a multitude of people who are hungering for truth.

Today, pray for the blessing of God, pray for the brokenness of God, and then watch as God uses you mightily!

As rivers flow through valleys and low countries, so the root of all holy actions is nourished by humility.

Thomas of Villanova

The Role of the Husband

In Ephesians 5:25–32, the role of the husband in marriage is outlined. In short, the husband is the initiator in the relationship. The husband is the one who is to nurture and cultivate the beautiful bride that the Lord has given him, just as Christ nurtures the church. Unfortunately, a lot of men are like potatoes, or "taters."

Some are spectators. They merely exist as observers in their homes. They come from work, sit in their chair, and shift into autopilot. Then there are the agitators. They never see anything good in their beautiful brides and constantly nitpick everything they do. Then there are the dictators. They see their home as their kingdom and their easy chair as their throne. They treat their kids like subjects and their wives like slaves. You might even call them supreme potent-taters.

But what is the biblical role of a husband? He is to be the initiator and the motivator of his marriage.

Men, God has given us the divine privilege of being the conduits through which He pours His love into the marital relationship. God grant us today the ability to be sensitive to our calling.

Marriage is more than finding the right person; it is being the right person according to God's Word.

R. Max

Train Up a Child

In Proverbs 22:6, we read, "Train up a child in the way he should go, And when he is old he will not depart from it." Let me give you a recipe for training up a child:

> If a child lives with criticism, he learns to condemn.
> If a child lives with hostility, he learns to fight.
> If a child lives with fear, he learns to be apprehensive.
> If a child lives with pity, he learns to feel sorry for himself.
> If a child lives with jealousy, he learns to be discontent.
> But:
>
> If a child lives with encouragement, he learns confidence.
> If a child lives with a balanced tolerance, he learns patience.
> If a child lives with praise, he learns to be appreciative.
> If a child lives with approval, he learns to live with himself and others.
> If a child lives with recognition, he learns to have goals.
> If a child lives with fairness, he learns justice.
> If a child lives with honesty, he learns what truth is.
> If a child lives with acceptance, he learns to love.

God grant us the opportunity and diligence to instill in our children those qualities in the second list and the alertness to avoid the first.

No man or woman ever had a nobler challenge or a higher privilege than to bring up a child for God; and whenever we slight that privilege or neglect the ministry for anything else, we live to mourn it in heartache and grief.

Vance Havner

Molding Our Children

It is not easy being a Christian parent in this century. Our nation is becoming more lax in its morals and ethics, and we are bringing up our children in a post-Christian era. Therefore, we need to recognize that war is being waged for the souls of our children. In light of that truth, it becomes essential that we begin training our children in the Lord from infancy. The greatest way of doing that is by emulating Jesus Christ for them when they are young and able to be molded.

As one poet wrote:

> I took a piece of plastic clay and idly fashioned it one day.
> And as my fingers pressed it still,
> it moved and yielded to my will.
> I came when days were past; the bit of clay was hard at last.
> The form I gave, it still bore;
> but I could change that form no more.
> I took a piece of living clay and touched it gently day by day.
> And molded with my power and art,
> a young child's soft, yielding heart.
> I came again when years were gone;
> it was a mind I looked upon.
> That early impress still he wore,
> and I could change that form no more.

May the Lord strengthen us today as we seek to train those whom He has entrusted to us.

I learned more about Christianity from my mother than from all the theologians of England.

John Wesley

Sowing Seed

As we read the parable of the sower in Matthew 13:1–23, we learn some important truths. First, only one of the four soils on which the seed fell produced fruit. In other words, not everyone will accept the gospel.

The seed is God's Word, and the four different soils represent four different types of men's hearts. Some hear the Word, but the devil snatches it away immediately. Another group of people seem to embrace the Word of God at first, but they abandon God when persecution comes, proving that they were never really saved. Still another group of people hear the Word and even seem to bear fruit; but in the end, they love the world more, and this, too, shows that they were never saved. Only the fourth soil, the fourth group of people, bore fruit. Only those who receive Jesus Christ as Savior and Lord are saved.

Finally, we learn from this parable that true salvation is not dependent upon the sower. The sower simply sowed the seed. You see, it is not our job to make people believe. That is the work of the Holy Spirit. Our job is simply to sow the seed. Our job is simply to get the Word of God out. In light of that, let's sow some seed today!

As seed is made for soil and soil for seed, so the heart is made for God's truth and God's truth for the heart.

Richard Glover

The Wedding Garment

In Matthew 22:1–14, Jesus told a parable of a wedding feast, symbolic of the kingdom of heaven. As this was a royal wedding, the king provided wedding garments for all of his guests. But there was a man who came to the wedding feast not wearing a wedding garment. This man wanted to come to the wedding on his own terms. He just figured, There are many spokes in the hub leading to God. I'll just come my way.

This man is what we could call a kingdom crasher— the one who says "I'll come my way, on my terms, when I want, and how I want." But what did the king do? He cast the man out. Why? Because this man wanted to enjoy the feast but not the terms of the king. He didn't want to wear the wedding garment.

There are people who will appear to accept the invitation into the kingdom of heaven. They will appear to be saved. But in the end, it will be evident that they were only kingdom crashers. And it will be evident because they are not wearing the wedding garment.

You ask, What is the wedding garment? It is the righteousness of Christ.

When you repent of your sins and trust Jesus as your Lord and Savior, He clothes you in His robes of righteousness and you are justified before God. And consider this: The invitation is for everyone, and the wedding garment is free. The only terms are that you give all that you are to Christ. In turn, He will give you all that He is!

If there is to be in our celestial garment but one stitch of our own making, we are all of us lost.

C. H. Spurgeon

April 10

Government and God

When Jesus said in Matthew 22:21, "Render therefore to Caesar the things that are Caesar's, and to God the things that are God's," He was emphasizing two important principles.

First, men are to honor and obey the governing authorities. Paying taxes is part of that. But there are Christians who say we shouldn't pay taxes to the government because it is wicked and corrupt. For the most part, it is. But Romans 13:1 tells us that all authorities are "appointed by God." To disobey our government is to disobey God.

Second, Jesus taught that men should honor and obey God. In other words, God wants the real you. He wants your worship. He wants your life! Jesus was saying that Caesar's image is on the coin, so give it to Caesar, but God's image is on man (Genesis 1:27). Therefore, give yourself to God!

As Christians, we have dual citizenship. As citizens of earth, we are to honor and obey the government. As citizens of heaven (Philippians 3:20), we are to honor and obey God.

In 1 Peter 2:17, Peter put it this way: "Fear God. Honor the king." God grant us the ability to live in such a way that we will be pleasing to Him.

Christianity promises to make men free; it never promises to make them independent.

William R. Inge

An Erroneous Gospel

The church today is under attack. We see it in the newspapers, on TV, and maybe even in person. But while there is a great attack from without, we need to be aware of the great attack from within.

In his book Authentic Christianity, Jeffrey Wilson said this:

Today Christianity is in a state of disarray and decay, and the condition is deteriorating year by year. The truth of God's Word has been watered down and compromised to reach a common denominator that will appeal to and accommodate the largest number of participants. The result is a hybrid Christianity, which is essentially man-centered, materialistic and worldly, and shamefully dishonoring to the Lord Jesus Christ. This shameful degeneracy is due in large part to the erroneous gospel that is presented by many today around the world.

God help us in these last days to be keenly aware of those who would desire to lure us away through man-centered, materialistic, worldly methods within the church. May God grant that we never lower His standard or water down His gospel. May we ever and always present the truth and do it in His love.

The middle of the road is a poor place to walk. It is a poor place to drive. It is a poor place to live.

Vance Havner

Beware of Leaven

In Matthew 13:33, Jesus said, "The kingdom of heaven is like leaven, which a woman took and hid in three measures of meal till it was all leavened." In this parable, leaven is the symbol of evil. Jesus referred to the teaching of the Pharisees and Sadducees in Matthew 16:6 as false doctrine.

In this parable, then, Jesus is saying that as the church grows, as the kingdom of heaven progresses, there will be leaven hidden within its midst. False doctrine will begin to permeate the church. Paul warned the Galatian church of this danger, writing: "A little leaven leavens the whole lump" (Galatians 5:9).

As Christians today, it is important that we be on our guard for leaven (false doctrine) that sweeps through the church. Do not entertain it; do not listen to it. Hebrews 13:2 tells us, "Do not forget to entertain strangers, for by so doing some have unwittingly entertained angels." The truth is, by entertaining strange doctrines, many have unwittingly entertained demons. So be on your guard! Use God's Word as your filter. If what you hear can't pass through there, reject it! Beware of leaven!

Any teaching which does not square with the Scriptures is to be rejected even if it shows miracles every day.

Martin Luther

Our Kinsman-Redeemer

In the book of Ruth, we are introduced to a man by the name of Boaz. His name means "standing in strength." He is the ga'al in Hebrew, or the "near kinsman" of Ruth. As the near kinsman, also called the "redeemer," Boaz redeems Ruth out of her poverty by purchasing her land and making her his bride. In the same way, Jesus Christ is our ga'al, our kinsman-redeemer; He is the one standing in strength. When we were poor and needy, He redeemed us and made us His bride.

As a kinsman-redeemer, Boaz provided several necessities for Ruth. He provided protection (Ruth 2:8). He provided sustenance (Ruth 2:9, 14). He provided comfort (Ruth 2:13). And he provided satisfaction (Ruth 2:14).

God provides us Christians with the same! First, He provides protection. Jude 24 says that "He is able to keep us from stumbling." Second, He provides for all of our physical needs (Philippians 4:19) as well as all of our spiritual needs; He is the Bread of Life (John 6:48), and He is our Living Water (John 7:38). Third, He comforts us: Psalm 94:19 says, "In the multitude of my anxieties within me, Your comforts delight my soul." And where do we, as believers, look for Christ's comfort? In His Word (Romans 15:4). Finally, our kinsman-redeemer satisfies us! Jesus said in John 4:14, "But whoever drinks of the water that I shall give him will never thirst."

Praise God that we serve one who is standing in strength and who gives us strength: the mighty God (Isaiah 9:6). He is our Protector, our Provider, our Comforter, and our Satisfier! We serve the Almighty God!

One Almighty is more than all mighties.

William Gurnall

Submitting One to Another

As a pastor of many years, I have come to the conclusion that almost every husband has memorized a least one verse in the Bible: Ephesians 5:22: "Wives, submit to your own husbands." If you listen to some men, you would think that this is carved in granite, at least in some homes. If some men had their way, it would be on a plaque over every doorway in the house. News flash! It is not in the original text!

At this point, if you are a man, your response may be "There goes my one and only verse!" If you are a woman, you may be singing, "Hallelujah!"

The verb submit as it is used in the text of Ephesians 5:22 is only implied from the previous verse which says, "submitting to one another." In other words, Paul starts out by setting the precedent for submission. Then in verse 22, he directs ladies to submit to their husbands, and in verse 25, he mandates that husbands submit by loving their wives.

The point is this: the marriage relationship is one of mutual submission in love. God grant that our marriages be biblical relationships! Then, and only then, will there be true harmony and joy.

> *One plus one equals one may not be an accurate mathematical concept, but it is an accurate description of God's intention for the marriage relationship.*
>
> *Wayne Mack*

Fishers of Men

In Mark 1:17, Jesus said to His disciples, "Follow Me, and I will make you become fishers of men." Then, as He departed from this earth, He commissioned them again to "go into all the world and preach the gospel to every creature" (Mark 16:15).

It is very clear that from beginning to end, Jesus was appointing His disciples to take the gospel to everyone. This command holds true for all of Christ's disciples today. We are all called to proclaim the gospel. We are all called to be fishers of men. Unfortunately, too many Christians are no longer fishers of men but rather keepers of the aquarium.

We often think that proclaiming the kingdom of God is reserved for those who have the gift of evangelism or for those who are called to be missionaries in foreign countries. Not so! We are all called to proclaim the truth. We are all called to be missionaries. Maybe we are not called to leave our country or to preach on street corners. But the fact is, wherever God has placed you, that is your mission field. That is your pond. Do the work of an evangelist there. Be a fisher of men there. If you need boldness, pray for it just as the early church did as recorded in Acts 4:29.

God help us not to be merely keepers of the aquarium but constant fishers of men. We need to take the gospel to a world that desperately needs the only way, the only truth, and the only life: Jesus Christ (John 14:6)!

The special person called to do missionary work is every person who is a member of the church of Christ. The call does not come to a chosen few, it is to every one of us.

Oswald Chambers

We Don't Have It, and We Can't Get It!

We often want God to use us, but we must realize that God cannot use us until we acknowledge that we have no resources within ourselves. In other words, God will not fill hands that are already full. We must come to the end of ourselves; then God can use us.

When Jesus saw the hungry crowd on the hillside, He told His disciples to feed them (John 6:1–14). In their own way, they did everything they could. But ultimately, they realized that they didn't have enough bread to feed the people and that they didn't have enough money to buy bread even if they could have. In desperation, they replied to Jesus, "We don't have it and we can't get it!" At that point Jesus did the miraculous—He fed the five thousand.

That is exactly where the Lord wants each one of us. God wants us to come to Him every day with the realization that we don't have it and we can't get it apart from His divine enabling! It is only then that God can use us and do great things through us.

God help us today as we come to the end of ourselves and realize that our strength can only come from Jesus Christ.

When God intends to fill a soul, He first makes it empty.
When He intends to enrich a soul, He first makes it poor.
When He intends to exalt a soul, He first makes it sensible to
its own miseries, wants, and nothingness.

John Ravel

Don't Stop Halfway

Words of encouragement have significant importance to each of us, whether they come directly from the Lord, through His word, or through His people. Even the apostle Paul needed a word of encouragement now and then. When he was near the end of his second missionary journey, Jesus actually came to him in a vision and said, "Do not be afraid, but speak, and do not keep silent; for I am with you" (Acts 18:9–10).

The story is told of a man back East who was shoveling snow from his driveway when two boys carrying shovels approached him.

"Shovel your snow, mister?" one of them asked. "Only two dollars."

The puzzled man looked at them and replied, "Can't you see that I'm doing it myself?"

"Sure," said the enterprising young men, "that's why we asked. We get most of our business from people who are already halfway through and feel like quitting."

In the same way, Satan wants us to quit. But God wants us to continue. Norman Vincent Peale once said, "It's always too soon to quit."

The next time we feel like quitting, or the next time we see someone else ready to quit, let's express encouragement through God's Word. When we are inspired to be faithful to the end, we will receive the crown of life (James 1:12).

Religion is not a matter of fits,
starts, and stops, but an everyday affair.

David Livingstone

Biblical Submission

In Colossians 3:18, the role of the wife is plainly stated: "Wives, submit to your own husbands, as is fitting in the Lord." However, I have often found that neither men nor women properly understand this directive.

The husband tends to view his wife as a glorified slave. In turn, she sees nothing countering this in Scripture and, as a result, becomes very frustrated. But marital submission does not mean inferiority. Rather, the role of the wife is submission because there must be structure. There must be one who makes the final decision, or else there will be anarchy. God simply chose the husband to take the lead role. But that does not mean that the woman is inferior.

Furthermore, marital submission is not a blind obedience. Submission is not an opportunity for the husband to do whatever he wants. Obviously, if a husband asks his wife to do something that violates Scripture, then she must refuse! But the ultimate role of the wife is to submit to her husband in love. This, however, is contingent upon the husband fulfilling his role of loving his wife as Christ loved the church. And when he does that, then it is very easy for her to submit to him.

May we then, as Ephesians 5:21 says, "[submit] to one another in the fear of God."

As God by creation made two of one, so again by marriage he made one of two.

Thomas Adams

April 19

Jesus Is Praying for Us

Matthew 14:22–24 says: "Immediately Jesus made His disciples get into the boat and go before Him to the other side, while He sent the multitudes away. And when He had sent the multitudes away, He went up on the mountain by Himself to pray. Now when evening came, He was alone there. But the boat was now in the middle of the sea, tossed by the waves, for the wind was contrary."

Do you see the picture? Here were the disciples—seasoned fishermen—struggling once again to keep their boat afloat. But we know that they are going to be just fine. Why? Because Jesus was on the mountainside interceding for them. What a beautiful picture!

Well, the fact is Jesus is doing that for you and me right at this very moment. Romans 8:34 says, "It is Christ who died, and furthermore is also risen, who is even at the right hand of God, who also makes intercession for us." Hebrews 7:25 says, "He always lives to make intercession for them."

Many times we think we are going down with the ship. Everything is falling apart. There is no hope. Be encouraged, however, because right at this very moment, Jesus Christ is praying for you!

If I could hear Christ praying for me in the next room, I would not fear a million of enemies. Yet the distance makes no difference; He is praying for me!

Robert Murray McCheyne

God's Will in the Storm

Did you know that you could be in the will of God and still go through trials? In Matthew 14:22, Jesus commanded His disciple to get into a boat and launch out for the other side. However, two verses later we read that they were struggling to stay alive in the middle of a storm. Now that's what I would call a trial. And yet it was God who placed them in it.

But wait a minute, I thought that when I gave my life to the Lord, everything would always be easy!

Hardly! Psalm 34:19 says, "Many are the afflictions of the righteous."

"But I thought it would be smooth sailing!" Jesus said in John 16:33. "In the world you will have tribulation."

The reality is all of us will have storms in life. In fact, many of the storms we go through are designed specifically by God. Why? So that He can stretch us spiritually and, in the process, conform us to the image of His Son.

Our perfect example of this is Jesus Christ. He was right in the center of God's will, but God the Father purposely allowed Him to die on the cross for our sins. And if Jesus went through trials, it won't be any different for His saints.

God grant us today to be faithful to Him in the midst of whatever trial He is allowing us to go through!

> *By afflictions God is spoiling us of what otherwise might have spoiled us. When He makes the world too hot for us to hold, we let it go.*
>
> *John Powell*

True Worship

In John 4:23, Jesus said, "But the hour is coming, and now is, when the true worshipers will worship the Father in spirit and truth; for the Father is seeking such to worship Him."

How do you define worship? There are those who would say that worship is something that must be carried out by an ordained priest. Others say that worship is sitting in a Gothic church, admiring the beautiful stained glass windows and the sweeping beauty of the architecture. Still others would say that worship can only take place within the structure of a certain liturgy. Conversely, there are others who would say that worship really takes place when there is no structure and people are totally free to run around and do whatever they feel like in the passion of the moment.

May I suggest to you that all of these descriptions are external and extraneous to true worship?

What, then, is worship? One of the best definitions ever given was stated by William Temple: "To worship is to quicken the conscience by the holiness of God, to feed the mind with the truth of God, to purge the imagination by the beauty of God, to open the heart to the love of God and to devote the will to the purpose of God."

May the Lord deliver us from external extremes, that we may devote ourselves to worshiping Him in spirit and in truth.

To worship God in spirit is to worship from the inside out.

Donald S. Whitney

The Miracle of New Life

There have always been critics of Christ's miracles. One was Robert Ingersol, a famous atheist who gave lectures attempting to disprove that Lazarus was raised from the dead. He said that it was a trick and that "Lazarus was a good friend of Jesus and pretended to have died. He was then dressed up in grave clothes by his friends and was secretly buried. Later, as the plan was arranged, Jesus would pass by the sepulcher, and he would give the clue by calling Lazarus's name. Lazarus would then come out of the tomb, and everyone would think that Jesus had performed a miracle and that he was really God."

Then, in an attempt to emphasize his point, he would ask the audience, "Can anyone tell me why Jesus said, 'Lazarus, come forth'?"

One day an old Christian in the back of the auditorium got up, straightened himself, and said, "Yes, I'll tell you why my Lord said, 'Lazarus, come forth.' It is because if He had not said, 'Lazarus,' every dead person in the whole graveyard of Bethany would have been coming out to Him!"

Praise God that Jesus did do miracles and that He is still in the business of doing miracles today—the greatest miracle being that of new life. When a person gives his or her life to Christ, the Bible tells us that a resurrection takes place. A miracle. We read in Ephesians 2:1, "And you He made alive, who were dead in trespasses and sins." Let us praise the Lord today for the miracle of new life!

Salvation excels all the miracles ever wrought.

William Plumber

False Teachers

Second Peter says, "But there were also false prophets among the people, even as there will be false teachers among you, who will secretly bring in destructive heresies" (2 Peter 2:1). Notice that Peter says that false teachers and false prophets bring in their heresies secretly. Jude 4 tells us that they creep in unnoticed. The point is this: as Christians, we must be discerning and always on our guard for false teachers and false doctrine in these last days!

Satan is a great student of theology, and those whom he uses will teach a lot of truth but lace it with subtle lies. Satan does more damage as an angel of light than he does as a lion. Instead of pulling up wheat, he sows tares.

Satan and his messengers are masters of deception. Obviously, these false teachers don't come into the church wearing trench coats, dark glasses, and villainous mustaches, or flashing their false prophet identification card. No! They come subtly, secretly, and deceptively. They seem to be the nicest people. They get along with everyone. They are loving and gentle. They promote unity, but the problem is they promote unity at any price. And as time goes by, they increasingly disregard the essential doctrines of the faith and lead men astray.

Christian, be on your guard! May God grant you divine discernment as you search for His truth!

Satan's most effective work is done when he deceives people into thinking all is well.

Will Metzger

Whatever It Takes!

In Philippians 2:5–8, we find some of the most profound verses in all of Scripture:

Let this mind be in you which was also in Christ Jesus, who, being in the form of God, did not consider it robbery to be equal with God, but made Himself of no reputation, taking the form of a bondservant, and coming in the likeness of men. And being found in appearance as a man, He humbled Himself and became obedient to the point of death, even the death of the cross.

The primary purpose of this passage is to show us how we are to live the Christian life: in humility. Never has there been a greater demonstration of humility than when Jesus came to this earth to die.

In verse 6 of this text, we see that Jesus did not regard His equality with God to be robbery. He had all the privileges and rights of God, but He did not have an attitude that selfishly clutched all His privileges. Think about it: He was God—infinite and perfect—yet He set aside all that heaven had to offer to associate with us.

Another purpose for this text is seen in verse 7 where we are told that He took the form of a servant. This means that Jesus literally took on the character of a servant! The only person who had the right to everything laid it all aside out of humility and had nothing. He became a servant.

Finally, verse 8 tells us Jesus humbled Himself "to the point of death even the death of the cross." The Bible tells us that man was in need of a substitute. And so, in the greatest expression of humility ever seen, Jesus took our place!

All God's thrones are reached by going downstairs.

G. Campbell Morgan

The Vine and the Branches

In John 15:1–2, Jesus declared: "I am the true vine, and My Father is the vinedresser. Every branch in Me that does not bear fruit He takes away; and every branch that bears fruit He prunes, that it may bear more fruit." In this passage, Jesus talks about two types of branches: those that bear fruit and those that do not. These branches represent two kinds of disciples: true disciples and false disciples. Is Jesus saying that we could be saved in Him but somehow fall out of our salvation? No!

First, those who are taken away are not believers to begin with, because every believer bears fruit (Ephesians 2:10, James 2:17, Matthew 7:15–20). Those who bear fruit are not taken away but pruned. Furthermore, Jesus said in John 6:37, "All that the Father gives Me will come to Me, and the one who comes to Me I will by no means cast out." John 10:28 says that true believers "shall never perish," and John 17:12 says that "none of them is lost."

To whom, then, is Jesus referring? Jesus is talking about people like Judas Iscariot, who appeared to be saved but in reality never was. Judas walked with Jesus for three years and was the treasurer for the disciples, but he was only superficially connected to Christ.

Thus, the thrust of this passage is this: Are you in Christ, through faith, bearing fruit? Or are you connected to Christ by mere association, bearing no fruit? The apostle Paul made the direct challenge: "Examine yourselves as to whether you are in the faith. Test yourselves. Do you not know yourselves, that Jesus Christ is in you?—unless indeed you are disqualified" (2 Corinthians 13:5). Today, examine your relationship to Christ and confirm that it is more than an association with Him. Confirm that it is faith in Him.

The way to test yourself, the way to test any man, is to look below the surface.

D. Martyn Lloyd Jones

God's Precious Word

When God gave us His Word, the Bible, He gave us a rare and wonderful gift. Yet there are many Christians who take their Bibles for granted.

There was once a blind French girl who was given a copy of the gospel of Mark written in braille. As she read and reread the book, she came to have faith in Christ, and the book became more precious to her with each reading. She read it so much that she developed calluses on her fingers, which eventually prevented her from feeling the raised dots. Still, she was so determined to read God's Word that she peeled the skin off of her fingers to make them more sensitive. In doing so, she permanently damaged the nerves. Devastated, she picked up the book to kiss it farewell, only to discover that her lips were even more sensitive than her fingers had been. Thereafter, she spent the rest of her days reading God's Word with her lips.

God help us to keep from ever allowing a speck of dust to collect on His Word. May we crave it, as Job said, more than our necessary food (Job 23:12).

> *The Word of the Lord is a light to guide you, a counselor to counsel you, a comforter to comfort you, a staff to support you, a sword to define you, and a physician to cure you. The Word is a mine to enrich you, a robe to clothe you, and a crown to crown you.*
>
> *Thomas Brooks*

God's Timely Selection

Acts 1:24–26 records that, after prayer and scriptural confirmation, the disciples chose a new apostle—a man by the name of Matthias—to replace Judas. While we don't know much about Matthias, there are some characteristics given that give us insight as to why God chose this man to be the twelfth apostle.

First, Matthias was a man of prayer. He was one of the 120 disciples in the upper room who prayed for ten days for the outpouring of the Holy Spirit.

Second, he was a faithful man. One of the criteria for being an apostle was having been with Jesus from the time of His baptism until the time of His ascension. This reveals something very important: Matthias was a man who did not despise the days of "small things." When the disciples were first chosen, he hadn't made the cut. Talk about disappointment! Talk about discouragement! But not for Matthias. He continued to follow Jesus to the end. He was faithful, and God rewarded him.

He didn't have any hidden agendas. If he had, he would have been long gone when, year after year, he was never chosen to be one of the Twelve. Matthias was simply following the Lord until the end because he loved the Lord. And when Judas removed himself, God chose Matthias as the twelfth apostle.

God is still looking for people to use today—people like Matthias, who are prayerful, faithful, and humble.

Go, labor on; spend and be spent—
Thy joy to do the Father's will;
It is the way the Master went;
Should not the servant tread it still?

Horatius Bonar

A Slow Leak

As we look at Peter's denial of Jesus, it is important to note that the apostle's fall was not a spontaneous act but the result of a series of backslidings.

As Paul Little said, "Collapse in your Christian life is seldom a blowout; it is usually a slow leak." The truth is, Peter denied Jesus on Friday morning because, to begin with, he was already a long way from Him. Every day we make hundreds of choices. We either sow to the Spirit or sow to the flesh. There is a constant battle raging for our affections. But if we are going to be victorious over sin, we are going to have to work hard at it.

The Christian life is a lot like gardening. To have a successful garden, you have to get on your hands and knees to cultivate, nurture, tend, and protect. But if you want only weeds to grow, you do not have to do anything! If you want a vibrant walk with the Lord, you are going to have to work hard at it. But if you want to fall as Peter did, just leave the old nature alone, and it will overtake you like a slow leak.

Today, may the Lord grant us steadfastness as we put our hands to the plow, tending to our Christian life and resisting the collapse of being overtaken by sin.

> *I am convinced that the first step towards attaining a high standard of holiness is to realize more fully the sinfulness of sin.*

J. C. Ryle

A Cross before a Crown

We live in a society that tells us to indulge ourselves. Do your own thing. Whatever you think is right, do it! We have been bombarded with values of self-indulgence, self-absorption, self-centeredness, and self-love. We are a narcissistic society; we are in love with ourselves. As a result, we don't think of self-denial but of self-gratification.

Unfortunately, this self-indulgent attitude has even crept into the church. Some Christians are more consumed with their material possessions than they are with dying to themselves and helping their brother in need. In fact, they actually come to church to get pumped up with the world's philosophy of acquisition: What's in it for me?

However, Jesus said in Luke 9:23, "If anyone desires to come after Me, let him deny himself, and take up his cross daily, and follow Me." It is self-deception to expect gain without pain, humility, service, and giving. But Jesus said that true discipleship involves a cross before a crown, pain before gain, suffering before glory, and sacrifice before reward.

True, down-to-earth Christianity accepts the cost of discipleship, knowing that the cross must come before the crown! God grant that in our lives!

The only thing we should do with self is consent to its crucifixion and cooperate with God in the process.

Vance Havner

Going by the Book!

In Nehemiah 8:8, we read, "So they read distinctly from the book, in the Law of God; and they gave the sense, and helped them to understand the reading."

This is what a pastor should be doing when he speaks from the pulpit: reading from the Bible, giving the sense of the Bible, and helping people to understand the Bible. Contrary to current trends in the church, the pulpit is not a place for personal opinions. The pulpit is not a place to comment on current events. And the pulpit is certainly not a place to promote one's personal agenda. Rather, the pulpit is the place where God's Word should be read, explained, and applied to the lives of the people.

Unfortunately, the church today is in an anemic condition because God's Word is not being taught. A majority of preaching today is nothing more than personal opinion laced with Scripture in an attempt to formulate a series of nicely packaged, positive messages. In reality, these messages are merely promoting a personal agenda rather than Christ's agenda. The result is a weak, ineffective church.

Let's pray for those who stand in our church pulpits today. Pray that they might do what Nehemiah and Ezra did: read the Book, give the understanding of the Book, and apply the Book to the lives of the people. God help us to go by the Book!

One of the highest and noblest functions of a man's mind is to listen to God's Word, so to read His mind and think His thoughts after Him.

John R.W. Stott

Self-Denial

In Luke 9:23, Jesus said, "If anyone desires to come after Me, let him deny himself, and take up his cross daily, and follow Me." The word deny in Greek means "to completely disown," or "to utterly separate." In other words, we are to disown ourselves. We are to separate ourselves from our previous lifestyles. Does that mean that we are to hate ourselves and lock ourselves up? No! What Jesus is talking about is self-denial. He wants us to be God-willed instead of self-willed.

The apostle Paul talks about the flesh in Romans 7:18, saying, "For I know that in me (that is, in my flesh) nothing good dwells." We need to recognize that in our humanity, we have nothing by which to commend ourselves before God. When Jesus says that the believer must "deny himself," He is telling us: "Die to your sinful lust. Come to an end of your own ambitions. Crucify self!"

He wants us to be lifted up to honor and obey our Lord. That can happen only when we consciously take up His cross on a daily basis and seek to let Him mold us according to His perfect plan.

May we walk in the Spirit today by coming to the end of our own ambitions, self-will, and self-sufficiency, and submit ourselves entirely to the lordship of Jesus Christ!

I used to ask God to help me. Then I asked if I might help Him. I ended up by asking God to do His work through me.

Hudson Taylor

Jesus Is Coming Soon

In Matthew 16, Jesus publicly criticized the Pharisees and the Sadducees because they didn't have a clue about the true spiritual aspects of life.

Jesus told them, "When it is evening you say, 'It will be fair weather, for the sky is red'; and in the morning, 'It will be foul weather today, for the sky is red and threatening.'" That is Meteorology 101. We can look at the sky and tell what the weather is going to be like. Jesus said, that's great, "but you cannot discern the signs of the times."

The natural man can foretell a lot of things. He can tell when interest rates will go up or down. He can read fashion trends. His technology can tell him when a hurricane will hit days before it comes to shore. And yet with all of the know-how man possesses, he is still blinded to the true signs of the times.

Christians can look at the world today and come to one conclusion: Jesus is coming back soon! However, the world tries to fool itself into thinking things are getting better when they are not.

Let's pray today for our unsaved friends who have been duped into thinking that the world is becoming a better place and that, therefore, they have no need of Christ. God wants us to share the truth of the gospel so that the lost may have the same hope we have. Jesus is coming soon!

> *So let our lips and lives express*
> *The holy gospel we profess;*
> *So let our works and virtues shine,*
> *To prove the doctrine all divine.*
>
> *Watts*

Victory over Death

The Scriptures tell us that three of the twelve disciples were most intimate with Jesus: Peter, James, and John. It is interesting to note that whenever Jesus went away for times of intimacy with the Father, these three men accompanied Him.

When Jesus came into the room where He was about to raise Jairus's daughter from the dead, Mark 5:37 says, "And He permitted no one to follow Him except Peter, James, and John the brother of James." Then in Mark 9, when Jesus was transfigured on the mountain, only these three were with Him. And in Mark 14, when Jesus went into the garden of Gethsemane to pray before His betrayal, we are told that He took Peter, James, and John.

As we study these events, we note that all three instances were associated with death. When Jesus raised Jairus's daughter from the dead, Jesus was showing His closest disciples that He had power over death. In His transfiguration, He was showing that He would be glorified in death. And as He prayed in the garden, He showed His willingness to suffer death to secure our victory.

Thanks be to Jesus for His victory over sin and death!

All praise to the Lamb, accepted I am,
Through faith in the Savior's adorable name;
In Him I confide, His blood is applied;
For me He has suffered, for me He has died.

Wesley

The Priority of Preaching

When the church was birthed, the first thing the apostles did was to worship God. Acts 2:4 says that they began speaking in tongues. People in the gathering were from diverse areas and spoke various dialects and languages. However, verse 11 tells us that they all understood the utterances: "We hear them speaking in our own tongues the wonderful works of God." In other words, the apostles were worshiping God in different languages.

Though the first thing the church did was to worship God, what immediately followed was preaching the Word of God. As a crowd assembled to hear the men praising God, Peter stood up and gave the first sermon.

The church needs to get back to its priorities: the worship of God and the teaching of God's Word. There are many churches today that set their priorities in other places. Some emphasize counseling. Some emphasize Sunday school. Some emphasize small groups. Some emphasize reaching the unchurched. Some emphasize specialty doctrines. Some emphasize experience. All of these have their place, and all of these have some importance. But all of them, when compared to the teaching of God's Word, are subordinate.

The book of Acts is the blueprint of the church, and as we look at the blueprint, we see the priority given to preaching. (Acts 4:2; 5:42; 8:5, 25, 35, 40; 9:20, 27; 13:5, 38, 42; 14:7, 21, 25; 15:36; 17:18; 20:7)

May God help us to keep our priorities straight!

> *Your works for God will always count,*
> *Although it may be small;*
> *For He marks well your faithfulness*
> *When you have given all.*
>
> *Dennis J. DeHaan*

Where Else Would We Go?

In John 6, we are told that when the majority of the people following Jesus realized the cost of true discipleship, they turned away and walked with Him no more. In light of that, Jesus asked the Twelve, "Do you also want to go away?" (John 6:67). Verse 68 tells us what happened: "But Simon Peter answered Him, 'Lord, to whom shall we go? You have the words of eternal life.'" I love that! Peter says: "Jesus, we're not going to leave you. You have the words of eternal life!"

Jesus had just said in verse 63 that "the words that I speak to you are spirit, and they are life."

Now Peter is saying: "Yes, Lord, Your words are the words of life, and so we are not going to leave You. We are going to stay as close to You as we can!" Also notice the question, to whom shall we go? The truth is, when true disciples look back at the world, there is really nothing there for them. The world is empty. It is unfulfilling. Why? Because no one person can satisfy the yearning heart like Jesus Christ—not Buddha, not Confucius, not Allah, not Krishna, not any perceived spiritual leader or any human being for that matter.

John Phillips wrote, "To turn away from Christ to the dead founder of one of the world's false religions, or to the lifeless sophistries of a pagan philosopher, or to one of the modern proponents of today's humanistic creeds, is to exchange light for darkness, life for death, hope for despair, heaven for hell."

Like Peter, each of us should say to the Lord today, Lord, I'm not leaving You. Where else would I go? Where else would I find such love? Such forgiveness? Such grace? Lord, You have the words of eternal life, and so I surrender my will and my way to You today!

My heart, my life, my all I bring
To Christ who loves me so;
He is my Master, Lord, and King,
Wherever He leads I'll go.

B. B. McKinney

From the Mountain to the Valley

When the disciples came down from the mountaintop experience of seeing Jesus transfigured, they hit opposition. As they came down from the mountain, they encountered a demon-possessed boy. They came down from the mountain of glory to the valley of need (Matthew 17:1–21).

Has that ever happened to you? You are just leaving an event where God has really spoken to you, your heart has been warmed, and as soon as you get into your car to leave, the devil bombards your thoughts. Then some guy on the road tries to run you over. You have left the mountaintop and hit the real world again.

Why does that happen? It's because Satan wants to steal your joy. He knows he can't steal your salvation, so he will do everything he can to steal the blessing, peace, and joy that come by walking in the Spirit.

So what should we do? Well, to be forewarned is to be forearmed. Christians need to be on guard, especially after mountaintop experiences, because Satan is going to do everything he can to discourage us and to rob us of our joy. Let us be on our guard and walk in the Spirit today and every day.

The prince of darkness grim—
We tremble not for him;
His rage we can endure,
For lo! His doom is sure.

Martin Luther

Persistent Prayer

In Matthew 7:7, Jesus said, "Ask, and it will be given to you; seek, and you will find; knock, and it will be opened to you." In the Greek, Jesus is literally saying keep asking, keep seeking, and keep knocking. When you do these things, the answers will be constantly coming. In other words, be persistent in prayer.

Probably one of the greatest examples of a persistent prayer life is that displayed by George Muller. George Muller was a godly man who lived in the 1800s. In his early life, he began praying for five of his friends to accept Jesus as their Lord. It was not until he had prayed for five years that the first man came to Christ. In another five years, two more accepted Christ as their Lord and Savior. After twenty-five years, the fourth man was saved. George Muller continued praying for the fifth friend until he died. A few months after Muller's death, the fifth man gave his life to Christ.

How long did George Muller pray for that fifth man to accept Christ? Fifty-two years! May the Lord grant us that kind of persistence in our prayers. May we not give up until God has brought the victory. May we all be encouraged today to keep asking, keep seeking, and keep knocking, so that God in His perfect timing might answer our request.

When we call out to You, O Lord,
And wait for answers to our prayer,
Give us the patience that we need
And help us sense Your love and care.

Spurgeon

Turn the Other Cheek

There is a true story about a soldier who was weak and could never really get it together as a soldier. He didn't fare well at soldiering. His sergeant abused him greatly. There came a time when he could not perform a specific function in his training. When he collapsed on the ground, the sergeant came over and pummeled and kicked his body as he lay limp. The young soldier was in much pain and had to be carried to the barracks.

The next morning, as the bugle blew reveille, calling for the first military formation of the day, the soldiers got up. The sergeant awoke and, reaching down for his boots, found them shined and polished to perfection. When he asked who had shined the boots, he was told it was the soldier he had kicked the night before. The sergeant went to the soldier and asked how he could have done that. The soldier replied, "Because the Lord has given me a love for you." And with that, the sergeant accepted Christ and became a Christian.

In Matthew 5:39, Jesus said, "But whoever slaps you on your right cheek, turn the other to him also." We might ask ourselves why. The answer is for the sake of God's kingdom. When we let the power of the indwelling Holy Spirit dominate our being, we will be able to do as that soldier did. We can be assured that Jesus will use our obedience to help accomplish his redemptive purpose for mankind.

God grant that we may be godly witness to those around us, no matter how severe the persecution.

> *Let me turn the other cheek*
> *As You so often did;*
> *Let me feel the joy of love*
> *When saying, "I forgive."*

Monroe

Childlike, Not Childish

In Matthew 18:3, Jesus said, "Assuredly, I say to you, unless you are converted and become as little children, you will by no means enter the kingdom of heaven."

When the disciples heard this, their jaws must have dropped to the floor. They had been constantly arguing among themselves as to which of them would be the greatest in the kingdom of heaven. The fact is, they were waiting for Jesus to say, "Peter is the greatest because I called him the rock." Or, "John is the greatest because he displays a lot of love." Or, "Matthew is the greatest because he left a profitable business to follow Me."

But no! Jesus was saying that the greatest in the kingdom would be a person who was childlike. Jesus was saying, "Those who are in the kingdom will display childlike characteristics." He did not say childish characteristics. The disciples were being childish as they argued about their greatness.

Those who enter the kingdom of heaven and are the greatest in God's eyes are those who are simple, trusting, unpretentious, helpless, innocent, humble, and dependent. We need to ask ourselves: Am I a child of God? Have I been born again, accepting Jesus Christ into my life as Lord and Savior? People will know it when you are His child, because you will display these childlike characteristics.

God, grant today that we not be childish but childlike as we display our Father's love.

There's so much wisdom to be learned,
So many ways for me to grow,
Lord, I would listen like a child,
And learn what you would have me know.

K. De Haan

May 10

The Lowliest Is the Loveliest

Have you ever been around someone who is truly humble? Did you notice a grace about them—a gentleness that seemed to pull you in? Truly, the lowliest Christian is the loveliest Christian.

Proverbs 29:23 says, "A man's pride will bring him low, but the humble in spirit will retain honor." That's why James wrote to the church, "God resists the proud, But gives grace to the humble" (James 4:6) and, "Humble yourselves in the sight of the Lord, and He will lift you up" (James 4:10). Peter said it very clearly in 1 Peter 5:5: "Be clothed in humility."

What is humility? As one man said, "True humility is not thinking badly of oneself; it is simply not thinking of oneself at all!" Some people act unreasonably unworthy, but God sees their action as a cover-up for self-promotion and pride. Humility is not caring if one gets credit for a task or service well done. Humility is being self-confident yet not arrogant or boastful about oneself. It is being seemingly insignificant to the world, while being assured that one is very important to Christ.

May we walk in humility, seeing others as better than ourselves (Philippians 2:3) and, as a result, drawing people through gentleness into the kingdom of God.

When all is done, renounce pride,
Self-praise and boasting scorn;
So shall you glorify the Lord
And thus Christ's name adorn.

Hallan

134

Make Me a Child Again

In Mark 10:14, Jesus said, "Let the little children come to Me, and do not forbid them; for of such is the kingdom of God."

Jesus was saying that the kingdom of God is full of people whose characteristics are those of children. As God's children, we Christians should be characterized by humility, dependency upon God, submission, childlike innocence, childlike faith, and childlike trust.

Let us not just pray the following prayer but consciously seek God's help in meeting the goal it indicates.

Make me, oh Lord, a child again,
so tender and frail and small,
In self possessing nothing, in Thee possessing all.
Oh Savior, make me small once more,
that downward I may grow;
And in this heart of mine restore the faith of long ago.

With Thee may I be crucified, no longer I that live.
Oh Savior, crush my sinful pride,
by grace which pardon gives.
Make me, oh Lord, a child again, obedient to Thy call,
In self possessing nothing, in Thee possessing all.

Anonymous

Inseparably Linked

One of the most glorious truths in the entire Bible is the fact that when we give our lives to Christ, we are inseparably linked with God from that point on through eternity. In John 14:20, Jesus said, "At that day you will know that I am in My Father, and you in Me, and I in you."

That is a glorious union: "I in you!" Paul said in 1 Corinthians 6:15: "Do you not know that your bodies are members of Christ? Shall I then take the members of Christ and make them members of a harlot?" Paul is saying if a Christian goes to bed with a prostitute, he is joining Christ with a prostitute. Why? Because once we accept Jesus as our Lord and He lives in us, we are inseparably linked with Him. The joy of this thought is that nothing can separate me from the love of God which is in Christ Jesus (Romans 8:38–39). Why? Because I am inseparably linked with my God!

The Bible tells us that Christ is the vine and we are the branches (John 15), that He is the head and we are the body (Ephesians 4), and that He is the bridegroom and we are the bride (Revelation 21).

Let's ask ourselves: Am I overcome with worries? Am I in the middle of a trial? Have I wondered if God is near? Rest assured that when we are Christians, God is not only near us but in us! Every minute of every day He is available to us to teach us, to love us, to dispense His mercy and grace. He is always there!

Oh, let us thank God today for His inseparable union with us through Christ!

Father, thank You for Your Spirit,
Fill us with Your love and power;
Change us into Christ's own image
Day by day and hour by hour.

Anonymous

The Battle Belongs to the Lord

Are you at a place of overwhelming circumstances and do not know what to do? Does it seem as if there is an armada of difficulties facing you, and you are not sure what to do? Then read 2 Chronicles 20 and see what Jehoshaphat, the King of Judah, did when he faced overwhelming problems. In verse 2, "some came and told Jehoshaphat, saying, 'A great multitude is coming against you.'" Verse 3 says he "set himself to seek the Lord, and proclaimed a fast." In verse 12, Jehoshaphat prayed to God and said, "We have no power against this great multitude that is coming against us; nor do we know what to do, but our eyes are upon You."

What was the outcome? God sent a prophet who said, "The battle is not yours, but God's" (verse 15).

Oh, what good words to hear! The overwhelming circumstances we face daily are not ours to fight, but God's. He does battle for us as we cast our cares on Him. Encouraged by the word of the Lord, Jehoshaphat sent the armies of Judah to the battlefield singing praises. As they went forth, God wiped out their enemy.

God grant us today to go out with joy and be led forth with peace, knowing that the battle belongs to the Lord!

Into His hands I lay the fears that haunt me,
The dread of future ills that may befall;
Into His hands I lay the doubts that taunt me,
And rest securely, trusting Him for all.

Christiansen

Signpost

William Barclay tells the story of an old man on his death bed who was very distraught. When asked what was bothering him, he said, "When we were boys at play, we reversed a signpost one day at a crossroads, and I've never ceased to wonder how many people were sent in the wrong direction by what we did." The story reveals this man's sensitive heart to sin and his desire to make things right.

Even though we can be sure that God forgave this man, a spiritual truth can be found in this story. The Bible teaches us that we are to be examples to the world. The way we live our lives is a signpost so others can learn the way.

What direction are you sending people? What do your coworkers see when they observe you at work? What do your friends see when your guard is down? What do your fellow Christians see when you are not at church? What does your spouse see that nobody else sees? What do your children see?

Thought provoking and scary, isn't it? We are living signposts. Every day we direct people in one of two directions: the right way or the wrong way, to heaven or to hell, to God or away from God.

Oh heavenly Father, we do desire to be godly signposts. Please help us to live our lives in such a way that whoever we come in contact with will be directed to you, Lord.

> *While passing through this world of sin,*
> *And others your life shall view,*
> *Be clean and pure without, within;*
> *Let others see Jesus in you.*
>
> *B. B. McKinney*

Hatred of Sin

When Chrysostom was arrested by the Roman emperor, the latter sought unsuccessfully to make the Greek Christian recant his faith. So the Emperor gathered his advisors to discuss what could be done to the prisoner.

"Shall I put him in the dungeon?" asked the emperor.

"No!" said one of his counselors. "For he would be glad to go. He longs for the quietness wherein he can delight in the mercies of his God."

"Then he shall be executed!" said the emperor.

"No," was the answer. "For he will also be glad to die. He declares that in the event of death, he will be in the presence of the Lord."

"What shall we do, then?" the ruler asked.

"There is one thing that will give Chrysostom pain," the counselor said. "To cause Chrysostom to suffer, make him sin. He is afraid of nothing except sin!"

Oh, may it be so with us! Christians, let us unite our hearts together for a great hatred of sin!

Terror by night nor arrow's flight
Can make my soul afraid;
Naught can alarm, no foe can harm,
When on Him I remain stayed.

Anonymous

The Sevenfold Glory of Christ

In Revelation 1:14–16, John describes the sevenfold glory of Christ as seen in his vision. First, John tells us that Jesus' head and hair were white as snow, alluding to the majestic purity of Christ and His perfect state at His second coming.

Second, His eyes were like fire. This speaks of the penetrating omniscience of God. Hebrews 4:13 says that everything is naked before God. When Christ returns, all men will be judged according to their works.

Third, His feet were like refined brass, referring to Christ's judgment. In the Bible, brass is associated with sin. The utensils used for temple sacrifices for sin were brass. When Jesus returns, we are told, He will tread the winepress of the fierceness and wrath of the almighty God (Revelation 19:15).

Fourth, His voice was like many waters. This speaks of Christ's commanding authority and power. Jesus said in Matthew 28:18, "All authority has been given to Me in heaven and on earth."

Fifth, He had seven stars in His hand, representing the leadership of the church. Those who lead Christ's church are His possession and are under His protection and sovereign control.

Sixth, a two-edged sword went out of His mouth. This is the sword that Christ will use against those who reject Him at his return. We now live in a day of grace. Anyone who calls upon the name of the Lord shall be saved (Acts 2:21). But those who reject Christ at His second coming will face His sword (Revelation 19:11–15).

Seventh, His countenance shone like the sun. This was the shekinah glory of God, much like John had seen briefly on the mountaintop in Matthew 17:2.

How wonderful it would be if we could have a fresh revelation of Jesus Christ as we review John's vision! May it be etched on our hearts.

> *Christ is our hope of glory*
> *And the glory of our hope.*
>
> *Anonymous*

One Another

In our relationship with fellow Christians, the biblical emphasis is on one another.

> "Be kindly affectionate to one another with brotherly love." (Romans 12:10)
> "Be of the same mind toward one another." (Romans 12:16)
> "Therefore let us not judge one another." (Romans 14:13)
> "Be like-minded toward one another, according to Christ Jesus." (Romans 15:5)
> "Receive one another, just as Christ also received us, to the glory of God." (Romans 15:7)
> "Admonish one another." (Romans 15:14)
> "Bearing with one another in love." (Ephesians 4:2)
> "Be kind to one another, tenderhearted, forgiving one another." (Ephesians 4:32)
> "In lowliness of mind let each esteem others better than himself." (Philippians 2:3)
> "Bearing with one another, and forgiving one another." (Colossians 3:13)
> "Love one another fervently with a pure heart." (1 Peter 1:22)
> "Be hospitable to one another." (1 Peter 4:9)
> "As each one has received a gift, minister it to one another." (1 Peter 4:10)
> "Be submissive to one another, and be clothed with humility." (1 Peter 5:5)
> "Consider one another in order to stir up love and good works." Hebrews (10:24)
> God help us to stop thinking about ourselves and start doing the "one anothers" in the Bible!

No man's life is for his private use.

Anonymous

Seek and Save

Of all Christ's titles, one of my favorites is the Good Shepherd (John 10:11). He is called "that great Shepherd of the sheep" in Hebrews 13:20 and the Chief Shepherd in 1 Peter 5:4. In relation to that, the Bible calls us sheep. When you really think about it, that suits us well.

Sheep are not very smart creatures. They often wander from the path, and the shepherd has to go out and find them before they stumble into a ditch or are attacked by a predator. A good shepherd is willing to lay down his life for his sheep. He will leave the ninety-nine and go after one missing sheep. He will seek diligently through brush and mountainous terrain to find it.

That is what Christ did for us! In Luke 19:10, Jesus said, "For the Son of Man has come to seek and to save that which was lost."

Are you off the path? Have you wandered from the sheepfold of Christ? Are you down in a ditch? Has your sin overtaken you and left you in the clutches of predators? Then cry out to the Good Shepherd. He is longing to bring you back into the sheepfold. If you have wandered from God, cry out to Him! He longs to seek, save, and restore those sheep that are lost.

But all thro' the mountains, thunder-riven,
And up from the rocky steep,
There rose a glad cry to the gate of heaven,
"Rejoice! I have found My sheep!"
And the angels echoed around the throne,
"Rejoice, for the Lord brings back His own!
Rejoice, for the Lord brings back His own."

Elizabeth G. Clephane

The Care of a Shepherd

In Matthew 18:12–13, Jesus said: "What do you think? If a man has a hundred sheep, and one of them goes astray, does he not leave the ninety-nine and go to the mountains to seek the one that is straying? And if he should find it, assuredly, I say to you, he rejoices more over that sheep than over the ninety-nine that did not go astray."

He Jesus is telling the disciples that it is absurd to think that a shepherd would not go out to find even one missing sheep.

How intense Christ's individual care is! He is not willing to part with a single one of us. Each of us is important to Him. This also shows that He has infinite patience with us. With all of the foolish things we do, Jesus doesn't say: "Okay, that's it! I've had it! You've strayed one too many times. I'm not coming after you anymore."

No! No matter how many times we fall, Jesus persistently comes to restore us. Often, He has been patiently trying to reach us for a very long time before we finally accepted Him as Lord and Savior.

We also see here Christ's rejoicing care. When we stray from the path, Christ seeks us, finds us, forgives us, and then rejoices over us!

Let us praise the Lord for His individual, patient, rejoicing care as the Good Shepherd!

There were ninety and nine that safely lay
In the shelter of the fold,
But one was out on the hills away,
Far off from the gates of gold—
Away on the mountains wild and bare,
Away from the tender Shepherd's care,
Away from the tender Shepherd's care.

Elizabeth G. Clephane

A Heavenly Father

Every day we have the privilege of praying to our Father in heaven. Think about it: we can actually pray to God as our personal Father! And because He's a heavenly Father, and therefore a perfect Father, we get to enjoy the benefits that a perfect, caring Father provides. Let's look at just few of those advantages.

He's a heavenly Father, so He's never moody. He's a heavenly Father, so we have divine protection. He's a heavenly Father, so we have divine guidance. He's a heavenly Father, so His love never grows cold. He's a heavenly Father; therefore, I can have divine peace and comfort in a world that is chaotic and falling apart. He's a heavenly Father; therefore, I can be assured that He will provide perfectly and abundantly for all of my needs.

Because we live in a fallen world, no earthly father can be perfect. They all make mistakes, but we still love them. However, we have a heavenly Father who is perfect.

Be encouraged today. Don't be reticent about asking God to listen. We can take those cares to the heavenly Father, who knows us inside and out and knows how to care for us perfectly.

More holiness give me, More striving within;
More patience in suffering, More sorrow for sin;
More faith in my Saviour, More sense of His care;
More joy in His service, More purpose in prayer.

More gratitude give me, More trust in the Lord;
More pride in His glory, More hope in His Word;
More tears for His sorrows, More pain at His grief;
More meekness in trial, More praise for relief.

Philip P. Bliss

Restoration

One of our responsibilities as Christians is to confront a brother overtaken in sin, and yet most Christians today treat such confrontation as a crime. They don't want to get involved. In other words, our preaching becomes separate from our practice. We will preach from the pulpit no tolerance for sin, but when it comes to real life, we have a great tolerance for sin in the lives of fellow believers. We will talk about it and preach about it. However, if a fellow Christian decides to live in sin—adultery, for example—we just turn our heads, mumble to ourselves about it being wrong in God's eyes, and decide that it's not our business.

Turning our heads in that situation is not biblical. Proverbs 27:5 says, "Open rebuke is better Than love carefully concealed." In other words, if we really love our brother, we will confront him.

Galatians 6:1 says, "Brethren, if a man is overtaken in any trespass, you who are spiritual restore such a one in a spirit of gentleness, considering yourself lest you also be tempted." So the spiritual man, the godly man, the man who is concerned for his brother, will confront his brother if he has fallen into sin—not so that he can kick him, but to restore him!

God help us to love our Christian brethren and be compassionate enough to take the time to get involved, to confront them, and to love them and see them restored.

Down in the human heart, Crushed by the tempter,
Feelings lie buried that grace can restore;
Touch by a loving heart, Wakened by kindness,
Chords that are broken will vibrate once more.

Fanny Crosby

Two or Three Gathered

You probably have heard Matthew 18:20 quoted many times in prayer meetings during your Christian walk. Jesus said, "For where two or three are gathered together in My name, I am there in the midst of them." However, the context of this verse has nothing to do with a prayer meeting. Jesus is referring to the two or three witnesses who go and confront a brother who is in sin. In other words, when a church implements church discipline, they have to take two or three witnesses. In effect, God says, "As you do it according to My Word, I am there in your midst while that confrontation of restoring a sinning saint is taking place."

This verse wouldn't make sense if it was referring to a prayer meeting. People often quote this verse and say, "Okay, Lord, there are two or three in this place, so we know you're in our midst." Well, what if there was only one of you? Would God not honor your prayers? Of course He would! What if there were one thousand of you? Does that mean that God is superabundantly in that place? No! The Bible declares that God is omnipresent and always attentive to the prayers of His people.

The point then is twofold: we need to keep Scripture in context, and God hears the prayers of His people, whether one or one thousand!

Power in prayer, Lord, power in prayer!
Here amid earth's sin and sorrow and care,
Men lost and dying, souls in despair;
O give me power, power in prayer!

Albert S. Reitz

Limitless Forgiveness

One of the hardest things for us to do is to forgive others. We see that in the world every day. Unfortunately, Christians struggle with it just as much as anyone else. On one occasion (Matthew 18:21), Peter really thought he had a handle on true forgiveness; so he said to Jesus: "How often shall my brother sin against me, and I forgive him? Up to seven times?" As he spoke, Peter really thought he understood forgiveness. He had been taught by the rabbis that you should forgive your brother up to three times.

You will agree that most men can't even forgive another person one time. According to what Peter had been taught, forgiving his brother three times was being spiritual. Peter doubled what he had learned and added one for good measure and then said, "How about this Lord: I'll forgive my brother seven times!" And I'm sure Peter was patting himself on the back thinking: "You've outdone yourself this time, Peter. My, you're spiritual!"

What was Jesus' response? "I do not say to you, up to seven times, but up to seventy times seven." In other words, our forgiveness of others is to be limitless because Christ's forgiveness of us is limitless.

When we forgive, we ride the crest of love's cosmic wave; we walk in stride with God.

L. B. Smedes

Don't Be a Statistic

No one has to tell us that divorce has become the great tragedy of the last half of this century. In the 1950s, the divorce rate was two per one thousand people. By the early 1970s, that figure had doubled. Today it has tripled: each year there are more than one million divorces in the United States alone. That means two million crushed lives, besides children, relatives, and friends. In fact, it would be surprising if any of us have not been directly or indirectly affected by divorce.

I could go on with all of the gory details and list a mass of statistics, but the point is, don't become a statistic. If you are married, don't let the devil rip you off. You may say, "Well, what can I do?" You can do plenty. First of all, your Christian bookstore is literally overflowing in books dealing with marriage. Better than that, God's Word is full of instruction. Try Ephesians 5. If your church offers a marriage course or seminar, sign up and get involved.

With the availability of all of those aids and more, it is obvious that marriages are not suffering because of a lack of knowledge. Rather, they are suffering from a lack of applying that knowledge. Simply put, marriage is work, and if we want our marriage to be all that God wants it to be, we are going to have to put Him in the center of it. Don't be a statistic; work at your marriage!

It seems preposterous that throughout our lives we train ourselves on how to be successful at most anything. We learn how to be the best in competitive sports, in careers, even in parenting, but we are negligent when it comes to educating ourselves on how to have a successful, happy marriage. With our focus on God, giving up self will come easier and we will find ourselves putting our spouse first over our own needs—then the marriage will succeed.

B. R. S.

Singleness

Are you single? In 1 Corinthians 7:32–33, Paul says, "He who is unmarried cares for the things of the Lord—how he may please the Lord. But he who is married cares about the things of the world—how he may please his wife."

Think about it! When you get married, you have a responsibility to your spouse; when you are unmarried, you have more time on your hands to serve the Lord. Admittedly, the Lord, in His perfect timing, will bring a spouse into your life; but until then, here are some suggestions to keep yourself pure:

Channel your energy into spiritual service. Get deeply involved at your church.

Keep yourself busy doing things with other Christians. "Idle time is the devil's playground."

Pray and stay. Pray daily and stay in God's world daily.

Don't allow yourself to be consumed with is-this-the-right-one syndrome. Serve God and trust Him to bring the most suitable candidate into your life in His perfect timing.

Be cautious where you go and what you allow your thoughts to take in.

Praise God and be content! He is in control and knows exactly what He's doing according to His plan for your life.

Be encouraged! There is so much that God can do through us during a season of singleness. We can use our singleness for God's glory, magnify Him in all we say and do, and reap the benefits!

Let the words of my mouth and the meditation of my heart
Be acceptable in Your sight,
O Lord, my strength and my Redeemer.

Psalm 19:14

Boldness

Boldness is something many Christians struggle with; yet it is something that can and should be possessed. Jesus was bold. The people said of Him in John 7:26: "Look! He speaks boldly!" Jesus was the personification of boldness. He never slinked or cowered when He was assaulted by His enemies. He always stood up for truth, and so should we as His children. The question is, how do we do it? How can we as believers grow in boldness? There are two ways.

First, abide in Christ. Spend time with Jesus. For example, we read in Acts 4:13: "Now when they [the Sanhedrin] saw the boldness of Peter and John, and perceived that they were uneducated and untrained men, they marveled. And they realized that they had been with Jesus." When you spend time with Jesus, when you abide in Christ, His life becomes part of yours, and the fruit of that is boldness.

Second, pray for boldness. We read in Acts 4:31, "And when they had prayed, the place where they were assembled together was shaken; and they were all filled with the Holy Spirit, and they spoke the word of God with boldness." The point is this: after they prayed for boldness, they received boldness. God wants us to be bold. The Bible says in 2 Timothy 1:7, "For God has not given us a spirit of fear, but of power and of love and of a sound mind." There is no fear in Christ, but His power and boldness are available to us.

When we need boldness to stand up for truth, we can abide in Christ and ask Him for it. He'll bestow it upon us as needed.

> *I love to tell the story;*
> *'Tis pleasant to repeat.*
> *It seems each time I tell it,*
> *More wonderfully sweet;*
> *I love to tell the story,*
> *For some have never heard*
> *The message of salvation*
> *From God's own Holy word.*
>
> *Katherine Hankey*

Sins That Are Blotted Out

In Acts 3:19, Peter preached to the crowd and said, "Repent therefore and be converted, that your sins may be blotted out."

That was good news to the Jews, because they had been taught that their sin was never blotted out; it was only covered, and even then, not for very long. Every time they sinned, they had to go to the temple and offer a sacrifice to atone for their sin. But invariably, as soon as they left the temple and climbed on their camel, someone would cut them off on the road. This probably caused them to sin in their heart, and they had to go back to the temple to make atonement for their sin. So sin was never blotted out; it was only covered for a while.

The term blotted out is not the idea of marking over but rather of erasure. Most ancient writing was done on papyrus; and the ink that was used contained no acid, as does our modern-day ink. As a result, the ink did not bite into the papyrus—it just sat on the surface. When you wanted to erase the writing, you simply took a damp sponge and wiped it out. No trace. That's exactly what Peter is saying: repent of your sins, be converted into Christ Jesus, and He will wipe your sins away as if they were never there.

No trace! That is why Paul says in Romans 8:1, "There is therefore now no condemnation to those who are in Christ Jesus." Why? Because their sins have been blotted out!

Jesus paid it all,
All to Him I owe;
Sin had left a crimson stain,
He washed it white as snow.

E. M. Hall

Total Surrender

In Matthew 19:16–22, we read about the rich young ruler who came to Jesus asking for guidance in what he needed to do to have eternal life. He listened to what Jesus had to say and even had some dialogue with Him, yet he went away sorrowful because he was not willing to part with his many possessions.

Upon the departure of the young man, Jesus turned to His disciples and said, "Assuredly, I say to you that it is hard for a rich man to enter the kingdom of heaven" (verse 23). Jesus was not saying that if we have money, we cannot enter heaven. He was, however, pointing to the area in this man's life that was more important than his relationship with God. It wasn't that this man had money; it was that money had him.

We need to consider this carefully. It may not be money in our life; it may be our spouse, it may be our job, or it may be a hobby. Whatever we set as a premium in our life over God is what Christ will want from us. Jesus always puts His finger right on the very thing that we make the priority in our lives and says, "That is what I want you to surrender to me as a token of your love!"

Sometimes God ask us to surrender something in our life, and we are reluctant about it. When that happens, we need to surrender it to Christ. We must take it to the foot of the cross as an idol in our life, and leave it there, never to pick it up again. Make it an offering and demonstration of our affection to Jesus Christ as our Lord.

May the Lord strengthen us as we step out in boldness and in total surrender.

> *All to Jesus I surrender,*
> *Lord, I give myself to Thee;*
> *Fill me with Thy love and power;*
> *Let Thy blessing fall on me.*
> *I surrender all, I surrender all,*
> *All to Thee, my blessed Saviour,*
> *I surrender all.*
>
> *J. W. Van DeVenter*

The Same Eternal Life

One of the most beautiful attributes of God is that He does not play favorites. He is no respecter of persons. To those who call upon Him, He distributes His love equally.

Jesus illustrated this in the parable of the workers in the vineyard in Matthew 20:1–16. He said the owner of a vineyard went out at various hours of the day to employ workers. At the end of the day, as agreed upon, he gave a day's wage (a denarius) to the men who had worked all day. But he also gave those who came in to work at various hours a day's wage. Jesus was illustrating the fact that everyone who gets saved receives the same eternal life.

Some people get the idea that those who come to the Lord at the end of their life are going to get a little shack in the corner of heaven. Like a celestial shantytown. Then those who were saved as teenagers and served the Lord their whole lives will be living in uptown heaven estates. It doesn't work that way. John 14:2 tells us that we will all be living in the Father's house.

Christians, be encouraged. All believers will receive the crown of life (James 1:12). All believers will receive the crown of righteousness (2 Timothy 4:8). All believers will receive the crown of glory (1 Peter 5:4).

There's a land that is fairer than day,
And by faith we can see it afar;
For the Father waits over the way
To prepare us a dwelling place there.

S. F. Bennett

Serve Others

I think we would all agree that we live in an egoistic, self-centered society. As a result, servanthood is a word that is hardly spoken and rarely demonstrated. In fact, if you do not promote yourself, toot your horn, or push yourself to the top, you are considered a little strange. Pride, self-esteem, self-reliance, and self-accomplishment are actually seen as virtues in our society.

The truth of the matter, however, is this: the more you promote yourself, the weaker all of your relationships become. Just look at a team sport. When you have people who want to promote only themselves, then team spirit and cohesiveness begin to fall apart.

How about the business world? When you have someone at work who wants to push his or her agenda for personal benefit, regardless of how it affects others, you are going to have chaos.

When self-fulfillment and self-gratification are the sole motivators, rather than humility and servanthood, there is going to be disunity, disharmony, division, envy, jealousy, anger, bitterness, and flat-out ruin. That is why Jesus taught us to be servants.

God grant us the ability today to serve one another, rather than ourselves!

> *Out in the highways and byways of life,*
> *Many are weary and sad;*
> *Carry the sunshine where darkness is rife,*
> *Making the sorrowing glad.*
> *Give as 'twas given to you in your need,*
> *Love as the Master loved you;*
> *Be to the helpless a helper indeed,*
> *Unto your mission be true.*
>
> *I. B. Wilson*

Everybody, Somebody, Anybody, Nobody

There were four people in the church whose names were Everybody, Somebody, Anybody, and Nobody. The church had responsibilities that needed to be filled, and Everybody was asked to help. Everybody was sure that Somebody would do it. Anybody could have done it. But do you know who did it? Nobody! It ended up that Everybody blamed Somebody, when Nobody did what Anybody could have done.

The church grounds needed some work, and Somebody was asked to help. But Somebody got angry about that, because Anybody could have done it just as well, and after all, it was really Everybody's job. In the end, the work was given to Nobody, and Nobody did a fine job. On and on this went.

Whenever work was to be done, Nobody could always be counted on. Nobody visited the sick. Nobody gave liberally. Nobody shared his faith. In short, Nobody was a very faithful member. Finally, the day came when Somebody left the church and took Anybody and Everybody with him. Guess who was left? Nobody!

If you are not involved in service to your church family, I encourage you today to become a servant there. Jesus said in Matthew 20:26, "But whoever desires to become great among you, let him be your servant."

To the work! To the work! We are servants of God,
Let us follow the path that our Master has trod;
With the balm of His counsel our strength to renew,
Let us do with our might what our hands find to do.

Fanny Crosby

Christ's Coronation

When monarchies of past ages coronated a king, they did so to highlight the majesty, glory, power, dignity, and office of the king. The new king would be dressed in royal splendor as he was paraded through the streets on a royal stallion. Yet when Jesus came into Jerusalem being heralded as the Messiah, He did not come in regal pageantry or earthly splendor. He purposely came through town on a lowly donkey. He came in humility.

Think about it: Everything Jesus had during His life was borrowed. He was born in a borrowed manger. He slept in a borrowed bed. He borrowed ships for traveling and preaching. He borrowed a donkey on His coronation day. And when He died, He was buried in a borrowed tomb. Jesus did not come in pomp, but rather in humility.

Therefore, Jesus' earthly coronation seems contradictory and inappropriate, because He is the King of kings and the Lord of lords. Why did Jesus live in such humility? He was showing us that He didn't come to be served, but to serve. And He didn't come in the might of arms, but in the strength of His love.

Let us thank the Lord that He was born and lived in humility and love. When He comes again, it will be to judge in power and great glory.

He left His Father's throne above,
So free, so infinite His grace!
Emptied Himself of all but love
And bled for Adam's helpless race.

Wesley

The Neos of God

When the Jews spoke of God's temple, they would speak of either the hieron or the neos. The hieron referred to the greater part of the temple site: the court of the Gentiles, the court of the women, the court of the Israelites, the court of the priests, and so on. The neos describes that which was the actual temple—the holy place and the Holy of Holies.

The Holy of Holies could be entered only by the high priest once a year to make atonement for the sins of the nation. It contained the ark of the covenant and was the place of God's glory and presence. When Jesus died on the cross, the veil that separated the Holy of Holies from the rest of the temple was torn from top to bottom, signifying that all men could now come into the presence of God through Christ. Jesus made atonement for our sins once and for all.

We read in 1 Corinthians 6:19, "Do you not know that your body is the temple of the Holy Spirit who is in you, whom you have from God?" The Greek word for temple in this passage is "neos." Paul is saying that when you give your life to Christ, your sins are forgiven—past, present, and future—and your body becomes the neos of God. Your heart literally houses the very presence of God!

Thank the Lord today for the overwhelming privilege of being the very neos of God!

Christ in you, the hope of glory.

Colossians 1:27

Unspiritual Paraphernalia

In Matthew 21:12, we find Jesus cleansing the temple, and doing so with indignant anger. He drove out all those who were selling things and ripping off God's people. God's house had become a place of pandering unspiritual paraphernalia instead of promoting prayer.

I believe that the Lord is still grieved over all the unspiritual merchandising that is being done to God's people today, all under the banner of Christianity.

For example, I read of a guy who will send you a tiny packet of honey. He says, "Fast with me so that your eyes can be enlightened. Then together we can break our fast with the honey. Sow a seed with me. Just send $77." Or how about the anointed plastic glove? "Wear your faith glove while you write out your best check now." Or you will be sent a black and white picture of Jesus: "Look at the eyes in the picture for about forty seconds under good light, and then blink your eyes, look up, and you will see Jesus the way I did when I saw Him in the Spirit." There are people who will send you sanitary wipes to anoint your eyes. There are faith handkerchiefs, prayer cloths, prayer rugs, depressions nails, special anointing oil, anointed water, anointed mantles, anointed pencils, and on and on.

The fact is, God wants a personal relationship with you, and you don't need all this unspiritual paraphernalia in order to walk with Him.

Take time to be holy, the world rushes on;
Spend much time in secret with Jesus alone;
By looking to Jesus like Him thou shalt be;
Thy friends in thy conduct His likeness shall see.

W. D. Longstaff

Living Water

After Jesus had given living water to the woman at the well, we are told in John 4:28 that she "left her waterpot [and] went her way into the city." This little detail expresses three wonderful truths.

Number one: It expresses fulfillment. This woman came looking for physical water, as she had every day of her life. However, now she had found living water that would satisfy her for eternity. Satisfied with Christ, she had all that she needed. Jesus said in Matthew 6:33, "But seek first the kingdom of God and His righteousness, and all these things shall be added to you."

Number two: This deserted waterpot speaks of leaving our old life behind and not looking back. In Luke 9:62, Jesus said, "No one, having put his hand to the plow, and looking back, is fit for the kingdom of God." This woman had left her past behind to follow only Christ. Similarly, in Luke 9:23, Jesus said, "If anyone desires to come after Me, let him deny himself, and take up his cross daily, and follow Me." When I come to Christ, I no longer want to do the things I used to do or hang around the people I used to hang around with. Once a person has been filled with living water, he doesn't want to go back to the old waterpots of this world.

Number three: The woman's going into the city shows us the response of a truly converted person. Once she was born again, she instinctively went into the city and shared her newfound faith. Having been filled with the water of life, she was compelled and eager to share it with everyone else.

Have you found the water of life? Have you tasted the living waters? Are you satisfied? Have you left behind the old waterpots of your past, or do you go back to them from time to time? Are you in love with Christ? And if you are, are you sharing Him with others? Praise the Lord for His living water, and may we take it to a parched world.

Your eternal destiny lies in your response to the Truth.

Author Unknown

Following Christ

Jesus declared in John 8:12, "He who follows Me shall not walk in darkness, but have the light of life." What does it mean to follow Christ?

People say that they follow Christ, yet in Matthew 7:22–23, Jesus says: "Many will say to Me in that day, 'Lord, Lord, have we not prophesied in Your name, cast out demons in Your name, and done many wonders in Your name?' And then I will declare to them, 'I never knew you; depart from Me, you who practice lawlessness!'" So we must understand what it really means to follow Christ. The New Testament Greek word used here, akolouthein, has four related meanings:

First, it was used to describe a soldier who followed his commanding officer's orders without reservation. The Bible teaches us that we are soldiers of Christ (2 Timothy 2:3–4). To follow Christ means to obey Him faithfully as our commander in chief.

Second, this word was used to describe a servant who was at the beck and call of his master. The Bible tells us that we are servants of Christ (Colossians 3:24). To follow Christ means to stop serving oneself and to serve others.

Third, it was used to describe a citizen who followed the law of the land. The Bible says that we are citizens of heaven (Philippians 3:20). To follow Christ means to obey His commands.

Fourth, it was used to describe a student who followed the principles of his teacher. The Bible tells us to study God's Word and to be doers of it (James 1:22).

Today, let us follow the Lord as soldiers, servants, citizens, and students.

Salvation is free, but discipleship costs everything we have.

Billy Graham

Nothing but Leaves

In Mark 11:14, Jesus cursed a fig tree because it had no fruit but only leaves. By cursing the fig tree, Jesus was illustrating the condition of the Jews. He had come to His own people, but they didn't know Him. The Jews had religion (leaves), but no fruit. A lot of people are like that—a lot of religion, but no inward change—and it amounts to nothing but leaves.

Contemplate the poet's words below.

Nothing but leaves, the Spirit grieves over wasted life,
Or sins committed while conscience slept,
Promises made but never kept,
Hatred battle and strife—nothing but leaves.
Nothing but leaves, no garnered sheaves of life's
fair ripened grain,
Words, idle words, for earnest deeds,
We sow our seeds, lo tares and weeds,
We reap with toil and pain—nothing but leaves.
Nothing but leaves, memory weaves
no veil to hide the past,
As we retrace our weary way,
Counting each lost and misspent day,
We find sadly at last—nothing but leaves.
And shall we meet the Master
so bearing our withered leaves?
The Savior looks for perfect fruit,
We stand before him humbled, mute,
Waiting the words he breathes—nothing but leaves.

Author Unknown

Not Another Excuse!

In Luke 14, Jesus told a parable about a man who held a great feast. But when it was time to come to the banquet, the people with one accord began to make excuses.

The first guy said he couldn't come because he had just bought some land, and he needed

to go to see it. Talk about a poor excuse! What kind of person would purchase property without seeing it first?

The second guy said he couldn't come because he had just purchased five oxen, and he needed to test them. Again, what kind of fool would buy five oxen without first making sure they weren't lame? That would be like buying a used car from Greedy Gary's Auto Utopia without taking it for a spin around the block.

The third guy said he couldn't come to the feast because he'd just gotten married. Well, no one ever told him he couldn't bring his wife.

All of these people made up crazy excuses to put off going to the feast, to put off the kingdom, to put off Christ. They treated the invitation as though it were a trivial thing. People today treat Christ's kingdom the same way—as if it were a trivial issue, when in fact accepting the invitation is the most important choice they can ever make.

If you have never given your life to Jesus Christ, don't make another excuse. Don't refuse the invitation. Instead, come to the greatest feast of all time. Give your life to Christ!

Take me as I am, Lord,
And make me all Your own;
Make my heart Your palace
And Your royal throne.

Anonymous

The Way, the Truth, and the Life

There are those who say there are many ways to God: If you are a Hindu, that is all right; if you are a Mormon, that is okay as well; if you want to seek God through crystals and guides, that is all right. But the truth is, it is not all right to seek God in those other ways! The only way to God is through the way—Jesus Christ.

A lot of people say they have truth. A lot of people spend their lives searching for truth. More times than not, what they find is only the truth they want to hear. However, the Bible tells us that righteousness and truth are the foundation of God's throne. The only and most pure form of truth that we really know is the truth—Jesus Christ.

Then there are those who say that life is climbing to the top of Mount Everest. Or life is having all the money you could ever need to buy anything you want. Or life is being at the top of your profession. The fact is, we will all die, and what will it profit a man if he gains the whole world but loses his soul?

The only true life is eternal life with Jesus Christ. In John 14:6, Jesus said, "I am the way, the truth, and the life." Without the way, there is no going. Without the truth, there is no knowing. And without the life, there is no living. Jesus is the way, the truth, and the life!

I must need go home by the way of the cross,
There's no other way but this;
I shall never get sight of the gates of light,
If the way of the cross I miss.
The way of the cross leads home,
The way of the cross leads home.
It is sweet to know as I onward go,
The way of the cross leads home.

J. B. Pounds

Did You Know?

Did you know there are three things that God cannot do?

God cannot lie. (Titus 1:2)

God cannot learn, because He knows all things. (Job 31:4)

God cannot make you love Him, because He has given you a free will.

Did you know that there are four things that God doesn't know?

God doesn't know a sin that He doesn't hate. (Proverbs 8:13)

God doesn't know a sinner whom He doesn't love. (John 3:16)

God doesn't know another way to heaven except through His Son. (1 Timothy 2:5)

If you have never given your life to Christ, God doesn't know a better time to receive Him than right now.

Psalm 95:8 says, "Today, if you will hear His voice: 'Do not harden your hearts.'" 2 Corinthians 6:2 says, "Now is the day of salvation." Draw near to Him, and open your heart to Him right now!

Jesus is tenderly calling thee home,
Calling today, Calling today;
Why from the sunshine of love wilt thou roam
Farther and farther away?
Jesus is pleading; O list to His voice,
Hear Him today, hear Him today;
They who believe on His name shall rejoice;
Quickly arise and away.

Fanny Crosby

Salvation Is Nontransferable

In Matthew 25, we find Jesus teaching by presenting the parable of the ten virgins. The five virgins who didn't have oil asked those who did for some of theirs. But the wise virgins, who had oil, said, "No, lest there should not be enough for us and you; but go rather to those who sell, and buy for yourselves."

In this parable, the oil represents salvation. Five virgins were saved and five were not. We are taught a very important spiritual principle here: salvation is a direct gift from God and is nontransferable.

That does not mean we can't share our faith with others. In that sense, God does use us as His agents to transfer His love and message to others.

What it means is that you cannot get to heaven based on another person's faith! A man cannot borrow a relationship with God; he must possess it himself. A person cannot borrow the character of Christ; he must be clothed in it. Someone cannot live on the spiritual revenue of someone else. Each individual must make an individual decision to trust Christ as his Savior and Lord!

Have you been to Jesus for the cleansing power?
Are you washed in the blood of the Lamb?
Are you fully trusting in His grace this hour?
Are you washed in the blood of the Lamb?
Are you washed in the blood?
In the soul-cleansing blood of the Lamb?
Are your garments spotless?
Are they white as snow?
Are you washed in the blood of the Lamb?

E. A. Hoffman

Channels of Blessing

In Acts 3, we see Peter and John healing a lame man at one of the temple gates. The thing that strikes me is the availability and the sensitivity of these two men. No doubt they had seen many other lame men along the road, and yet they were sensitive at this point. Their alertness to hear the Holy Spirit and be available made them a channel by which God would work.

We are often in such a rush that we are neither sensitive nor available to God. There are people, both inside and outside the church, who are lame with hurt and need our touch. There are people lame with defeat who need our prayers. We need to be sensitive to those people and come to their aid. We need to be sensitive to those crying out for help in the world. The world is searching for purpose. The world is reaching out for help, and God is looking for hands to use.

God help us to be channels of blessing to those in need.

Is your life a channel of blessing?
Are you burdened for those who are lost?
Have you urged upon those who are straying?
The Saviour who died on the cross?

Make me a channel of blessing today,
Make me a channel of blessing I pray,
My life possessing, my service blessing,
Make me a channel of blessing today.

Harper G. Smith

Christian Evidence

In his book Protestant Christian Evidences, Bernard Ramm writes a series of answers to a question that he asked. The question: "If God became incarnate, what kind of man would he be?"

Here are six of his answers in abbreviated form:

1. If God became incarnate,

2. We would expect Him to be sinless.

3. We would expect Him to be holy.

4. We would expect His words to be the greatest words ever spoken to man.

5. We would expect Him to exert a profound power over human personality.

6. We would expect Him to perform supernatural doings.

7. We would expect Him to manifest the love of God.

Bernard Ramm concludes, "Of all the human beings who ever lived, Jesus Christ alone meets all those criteria."

The Bible states that Jesus was 100 percent man and at the same time 100 percent God. The life that Jesus lived is evidence that He alone is who He said He was: the Son of Man and the Son of God!

Fairest Lord Jesus, Ruler of all nature,
O Thou of God and man the Son;
Thee will I cherish, Thee will I honor,
Thou, my soul's glory, joy and crown.

Author Unknown

Pharisees

In his commentary, William Barclay explains the religiosity of the Pharisees by pointing out no fewer than six different kinds of Pharisees. See if you recognize any similarities to the people of today:

There was the shoulder Pharisee. He would wear his good deeds literally written on his shoulders, so everyone could see them and admire his piousness.

There was the wait-a-little-while Pharisee. This guy would always come up with a spiritual reason why he could not do something.

There was the bruised and bleeding Pharisee. This guy said it was a sin to look upon a woman in public, so in order to keep himself from sinning, he shut his eyes. Consequently, he bumped into walls of obstructions. Later, he displayed his bruises as spirituality.

There was the hump-backed Pharisee. This guy displayed his piousness by slouching over in a humpback position, to appear holy when walking in public.

There was the ever-reckoning Pharisee. This man kept a ledger of all of his good deeds and believed that for every good deed he did, God was indebted to bless him in return.

There was the fearing Pharisee. He was in constant fear of divine judgment, and while he did everything he could to make sure the outward visage of his life was in order, he did nothing about his heart.

As we look at the different types of Pharisee, we realize that there are people today who fit into these categories. May God grant us boldness to share His love with these individuals and humility that, in the process, we ourselves don't become like the Pharisees in our walks with the Lord.

> *He is able, more than able,*
> *to accomplish what concerns me today;*
> *He is able, more than able,*
> *to handle anything that comes my way.*

> *Rory Noland and Greg Ferguson*

Zero Tolerance

Today more than at any other time in the history of the church, pagan religions and cults are successfully infiltrating Christian cultures. False doctrines and false prophets are flourishing at an alarming rate. Unfortunately, our nation has opened up the floodgates to paganism and false doctrine, and those who call upon the Lord need to be discerning.

Scripture warns us of these things. Paul said in 1 Timothy 4:1, "Now the Spirit expressly says that in latter times some will depart from the faith, giving heed to deceiving spirits and doctrines of demons." Peter said in 2 Peter 2:1, "But there were also false prophets among the people, even as there will be false teachers among you, who will secretly bring in destructive heresies, even denying the Lord who bought them, and bring on themselves swift destruction." John calls them antichrists in 1 John 2:18. Jude calls them filthy dreamers, brute beasts, spots, clouds without water, trees whose fruit withers, twice dead, raging waves of the sea, wandering stars, murmurers, complainers, and those who do not have the Spirit.

In light of that, it behooves us as Christians to be very discerning at all times. We need to have zero tolerance for false doctrine and to be on our guard lest we develop a divided heart.

If I'm to be whom You desire all throughout my life,
A vessel unto honor, Lord, to Thee,
And before Your throne to hear You say
that I have done my part,
Lord I need an undivided heart.
If I'm to live in truth and love to glorify Your name;
If for a living sacrifice to be.
And to share the joy, the grace
and peace Your Spirit does impart,
Lord I need an undivided heart.

Dan Marks

Our Hope

As Christians, we are fascinated, motivated, and excited when we discuss the coming of our Lord. It is our hope; it is our joy. Why? Because when Jesus returns to earth, He is going to bring in His millennial and eternal kingdom. So we get excited when we start talking about the second coming of Jesus. But it seems that very often, unbelievers are fascinated as well.

There are a couple of reasons for the unbelievers' fascination. First, God has placed a void in every man's heart that only He can fill, and the very mention of the return of Christ meets with that natural pull that God created in each of us. Second, unbelievers see the world falling apart at the seams, and as they hear you share the truths that are in the Bible and see the incredible exactness by which those are prophesied, they are pricked in their hearts. A curiosity is sparked.

Christ's coming is our hope and joy, and we need to share that hope with others. We need to tell them that through faith in His name, they may have that hope as well.

When the trumpet of the Lord shall sound,
And time shall be no more,
And the morning breaks, eternal, bright and fair;
When the saved of earth shall gather
And our work on earth is done,
When the roll is called up yonder, I'll be there.

James M. Black

Our Heavenly Inheritance

If you were to stop and contemplate your heavenly inheritance, you might wonder what it includes. What does Scripture say? Here is just a sampling described by Jesus in the book of Revelation:

"To him who overcomes I will give to eat from the tree of life, which is in the midst of the Paradise of God." (Revelation 2:7)

"He who overcomes shall not be hurt by the second death." (Revelation 2:11)

"To him who overcomes I will give some of the hidden manna to eat. And I will give him a white stone, and on the stone a new name written which no one knows except him who receives it." (Revelation 2:17)

"And he who overcomes, and keeps My works until the end, to him I will give power over the nations . . . and I will give him the morning star." (Revelation 2:26–28)

"He who overcomes shall be clothed in white garments, and I will not blot out his name from the Book of Life; but I will confess his name before My Father and before His angels." (Revelation 3:5)

"He who overcomes, I will make him a pillar in the temple of My God, and he shall go out no more. I will write on him the name of My God and the name of the city of My God, the New Jerusalem, which comes down out of heaven from My God. And I will write on him My new name." (Revelation 3:12)

"To him who overcomes I will grant to sit with Me on My throne, as I also overcame and sat down with My Father on His throne." (Revelation 3:21)

> *Oh! What an overwhelming blessing that awaits us in our Father's house!*
> *Let it be said of us that the Lord was our passion,*
> *That with gladness we bore every cross we were given;*
> *That we fought the good fight, that we finished the course,*
> *Knowing within us the power of the risen Lord.*
>
> *Steve Fry*

Do You Have Oil?

In the parable of the ten virgins (Matthew 25), we are told that five virgins were shut out of the wedding feast and only five were allowed in. The amazing thing in this parable is the similarities between these women. They each had an invitation to the wedding. They each had an interest in the wedding; otherwise, they wouldn't have waited. And they each had a lamp. What was the difference? Five had oil and five did not! In other words: five were saved, and five were not.

The point Jesus was making is that there are those who appear to be Christians. They walk like, talk like, and act like Christians. They love to associate with Christians. They would never think of saying anything against the church. But they only have an external association with Christ.

When Christ returns as the Bridegroom coming for His bride (the church), there will be people we thought were Christians but in reality were never born again.

When Jesus exhorts His disciples at the end of this parable to be ready, what is He saying? Precisely this: Make sure that I am your Lord! Make sure that there is a change in your heart!

You are deserving of all the praises, Lord.
And I am yearning to be in Your presence once more.
Deep inside, my heart is burning; I want to
give You more;
For You're the only one that I adore.
How great You are. How great You are.
You are the mighty King and You've come to
reign in me.
How great You are! How great You are!

Shannon Fogal Wexelberg

Flattery

In Matthew 22, we read that the Herodians and the Pharisees came to Jesus, trying to entrap Him with a question regarding taxes. Leading up to it, they said in verse 1,: "Teacher, we know that You are true, and teach the way of God in truth; nor do You care about anyone, for You do not regard the person of men." In other words, You're not a man-pleaser.

These men were attempting to flatter Jesus. They were trying to butter Him up before entrapping Him. They were not sincere. If they had really believed that He was true and taught the truth, why hadn't they given their lives to Him? They were using one of the devil's favorite deceptions—flattery. Flattery is evil, because it laces truth with lies.

As Christians, we are told to speak the truth in love (Ephesians 4:15). When we say things to other people that may be true, it is sin when our purpose for saying them is to get something in return. We are called to speak the truth in love, not the truth for our gain!

God grant us the ability to genuinely encourage one another in the faith—not for personal gain, not so people will think that we are really generous, not so that we can butter them up to secure a favor, but simply to encourage them in God's agape love!

He's the God of the meek and lowly,
He's the God of the rich and the poor,
He's the great God of the universe,
He's my God forevermore.

Wagoner

Building Walls

When Nehemiah was allowed to go to Jerusalem and rebuild the walls, God had already brought His people back there from exile some ninety years earlier. The problem was that they had done nothing to rebuild the walls. The temple was built, but the walls of God's city were in shambles.

Unfortunately, this is true of many Christians' spirituality today. God has saved them, redeemed them, and brought them into a right relationship with Himself. However, there are things in their lives that they keep leaving undone but that God wants them to build up.

Just because we are saved does not mean we can put our life on cruise control; it doesn't mean we can just "abide and glide." No! Instead, our lives should be marked by continual striving toward godliness and holiness.

Don't live in "sloppy agape." Don't abide and glide. Rather, set your mind to build up the walls of our most precious faith!

Living for Jesus a life that is true,
Striving to please Him in all that I do,
Yielding allegiance, glad-hearted and free,
This is the pathway of blessing for me.

O Jesus, Lord and Savior, I give myself to Thee;
For Thou, in Thine atonement,
didst give Thyself for me;
I own no other Master; my heart shall be Thy throne;
My life I give, henceforth to live, o Christ,
for Thee alone.

T. O. Chisholm

The Good Hand of God

When Nehemiah was allowed to go and rebuild the walls of Jerusalem, he said that the king granted his request "according to the good hand of my God upon me" (Nehemiah 2:8). Nehemiah gave the credit to God. Nehemiah did a lot of preparation; he did his homework. But he didn't say, "Yes, the king granted my request because I was a wise businessman and did my homework." No!

Nehemiah had the proper perspective. He realized that nothing could have been accomplished outside of God's good hand being upon him. Oh! How important it is that we give God the glory and not take credit ourselves, whenever He does anything through us.

Psalm 115:1 says, "Not unto us, O Lord, not unto us, But to Your name give glory." God will not use a man or woman in the capacity that He did Nehemiah if they want to take the glory themselves. Nehemiah, like all praying, humble men, did not ascribe his success to his own ingenuity but realized that in all issues of his life, it was the controlling hand of God that directed him.

Let us give God the glory for all that He has done in our lives. Let us give thanks for His good hand upon us!

To God be the glory, great things He hath done;
So loved He the world that He gave us His Son,
Who yielded His life, an atonement for sin,
And opened the life gate that all may go in.
O perfect redemption, the purchase of blood,
To every believer the promise of God;
The vilest offender who truly believes,
That moment from Jesus a pardon receives.
Praise the Lord, praise the Lord,
Let the earth hear His voice!
Praise the Lord, praise the Lord,
Let the people rejoice!
O come to the Father, through Jesus the Son,
And give Him the glory, great things He hath done.

Fanny Crosby

The Good Work

Once Nehemiah came to Jerusalem and shared with the people his burden to rebuild the walls, we read in Nehemiah 2:18, "they set their hands to this good work." Some translations say, "They set themselves to work heartily." In other words, there was great determination. They were generous, competent, courageous, self-denying, devoted, and resolute! Their mindset was, Let's see it through to completion. Let's do it! O God, that every member of Christ's church would have a desire to rise up and build—that every believer in Christ would set their hands to serve. If only we would all be generous, competent, courageous, self-denying, devoted, and resolute servants for Jesus Christ!

Are you steadfast in your service for God? Are you generous and resolute in that which you give Him? Have you set your hands to do the good work?

May we be like those of Nehemiah's day who rose to the occasion and did the good work!

> *To the work! To the work! We are servants of God,*
> *Let us follow the path that our Master has trod;*
> *With the balm of His counsel our strength to renew,*
> *Let us do with our might what our hands find to do.*

Fanny Crosby

True Citizenship

When we travel to another country, we're asked at customs, "Where is your citizenship?" Our response is usually "The United States." But in God's eyes, the Christian's response should be "Heaven."

The Bible tells us in Philippians 3:20, "For our citizenship is in heaven." As Christians, we are no longer obligated to earthly things but heavenly things. Ephesians 2:6 tells us that we are seated in heavenly places in Christ. We have died to this world, and we have been raised in Christ!

Do you perform your job at work as though you are a citizen of heaven or a citizen of earth? Do the words that leave your mouth have the accent of heaven or the accent of this world? If someone examined your relationship with the Lord, would they say that you are an alien or a citizen?

We are citizens of heaven! God grant us the ability to live our lives accordingly.

It may not be on the mountain's height,
or over the stormy sea;
It may not be at the battle's front
My Lord will have need of me;
But if by a still, small voice He calls to paths
I do not know,
I'll answer, dear Lord, with my hand in Thine,
I'll go where You want me to go.

I'll go where You want me to go, dear Lord,
O'er mountain or plain or sea;
I'll say what You want me to say, dear Lord,
I'll be what you want me to be.

Mary Brown

Encourage One Another

In 1 Thessalonians 5:11, we are exhorted to "comfort each other and edify one another." In Hebrews 10:24–25, we are commanded to meet regularly as God's people; one of the reasons stated is to encourage one another.

God's Word tells us that it is important for us to lift up and encourage one another. There have been times in my own Christian walk when I've felt like quitting. Sometimes responsibilities and pressures can weigh us down, and it has been in those times that a little word of encouragement has brightened my eyes and given me hope and strength. Remember this: God will use individuals in your life to encourage you and get your thinking back on track.

There are things we can do to help motivate ourselves, too, when the need arises and no one is around. I am reminded of an elderly friend who keeps things like thank-you notes, greeting cards, and mementos from special events. She tells me that recalling the people who were part of these treasures encourages her to recall their love and friendship. When she starts feeling lonely and depressed, she pulls out her box of memories and is encouraged. That is why the Bible says in Proverbs 12:25, "Anxiety in the heart of man causes depression, But a good word makes it glad."

Let us make it our goal today to encourage those who come across our path, especially those of our own household.

Consider what the Lord has done
Through those who've shown you love;
Thank them for their faithful deeds,
For blessings from above.

Spurgeon

The Parable of the Talents

In the parable of the talents (Matthew 25:14–30), Jesus illustrated how those who would, and some would not enter into His kingdom. The first two men doubled the talents that the master gave them. This represents that they are not saved by good works, but their good works manifest the inward transformation of salvation. On the other hand, the third man produced nothing. In fact, he buried his talent. This man illustrates to us an external association with the master but no changed life. He produced no labors because he had no inward change. He had no love for the master; otherwise, he would have at least put the talent in the bank.

Take note: The third man was not shut out of the kingdom because he committed a heinous crime. He didn't embezzle or misuse his master's talent; he simply buried it. If you are not a Christian, don't squander your opportunity. Today is the day of salvation.

> *Give me a faithful heart, likeness to Thee,*
> *That each departing day henceforth may see*
> *Some work of love begun, some deed of kindness done,*
> *Some wanderer sought and won something for Thee.*

S. D. Phelps

June 25

You Did It to Me

There once was a man called Martin of Tours. He was a Roman soldier who had been converted to Christianity during its early years. One day as he was entering a city, a beggar asked him for some money. Martin had no money, but noticing that the man was shivering in the cold, he took off his soldier's coat and gave it to him.

That night, Martin had a dream. In his dream, he saw the heavenly places, the angels, and in the midst of them, Jesus Christ. As he continued to look, he noticed that Jesus was wearing a Roman soldier's coat. In his dream, he asked Jesus why He was wearing that battered old coat. "Who gave it to you?" Martin asked. Jesus replied, "You did."

Matthew 25:34–40 tells us this about the time when Jesus comes again to set up His kingdom:

> "Then the King will say to those on His right hand, 'Come, you blessed of My Father, inherit the kingdom prepared for you from the foundation of the world: for I was hungry and you gave Me food; I was thirsty and you gave Me drink; I was a stranger and you took Me in; I was naked and you clothed Me; I was sick and you visited Me; I was in prison and you came to Me.'
>
> Then the righteous will answer Him, saying, 'Lord, when did we see You hungry and feed You, or thirsty and give You drink? When did we see You a stranger and take You in, or naked and clothe You? Or when did we see You sick, or in prison, and come to You?' And the King will answer and say to them, 'Assuredly, I say to you, inasmuch as you did it to one of the least of these My brethren, you did it *to Me.*'"

Lord, let us live out these truths in our lives!

> *Make me a blessing, make me a blessing,*
> *Out of my life may Jesus shine;*
> *Make me a blessing, o Savior, I pray,*
> *Make me a blessing to someone today.*
>
> *Ira B. Wilson*

Let Me Hold Lightly

As Christians, it is important that we keep our perspectives heavenbound rather than earthbound. The world is telling us to consume things and then purchase more—to cling to the things of this world.

However, Jesus said in Matthew 6:19–20, "Do not lay up for yourselves treasures on earth, where moth and rust destroy and where thieves break in and steal; but lay up for yourselves treasures in heaven."

Let me hold lightly things of this earth;
Transient treasures, what are they worth?
Moths can corrupt them, rust can decay;
All their bright beauty fades in a day.
Let me hold lightly temporal things—
I, who am deathless, I, who have wings!

Let me hold fast, Lord, things of the skies;
Quicken my vision, open my eyes!
Show me Thy riches, glory, and grace,
Boundless as time is, endless as space . . .
Let me hold lightly things that were mine—
Lord, Thou dost give me all that is Thine!

M. S. Nicholson

June 27

An Intercessor

The apostle Paul wrote in Philippians 1:3–4, "I thank my God upon every remembrance of you, always in every prayer of mine making request for you all with joy." One of the overriding traits in the life of Paul is that he was a man of prayer. And not just any prayer! He was a man who constantly interceded for others. He was a mighty man of intercessory prayer!

Remembering the kind of man Paul was reminds us that God is still looking for men and women who will be mighty in prayer.

Let this prayer be yours today:

Make me an intercessor, one who can really pray,
one of the Lord's remembrances, by the night as
well as day.
Make me an intercessor, in Spirit-touch with Thee,
and give the heavenly vision, praying to victory.
Make me an intercessor; teach me how to prevail,
to stand my ground and still pray, though powers of hell
prevail.
Make me an intercessor, sharing Thy death and life,
in praying claiming others, victory in the strife.
Make me an intercessor, willing for deeper death,
emptied, broken, then made anew, and filled
with living breath.
Make me an intercessor, reveal this mighty thing,
Thy wondrous possibility of paying back my King.
Make me an intercessor, hidden, unknown, set apart,
thought little of by those around, but satisfying
Thy heart.

Unknown

The Wonders of the Cross

The cross of Christ is the core of redemptive truth for us as Christians. C. H. Spurgeon put it this way: "Leave out the cross, and you have killed the religion of Jesus. Atonement by the blood of Jesus is not an arm of Christian truth; it is the heart of it." In other words, it is the heart of Christianity. The cross is the main event in the life of every believer. Every person, before he is born again, must be taken to the cross.

H. C. Trumbull said, "Calvary shows us how far men will go in sin, and how far God will go for man's salvation." Christ's death on the cross is not the end of the story; it is the theme of the story. It is the focal point of all Scripture. It wasn't nails that kept Him on the cross. It was His love for you and me!

Let us be reminded of our most precious faith—a faith that is rooted and grounded in the fact that Jesus Christ died on the cross for our sins, that sinful man might be brought near to the Most Holy God. Let us refresh ourselves in the wonder of our salvation!

Alas! And did my Savior bleed and did my Sovereign die?
Would He devote that sacred head for sinners such as I?
Was it for crimes that I have done He groaned upon the tree?
Amazing pity! Grace unknown! And love beyond degree!
But drops of grief can ne'er repay the debt of love I owe;
here, Lord, I give myself away
'Tis all that I can do!
At the cross, at the cross, where I first saw the light,
and the burden of my heart rolled away.
It was there by faith I received my sight,
and now I am happy all the day!

Watts and Hudson

Unrestrained Worship

In John chapter 12, we are introduced to one of the most beautiful expressions of worship ever told in the Gospels' accounts. In verse 3 we read: "Then Mary took a pound of very costly oil of spikenard, anointed the feet of Jesus, and wiped His feet with her hair. And the house was filled with the fragrance of the oil."

The next verses actually tell us that the perfume was worth a year's wages. Mary was so absolutely adoring in her worship that she lost all sense of restraint. Oh, the beauty of her worship! She took all that she had and poured it on Jesus. This was an act of uncalculated worship. She didn't sit down and think, "Now if I pour this oil on Jesus, I'm going to be short a year's wages." She didn't sit down and think, "What will others think about me?" No! She simply gave lavishly.

Love doesn't think of how little it can decently give; love gives to the utter limits. So often, our attitude in giving to God is "Now let's see, how much can I part with this week and still get by comfortably?" We know very little of the kind of worship that is not driven by economics.

Our worship should be "Lord, I love you so much, and I am so grateful for what you have done in my life, that I just can't help but give you my all!" That was Mary. Mary is the example of unmitigated, unrestrained, magnanimous love that pours out its heart in worship with no thought of return. Mary was simply so overwhelmed in her worship of her Lord that she gave extravagantly.

May we all learn how to give our all in our worship to Him, as Mary did!

Give as 'twas given to you in your need.
Love as the Master loved you;
Be to the helpless a helper indeed,
Unto your mission be true.
Wilson

At the Master's Feet

The study of Mary and Martha, the sisters of Lazarus, is a wonderful study. Mary is mentioned three times in the Gospels, and each time we find her at the feet of Jesus.

First, in Luke 10:39 she is introduced as Martha's "sister called Mary, who also sat at Jesus' feet and heard His word." Second, in John 11 Mary was notified that Jesus had come to her brother's tomb. We read in verse 32, "Then, when Mary came where Jesus was, and saw Him, she fell down at His feet." Finally, John 12:3 records, "Then Mary took a pound of very costly oil of spikenard, anointed the feet of Jesus, and wiped His feet with her hair." Mary was a deeply spiritual woman. She found out that the blessing of God is found at the feet of Jesus.

Have you made the same discovery? Do you spend time in daily devotion at the Master's feet? Do you spend time in prayer listening for the Master's call?

God help us to learn the lesson of Mary and sit at the Master's feet!

What can I give to Jesus, Who gave Himself for me?
How can I show my love for Him,
Who died on Calvary?
I'll give my life to Jesus, and calmly, gladly rest
Each future hope and fond desire upon
His loving breast.
I'll give my voice to Jesus, and seek through
all my days
My every talent consecrate to sing His joyous praise.
I'll give my strength to Jesus, of head, of heart,
and will;
Go where He sends and ever strive His
purpose to fulfill.

Anonymous

Building and Battling

Building and battling are part and parcel of the Christian walk. Jude 20 talks about "building yourselves up on your most holy faith." The second epistle of Peter says, "Add to your faith" (2 Peter 1:5).

We are called to build upon our faith in Jesus Christ. There is no neutrality in our walks; either we are building or we are allowing our walk to slide.

Furthermore, we are all called to battle. If we are Christian, we are in the Lord's army. This is not the reserves, nor is it a four-year tour of duty. It is a lifetime involvement. Those who do not recognize that we are in constant spiritual warfare are going to have a hard go of it.

According to 2 Timothy 2:3, we should "endure hardship as a good soldier of Jesus Christ." Romans 13:12 says, "Let us cast off the works of darkness, and let us put on the armor of light." The fact that we are told to put on armor tells us that we are soldiers. And the fact that we are soldiers points out that we are in a battle.

How are you getting along in building and battling? May the Lord strengthen us today as we put on the armor of light to fight against the enemy and at the same time build up our most holy faith.

> *Onward, Christian soldiers, marching as to war,*
> *With the cross of Jesus going on before!*
> *Christ, the royal Master, leads against the foe;*
> *Forward into battle, see His banner go.*
>
> *Like a mighty army moves the church of God;*
> *Brothers, we are treading where the saints have trod;*
> *We are not divided; all one body we,*
> *One in hope and doctrine, one in charity.*
>
> *Sabine Baring-Gould*

Don't Fizzle Out

In Nehemiah 4:6, we read that the Israelites built the wall of Jerusalem to half its height in remarkable time because "the people had a mind to work." Yet soon after that, some of them began to complain and say that they could not finish the work, as there was too much rubbish. How often do we feel like giving up when we're already halfway done? How many of us have projects that are halfway done but have sat in the garage for months, or maybe even years?

If we think about this concept from a spiritual standpoint, we may find that many of us started out doing something for the Lord that we knew He was calling us to do, but we never finished it. Maybe we got discouraged or spiritually fatigued in the middle of the work, and we just gave up.

The enemy wants us to fizzle out, but God wants us to keep building. He wants us to keep pushing on for His kingdom. Don't be overcome by the rubbish, as some of the people were in Nehemiah's day. Instead, set your mind and our heart to do God's will. When we refresh ourselves in God's strength, He will divinely enable us to see the task to completion.

Though the apostle Paul had many reasons to be discouraged and to give up many times in his service to the Lord, he never did. He realized that his strength was in the Lord. Thus, he could pen these glorious words: "I can do all things through Christ who strengthens me" (Philippians 4:13).

Christians, don't fizzle out! Be strengthened in the Lord's might!

My soul, be on thy guard; ten-thousand foes arise;
The hosts of sin are pressing hard,
to draw thee from the skies.
O watch and fight and pray; the battle never give over;
Renew it boldly every day, and help divine implore.

George Heath

Do You Hear the Lord?

Jesus said in John 10:4 that the sheep follow their shepherd "for they know his voice." Sheep have keen perception and acute hearing. Sheep quickly become accustomed to the master's voice and follow him and him alone. Even if a stranger were to come up and say the same words the shepherd says, the sheep would not follow him. That speaks of the special relationship each shepherd has to his sheep.

What is true of sheep is true of us as believers. When a person is born again, he has the capacity to hear from God for the very first time. The Bible says in Isaiah 30:21, "Your ears shall hear a word behind you, saying, 'This is the way, walk in it.'"

Jesus communicates with His sheep. Primarily, He speaks through His Word. The Bible is full of God's love letters to us. He also provides guidelines, directives, and desires for our lives. We are told in 2 Timothy 3:16, "All Scripture is given by inspiration of God, and is profitable for doctrine, for reproof, for correction, for instruction in righteousness." To the unbeliever, the Bible is a closed book (1 Corinthians 2:14). However, the believer can still hear the Lord speaking today.

The Lord also speaks to us through circumstances. God is faithful to line up circumstances in our lives so we will hear Him loud and clear. God speaks to us through His creation. We read in Psalm 19:1–3: "The heavens declare the glory of God; And the firmament shows His handiwork. Day unto day utters speech, And night unto night reveals knowledge. There is no speech nor language Where their voice is not heard." Our Good Shepherd speaks to us! The question is, are we listening? God help us today to listen to what the Lord would have to say to us.

When God says, "Trust me on this one," we can believe Him because He knows what He is doing.

B. R. S.

The Belt of Truth

In Ephesians 6:10–14, we read:

> Finally, my brethren, be strong in the Lord and in the power of His might. Put on the whole armor of God, that you may be able to stand against the wiles of the devil. For we do not wrestle against flesh and blood, but against principalities, against powers, against the rulers of the darkness of this age, against spiritual hosts of wickedness in the heavenly places. Therefore take up the whole armor of God, that you may be able to withstand in the evil day, and having done all, to stand. Stand therefore . . .

Notice how the apostle Paul says stand four times. The enemy wants us to fall. God wants us to stand. How do we do it? How do we stand firm and resolute in our faith in a world that hates us and in a battle where the devil wants to devour us? The Bible says we do it by putting on the whole armor of God.

The first piece of armor is the belt of truth. Ephesians 6:14 words it as "having girded your waist with truth." What is the most solid foundational truth we have? It is God's Word. Jesus said in John 17:17, "Your word is truth." If we want victory in our life, the first thing we need to do is make God's Word our foundation. As the belt wrapped around the Roman soldier's armor, so the Word of God must wrap around our life.

Let us strive to make God's Word our belt of truth.

How firm a foundation, ye saints of the Lord,
Is laid for your faith in His excellent Word!
What more can He say than to you He hath said,
To you who for refuge to Jesus have fled?

Unknown

The Breastplate and the Cleats

As we look at the armor of God talked about in Ephesians 6, we see that the second piece of equipment is found in verse 14: the breastplate of righteousness. The Roman soldier wore a breastplate to protect his vital organs. It was a crucial piece of equipment to keep him alive in the battle zone.

The Bible tells us in Isaiah that our own righteousness is as filthy rags. We will fail miserably in spiritual warfare if we try to go against the enemy in our own power. Our only strength and ability to stand is in the righteousness of Christ.

The devil will try to get us to succumb to unrighteousness, which is our natural bent. The only way we can even hope to fight against him is in the righteousness of Christ. It is Christ's righteousness that covers and protects our hearts.

The third piece of equipment is the cleats of peace. Ephesians 6:15 talks about "having shod your feet with the preparation of the gospel of peace." In order to hold their ground in hand-to-hand combat, Roman soldiers would wear sandals with nails driven through them. We might call them ancient cleats.

Thus, the apostle Paul is encouraging us to put on Christ's cleats of peace so we won't slip in the battle. Stand firm on the gospel of peace, which is the message and hope of Christ.

God grant us success in the battles of today!

Soldiers of Christ, arise, and put your armor on,
Strong in strength which God supplies through His eternal Son;
Strong in the Lord of hosts, and in His mighty power,
Who in the strength of Jesus trusts is more than conqueror.

Charles Wesley

The Recipe for No Persecution

There is a story about a Christian man who was starting a new job. He told his wife that he was concerned about working at his new place of employment because he had heard that all of the people there were profane and ungodly. When he arrived home at the end of his first day, his wife asked him, "How was your day at work, dear?" "Terrific," he replied. "Nobody knew I was a Christian."

What a sad indictment! This man didn't want to be persecuted for his faith. But Jesus said in Matthew 5:10, "Blessed are those who are persecuted for righteousness' sake." Jesus was saying, You are blessed when you stand up for me!

Here is a recipe for avoiding persecution:

1) Mimic the world's standard and by no means ever criticize it.

2) Don't talk about the gospel, especially regarding people's need for repentance.

3) Laugh at the world's jokes and enjoy its entertainment.

4) Smile when the world mocks at God and takes His name in vain.

5) Be ashamed to make a stand for Jesus.

If we do all five of these, it is virtually guaranteed that we won't be persecuted. But then again, neither will we experience the joy of the Lord.

Just live your life before your Lord, it matters not what others do—
Your actions will be weighed by Him who metes out judgment just and true.

Rae

Wash Yourself, Anoint Yourself, Dress Yourself

In the book of Ruth, there came the day when Ruth was to present herself to her kinsman-redeemer, Boaz. Before she did, Naomi gave her some practical advice: "Wash yourself and anoint yourself, put on your best garment" (Ruth 3:3).

These are three practical things that each of us ought to do in relationship with our Kinsman-Redeemer, Jesus Christ. First, we ought to wash ourselves. Second Corinthians 7:1 says, "Therefore, having these promises, beloved, let us cleanse ourselves from all filthiness of the flesh and spirit, perfecting holiness in the fear of God"—meaning, we should strive to live a holy life. Second, we ought to anoint ourselves. 1 John 2:20 tells us that we "have an anointing from the Holy One." As Christians, we have an anointing by the Holy Spirit. We are commanded in Ephesians 5:18 to be "filled with the Spirit." Thus, we act of our own will and submit to the Spirit's leading. Third, we need to dress ourselves. Ephesians 4:22–24 tells us that we need to "put off" the old garments of our former life and "put on" the new garments of our new nature. Just as we decide each day what we are going to wear physically, we need to choose our spiritual garments.

May Naomi's words speak into our hearts today: wash yourself, anoint yourself, dress yourself! Walk in holiness, in the Spirit, and according to your new nature!

Ready for service, lowly or great, ready to do His will.

Anonymous

Self-Distrust

We often think of the disciples as model believers, men of superlative faith. On the last night of our Lord's life on earth, however, instead of faith, loyalty and friendship, they displayed fear, embarrassment, and impotence.

In Matthew 26:31, Jesus had told them that they would desert him. But in verse 35 we read, "Peter said to Him, 'Even if I have to die with You, I will not deny You!' and so said all the disciples." In other words, Listen, Lord, you're mistaken. We'll be with you till the end. We're strong. We'll never stumble. We'll never be ashamed of you.

Well, what happened? We read in verse 56 that they all forsook Him, and later Peter denied knowing Him at all. The problem with the disciples was that they trusted in their own strength. They mistook their good intentions for spiritual maturity. They were proud and self-reliant.

The first step to spiritual maturity is realizing our own spiritual deficiency. Believers who claim to be wise and who rely upon their own abilities are only displaying how weak and immature they really are. Humility and meekness are the strengths of the believer. Paul said in 2 Corinthians 12:10, "For when I am weak, then I am strong."

May we learn the lesson of self-distrust and understand that our only source of strength is in Christ alone!

Create in me a clean heart, O God,
And renew a right spirit within me.
Cast me not away from Thy presence, O Lord,
And take not Thy Holy Spirit from me.
Restore unto me the joy of Thy salvation,
And renew a right spirit within me.

Anonymous

Christ Knows the Worst

One of the most glorious truths that we can ever learn about our Lord's love for us is this: He knew the worst about us before He even saved us. Therefore, whatever we do after salvation is not going to surprise Him. Jesus chose His disciples knowing that one of them would betray Him. Yet as we look at our Lord's life, we see that he was always reaching out to Judas. Tragically, Judas rejected Him.

Jesus loved His other disciples to the end as well. He chose them even knowing that they would desert Him in His hour of need. Jesus even chose Peter to be the leader of the disciples knowing that Peter would curse his very association with Him.

Jesus chose each of us knowing that we would from time to time be ashamed of our association with Him. Jesus knew the worst of us before He saved us. Does that mean that we should sin? Certainly not! Rather, it motivates us not to sin, because we know we have a Savior who has unfathomable love toward us.

The apostle Paul put it this way in Romans 5:20: "But where sin abounded, grace abounded much more." Corrie ten Boom said, "There is no well of sin so deep that the love of God is not deeper still."

Let us thank our Lord today for His incredible, immeasurable love!

Grace, grace, God's grace,
Grace that will pardon and cleanse within;
Grace, grace, God's grace,
Grace that is greater than all our sin.

J. H. Johnston

The Sorrow of Christ

When Jesus was praying in the garden of Gethsemane the night before His death, we read in Matthew 26, He became sorrowful, even unto death. Look at the events He knew would happen:

One of His own disciples would betray Him. All the others would desert him. Peter, the one in whom He had invested the most, would empathetically deny Him and curse his very association with Him.

He would be rejected by His own people. He came to be Israel's Savior, its Messiah, but He was rejected. Jew and Gentile alike would sentence Him to death in the name of God. Jesus, who alone is just, would suffer the injustice of man. He would experience physical pain as His beard was plucked out, His face punched and spit upon, His back scourged, and His head crowned with thorns, and then He would die an excruciating death on a cross. He, the sinless God, who would take on all the repulsive sin of man.

More than all of those things, He knew He would be separated from the Father while being the atonement for sin. You see, God's holiness cannot dwell with sinfulness. So a union that had existed for eternity would be broken as Jesus became our sin.

In light of those factors, it is no wonder that Jesus actually began to bleed from His sweat glands.

Why did Jesus go through all of this? Because He loved man; because He loved us. May our hearts be warmed today as we consider our Lord's love for us!

Alas, and did my Savior bleed
and did my Sovereign die?
Would He devote that sacred head
for sinners such as I?
Was it for crimes that I have done
He groaned upon the tree?
Amazing pity, grace unknown, and love beyond degree!

Isaac Watts

Warring in the Spirit

While Jesus was being arrested in the garden of Gethsemane, John 18:10 tells us, Peter drew his sword and cut off the ear of the high priest's servant. Just prior to Peter's impetuous act, the other disciples had asked Jesus whether He wanted them to use their swords. However, Peter didn't wait for instructions, and away he went, hacking into the crowd. Immediately, Jesus rebuked him—and then healed the young man's ear.

The spiritual lesson here is very clear: It is important that we wait for the Lord's instructions before we step out in the flesh and cause our own demise. Second Corinthians 10:3–4 says: "For though we walk in the flesh, we do not war according to the flesh. For the weapons of our warfare are not carnal but mighty in God for pulling down strongholds." Because Peter had failed to fight in the Spirit through prayer earlier, he now tried to fight in the flesh, and it reaped a disastrous harvest.

May we find victory today in warring in the Spirit through prayer. May we await the Lord's instructions instead of taking matters into our own hands and bringing about our own ruin.

> *Breathe on me, Breath of God,*
> *Fill me with life anew,*
> *That I may love what Thou does love,*
> *And do what Thou would do.*
> *Breathe on me, Breath of God,*
> *Until my heart is pure,*
> *Until with Thee I will Thy will,*
> *To do and to endure.*
> *Breathe on me, Breath of God,*
> *'Til I am wholly Thine,*
> *'Til all this earthly part of me*
> *Glows with Thy fire divine.*
>
> *Edwin Hatch*

Twelve Legions

Peter tried to take matters into his own hands by hacking away at the crowd at Jesus' arrest in Gethsemane. "So Jesus said to Peter, 'Put your sword into the sheath. Shall I not drink the cup which my Father has given Me?'" (John 18:11). Jesus was saying, Listen, Peter, if I need your help, I'll let you know, but it's doubtful that I'll need your puny sword. Why would Jesus say that? Jesus had the command of at least twelve legions of angels. A Roman legion consisted of 6,000 soldiers. Twelve legions of angels would be 72,000 angels!

How powerful are angels? Incredibly powerful, as seen in 2 Kings 19:35, where we are told that one angel slew 185,000 Assyrian soldiers in one shot. If you multiply that destruction by 72,000, you have enough in your arsenal to destroy the inhabitants of the earth at least two times. So Jesus was telling Peter, Listen, if I want to destroy these guys, I can do it in an instant. But this is the plan for redemption.

God is in control of every situation of our lives. If He needs our help, He'll let us know. We don't need to step out in the flesh and fight battles on our own. Rather, we need to realize that the battle belongs to the Lord and that He will deliver in His time, according to His perfect plan.

> *They bound the hands of Jesus in the garden*
> *where He prayed,*
> *They led Him through the streets in shame.*
> *They spat upon the Savior, so pure and free from sin,*
> *They said "crucify Him, He's to blame."*
>
> *He could have called ten-thousand angels*
> *To destroy the world, and set Him free.*
> *He could have called ten-thousand angels*
> *But He died alone, for you and me.*
>
> *Unknown*

The Gates of Hades

In Matthew 16:18, Jesus said that the gates of Hades would not prevail against the church He would build. We often take this verse as reflecting God's protection for the saints: Hades' gates can't come against us. But that is not what Jesus was saying. Gates are not offensive weapons.

A gate is something that keeps people shut in or shut out. The gates of Hades are the gates that close men in hell. Jesus was saying, Because I will die on the cross and rise victoriously, I will therefore build My church, and I will build up My saints. Because the gates of Hades were not able to hold Me, neither will they be able to hold those for whom I died—those who place their trust in Me! Do you see the powerful truth in that statement?

Because Jesus has conquered sin, death, and hell, the gates of Hades can neither prevail against us nor hold even one of God's children in. We are released from the penalty of sin.

If the Lord had not been on our side,
All our enemies would have swallowed us alive.
If the Lord had not been on our side,
All the raging waters, and the mighty flood,
Would have swept over us.
If the Lord, If the Lord, If the Lord
Had not been on our side.
Blessed be the Lord, Who has not given us up,
The Lord who is our help,
Maker of heaven and earth.

Rob Mathes

Spiritual Failure

Six events lead up to Peter's denial of Jesus.

First, in Matthew 16, Peter received a revelation from God that Jesus was the Christ. But no sooner had Jesus commended Peter than Peter took Jesus aside and rebuked Him. Spiritual pride!

Peter's second downfall was self-confidence. After Jesus told His disciples that they would all flee once He was arrested, Peter said, in effect, "Even if all of these guys do, I never will!" Self-confidence!

Peter's third step to spiritual failure is found in the Garden of Gethsemane when Jesus asked him to pray. As Jesus retreated to pray, Peter retreated to sleep. Zero devotion!

Peter's fourth descent came when Jesus was arrested. Peter started slicing into the crowd with his sword. You see, because he was proud, because he was self-confident, because he didn't pray, he tried to take matters into his own hands—impulsiveness motivated by the flesh.

Peter's fifth decline is found in a single verse. Matthew 26:58 records, "But Peter followed Him at a distance." The moment you start following Jesus at a distance, you are in trouble.

Peter's sixth step was that He warmed his hands at the enemy's fire. By this time, Peter was long gone. Moments later, he denied his Lord.

May the Lord speak to our hearts today and help us never to underestimate the power of one single sin. For one sin can lead to another, and the results will be tragic!

Change my heart, oh God, Make it ever true.
Change my heart, oh God, May I be like you.
You are the potter, I am the clay,
Mold me and make me, this is what I pray.

Eddie Espinosa

From Lameness to Leaping

In Acts 3, we have the account of a lame man's healing. As Peter and John were walking into the temple, they came across the man asking for alms. The man had been unable to walk for the forty years since his birth. In verse 6, Peter says: "Silver and gold I do not have, but what I do have I give you: In the name of Jesus Christ of Nazareth, rise up and walk." At that moment, the man was completely healed, and from that time on, he followed the apostles.

Here we have a good picture of our lost condition before Christ, and of what Christ does for us spiritually when we are saved. This man was born lame. The Bible tells us that we are born paralyzed in sin such that we cannot walk in a way pleasing to God. This man was laid by the entrance to the temple but never once was able to go in. The Bible tells us that no matter how close we get to the kingdom of heaven, if we are not born again, we will not enter into it. This man was poor; his whole existence was bound up in trying to acquire enough to get by—by begging. Man, in his lost condition, tries to fulfill himself with material things but is bankrupt without God.

The beautiful thing is that when this man was healed, he did not expect it; he wasn't deserving of it; he couldn't even buy it. But it was freely and instantaneously given. Likewise, salvation is freely given to us. We weren't expecting it; we were still in sin. But Christ came after us. We did not deserve it, nor could we have bought it if we had wanted to, but Jesus came to us while we were still sinners. And when we are born again, it is instantaneous and complete!

Let us thank God today and every day for the free gift of salvation!

White as snow, white as snow,
though my sins were as scarlet,
Lord, I know, Lord, I know that I'm clean and forgiven.

Leon Olguin

Heartburn

Just after Jesus' resurrection, two disciples were walking along the road to Emmaus. In Luke 24:15–16, we read: "So it was, while they conversed and reasoned, that Jesus Himself drew near and went with them. But their eyes were restrained, so that they did not know Him." As they were talking with Jesus, they told Him that they had been hoping that Jesus of Nazareth would redeem Israel.

At that point, verses 25–27 tell us that "[Jesus] said to them, 'O foolish ones, and slow of heart to believe in all that the prophets have spoken! Ought not Christ to have suffered these things and to enter into his glory? And beginning at Moses and all the Prophets, he expounded to them in all the Scriptures the things concerning Himself.'"

As they came to the village, the two men constrained Jesus to come in and eat with them. Jesus did so. And when at the meal He took the bread and blessed it and broke it, suddenly their eyes were opened— and Jesus vanished.

Then, we read, "they said to one another, 'Did not our heart burn within us while He talked with us on the road, and while He opened the Scriptures to us?'"

What these guys got here was a good case of heartburn! As the Scriptures were opened, their hearts burned. Let us seek the Lord in His Word and get a good case of heartburn!

Christ the Lord is risen today, Alleluia!
Sons of men and angels say, Alleluia!
Raise your joys and triumphs high, Alleluia!
Sing, ye heavens, and earth, reply, Alleluia!
Lives again our glorious King, Alleluia!
Where, O Death, is now thy sting? Alleluia!
Dying once He all does save, Alleluia!
Where thy victory, O Grave? Alleluia!

Charles Wesley

What Then Shall I do with Jesus?

When Jesus stood before Pilate and was found to be innocent, Pilate had the authority to release Him. However, the crowd didn't want Jesus released; rather, they wanted Barabbas released. Pilate then asked the crowd in Matthew 27:22, "What then shall I do with Jesus who is called Christ?" And though Pilate did not know it at the time, that is the most important question every human being since then inevitably has had to ask himself. What then shall I do with Jesus who is called the Christ?

The answer to that question will determine our eternal destiny. We must either accept Jesus as our Lord and Savior or reject Him as the crowd did, saying, "Crucify Him, crucify Him!" (Luke 23:21). We may not verbally yell out those words, but to reject Jesus Christ is to cry out from our hearts, "Crucify Him, crucify Him!" It is like saying inwardly, I don't want Him, I despise Him, and I reject Him. It is saying in our hearts, I am the master of my own life, and I will not have Jesus rule over me.

Those are frightful words! The only right response to Pilate's question is to embrace Jesus as our Lord and to say, as the centurion did at His cross, "Truly this was the Son of God!" (Matthew 27:54).

My life, my love I give to Thee,
Thou Lamb of God who died for me;
O may I ever faithful be,
My Savior and my God!
O Thou who died on Calvary,
To save my soul and make me free,
I'll consecrate my life to Thee,
My Savior and my God!
I'll live for Him who died for me,
How happy then my life shall be!
I'll live for Him who died for me,
My Savior and my God!

Ralph E. Hudson

My Sins

Because we are separated from the events of Jesus' cross by about two thousand years, we are apt to think that had we been there, we would have not deserted our Lord as His disciples did. We might think that we would have hung around and that we would not have mocked our Lord but rather stood up for Him. We might even think that we would have been there at the foot of His cross to support Him in His pain.

The truth is, had we been there on that dark morning, we would have fallen as miserably as everyone else did. For it was our sins that nailed Jesus to that cross.

Let us thank the Lord today for loving us, even when we miserably failed Him.

'Twas I that shed the sacred blood;
I nailed Him to the tree;
I crucified the Christ of God;
I joined the mockery.

Of all that shouting multitude
I feel that I am one;
And in that din of voices rude
I recognize my own.

Around the cross the throng I see,
Mocking the sufferer's groan;
Yet still my voice it seems to be,
As if I mocked alone.

Horatius Bonar

How Far Will God Go?

H. C. Trumbull once said, "Calvary shows us how far men will go in sin and how far God will go for man's salvation." Oh, how true those words are! Calvary does show us how far men will go in sin by placing the very Son of God on the cross. And it was a cruel cross!

Matthew 27 gives us an account of the cruelties Jesus suffered. The soldiers stretched Jesus' arms taut around a beam and then whipped His back with a scourge containing bits of bone and metal designed to rip the flesh open. Then they beat Him in the face, caned Him on the head, spit on Him, and mocked Him. And after that, they led Him through the streets to humiliate Him in front of everyone. Jesus experienced not only the cruelty of the soldiers but the cruelty of the thieves on either side of Him as well, as they jeered at Him. Then the populace of Palestine chimed in as they wagged their heads and said, "If You are the Son of God, come down from the cross." Then the religious leaders added to the cruelty of His cross by coming up to Him one last time to mock Him to His face.

If Jesus had saved Himself, He couldn't have saved us. Truly, Calvary shows us how far men will go in sin, but the beautiful thing is, that same cross shows us how far God will go for man's salvation.

For it wasn't those nails that held Jesus to that cross, but His *love* for you and me!

> *I will sing of my Redeemer and*
> *His wondrous love to me;*
> *On the cruel cross He suffered from the curse*
> *to set me free.*
> *I will praise my dear Redeemer,*
> *His triumphant power I'll tell,*
> *In His boundless love and mercy,*
> *He the ransom freely gave.*
>
> *Philip P. Bliss*

Follow Me

In John 13:15, Jesus said, "For I have given you an example, that you should do as I have done to you." Jesus said this when He was in the upper room with His disciples washing their feet. He was showing them they needed to care for one another, love one another, and serve one another.

The point is that Jesus always set the perfect example. He is our supreme example to follow. Throughout the Scriptures, God has given other examples as well, frail though they may have been in their human strength. He uses Abraham, Moses, Nehemiah, David, Stephen, and others to teach us.

If there was one man in the New Testament who best revealed what following Jesus' example can mean to our lives, though, it was the apostle Paul. In fact, Paul said in 1 Corinthians 4:16, "Therefore I urge you, imitate me." The word imitate literally means to mimic. Wait a second! How could Paul actually encourage people to mimic his life? The answer is found in Paul's second exhortation in the same book. Chapter 11 begins with him saying, "Imitate me, just as I also imitate Christ." He was saying that to the degree that he was an example of Jesus Christ, believers should follow his example.

May we likewise pattern the life of Christ and say to others, "Imitate me; mimic me; and follow my example, because I follow Christ!"

While passing thru this world of sin,
And others your life shall view,
Be clean and pure without, within,
Let others see Jesus in you.
Keep telling the story, be faithful and true,
Let others see Jesus in you.

B. B. McKinney

Anger

Anger is a sin that everyone must deal with. Ephesians 4:31 says, "Let all bitterness, wrath, anger, clamor, and evil speaking be put away from you." Colossians 3:8 says, "But now you yourselves are to put off all these: anger, wrath . . ." Anger is a sin. However, we do see Jesus angry in Mark 3:5, when religious leaders were trying to say that He had broken the Sabbath by healing a man's hand. Then in John 2:13–16, we see Him overturning the tables of the money changers in the temple and making a whip and driving them all out.

What about that specific kind of anger? It is righteous anger! Jesus was angry at the sin, but He still loved the sinners. He proved it by going to the cross for those same people.

The question is, how do we know whether our anger is righteous or sinful? To help answer that we must ask ourselves, Am I reacting this way because I'm hurt, threatened, or jealous? If we are, that is sin!

Most of the time when we are angry, it is probably because we have been hurt, or because things aren't going the way we think they should. So we get angry at that! But if we want to get angry about something, let it be about our sin.

Today, let us pray for hatred toward our own sin, and let us ask God to forgive us!

When anger springs up in my heart, dear Lord, because of the evil I see,
Just help me to channel the wrath that I feel, and do something noble through me.

J. D. Branon

The World and the Believer

James said in James 4:4: "Do you not know that friendship with the world is enmity with God? Whoever therefore wants to be a friend of the world makes himself an enemy of God." Jesus put it this way in Luke 16:13: "No servant can serve two masters; for either he will hate the one and love the other, or else he will be loyal to the one and despise the other. You cannot serve God and mammon."

Every day in the life of the believer, decisions of abstinence must be made. Christians can't do all of the things that people in our society do. We can't drink the same alcoholic beverages they do. We can't watch the same seductive movies they do. We can't listen to the same demoralizing music they do. We can't go to the same places they do. Therefore, believers are constantly making decisions of abstinence.

We don't want to be legalistic, but if we are going to be the salt and light that Jesus commanded us to be, there needs to be a separation from the world. Allan Redpath put it this way: "Your Christian experience is valueless, regardless of what you believe, unless it leads you to a standard of conduct that is in violent opposition to a lot that goes on in the world today."

God help us to live in the world and reach out to others in the world, but to not become part of the world!

In this world but never of it,
Help me, Lord, to live this day,
Free from all that would entangle,
Of the dazzle and array.

Graves

God Is in Control

Look at the life of our Lord. See all of the prophecies that were fulfilled in His death, burial, and resurrection. We come to the awesome conclusion that only the divine providence of God could have brought everything to pass so perfectly.

Jesus was crucified, yet none of His bones were broken. The soldiers divided His garments. His side was pierced. He was buried in a rich man's tomb. And on and on go the prophecies that were fulfilled. God was in complete control of every situation surrounding the life, death, burial, and resurrection of Jesus Christ.

These facts give us great hope. Since Christ did rise in fulfillment of Scripture, everything He said will come to pass. That tells us that we are ultimately going to heaven. It also tells us that God is in control of every circumstance in our lives and that He'll never leave us or forsake us (Hebrews 13:5). All things do work together for good to those who love God and are called according to His purpose (Romans 8:28).

Great is Thy faithfulness, O God my Father,
There is no shadow of turning with Thee;
Thou changest not, Thy compassions, they fail not;
As Thou hast been Thou forever will be.

Great is Thy faithfulness! Great is Thy faithfulness!
Morning by morning new mercies I see;
All I have needed Thy hand hath provided;
Great is Thy faithfulness, Lord unto me!

Thomas O. Chisholm

Things Don't Just Happen

Isaiah 46:9–10 says: "For I am God, and there is no other; I am God, and there is none like Me. Declaring the end from the beginning, and from ancient times things that are not yet done, Saying, 'My counsel shall stand, and I will do all My pleasure.'" This speaks of God's sovereign rule and divine providence.

God's providence could be defined as follows: God's independent and sovereign rule to bring to pass His designed will through normal and natural circumstances. God takes every circumstance of the lives of every person that has lived or will live, and He combines those circumstances with their ambitions, talents, gifts, and abilities. Then He orchestrates those with seemingly random choices, actions, plans, and decisions we make. He uses every single one of these to accomplish His divine, redemptive purpose for mankind. Things don't just happen.

Things don't just happen to children of God,
They're part of a wonderful plan.
The troubles, reverses, the sorrow, the rod,
Are strokes of the Great Sculptor's hand.

Things don't just happen to children of God,
The blueprint was made by His hands,
He designed all details to conform to His Son,
So all things that happen are planned.

No matter what happens to those called His own,
Events that are awful or grand,
Every trial of your life He sends from His throne,
Thing don't just happen, they're planned.

Jerry Brooks

Bring the Book!

In Nehemiah 8:1 we read, "Now all the people gathered together as one man in the open square that was in front of the Water Gate; and they told Ezra the scribe to bring the Book."

Whenever and wherever there has ever been a true revival, it has always been when God's people have brought the Book—God's Word. John Flavel once said, "The scriptures teach us the best way of living, the noblest way of suffering, and the most comfortable way of dying." Acts 20:32 tells us that the Word of God is that "which is able to build you up."

The reason why there was spiritual success in the days of young King Josiah is because Shaphan, a scribe, found the Book; and when he found it, he brought it to Josiah, and he and the people of Judah set their hearts toward God (2 Kings 22).

Again, revival always begins with bringing the Book. It continues when we obey the Book! We can get the Book, we can read it, and we can even love it. But do we obey it?

God help us to bring the Book, read the Book, and most importantly, obey the Book! (See James 1:22–25.)

> *Great God, with wonder and with praise*
> *On all Thy works I look!*
> *But still Thy wisdom, power, and grace*
> *Shine brightest in Thy Book.*
>
> *Watts*

Stepping Stones

Peter was given a revelation from God when he declared to Jesus, "You are the Christ" (Matthew 16:16). Nevertheless, as Jesus begins to unfold His plan of going to the cross, Peter took Jesus aside and rebuked Him. At that moment, Jesus looked at Peter and said in verse 23, "Get behind Me, Satan! You are an offense to Me." That word offense means "stumbling block". Peter "the stone" was now Peter "the stumbling block." At one moment, Peter was receiving revelations from God, and the next moment, he was listening to the lies of the devil.

What led Peter into that trap? Pride! Before we jump all over Peter, we will do well to take inventory of our own lives. How often is it that we have learned some wonderful truth about God, or God has used us in some small way, and we begin to think that we have really arrived? That is spiritual pride. The moment we think we have arrived is the moment we have departed. Oh, how we must be on our guard for spiritual pride!

Let us pray for humility and that we might be stepping stones for God's kingdom rather than stumbling blocks.

More like the Master I would ever be,
More of His meekness, more humility;
More zeal to labor, more courage to be true,
More consecration for the work He bids me do.

Take Thou my heart, I would be Thine alone;
Take Thou my heart, and make it all Thine own;
Purge me from sin, O Lord, I now implore,
Wash me and keep me Thine forevermore.

Charles H. Gabriel

The Resurrection

Jesus said in John 11:25: "I am the resurrection and the life. He who believes in Me, though he may die, he shall live." Then in John 14:19, He says, "Because I live, you will live also." Jesus went on to prove those statements by rising from the dead three days after His crucifixion. The resurrection of Jesus Christ is the cornerstone of our faith.

As Paul said in 1 Corinthians 15:17, "If Christ is not risen, your faith is futile; you are still in your sins!" Then, in verse 20, the apostle states: "But now Christ is risen from the dead." The fact that Christ has risen from the dead proves some wonderful things:

Jesus is God. Only God has the authority to lay down His life and take it back again.

Everything Jesus taught and said is reliable and true. His resurrection, therefore, validates all of Scripture.

Jesus was victorious over sin, death, and hell at the cross. Therefore, faith in Him assures us of a heavenly inheritance.

We have not only a hope for the future but also strength to live now. This hope gives us great anticipation, which brings glorious joy.

Let us thank the Lord for His resurrection. Because He lives, we will, too.

Alas, and did my Savior bleed,
and did my Sovereign die?
Would He devote that sacred head
for sinners such as I?
Was it for crimes that I have done,
He groaned upon the tree?
Amazing pity, grace unknown, and love beyond degree!
But drops of grief can ne'er repay
the debt of love I owe;
Here, Lord, I give myself away, 'tis all that I can do.

Isaac Watts and Ralph Hudson

Removing the Stones

When the women came on Sunday morning to visit Jesus' body in the tomb, we read in Mark 16:3, they asked themselves, "Who will roll away the stone from the door of the tomb for us?" They were coming to anoint a dead body, but Jesus had risen. They had come seeking the body of Jesus, expecting the obstacle of the stone. But He had removed the stone! He had risen!

This teaches us a spiritual principle. There will always be obstacles when we are serious about seeking Jesus. There are always large stones creating barriers when we want to seek Christ. Indeed, there will be stones of many sizes that the devil will use to try to divert us. He will try to discourage us. He will try to seal off access to Christ. He will roll the stone of busyness in our way. Many Christians say, "I don't know where the time goes, but I haven't had time to seek the Lord today." Numerous Christians get so discouraged in the heat of spiritual warfare that they feel like giving up. But He will roll away the great stone of spiritual warfare from the path. We need to remember this: Yes, there will be obstacles in our way when we want to seek Jesus; but for those who are persistent in the pursuit, Jesus always has a way of rolling those stones away.

God help us to be relentless in our daily pursuit of Him and, along the way, to find those stones of discouragement rolled away.

At the cross, at the cross where I first saw the light,
And the burden of my heart rolled away,
It was there by faith I received my sight,
And now I am happy all the day!

Isaac Watts and Ralph Hudson

July 29

The Priority of the Church

In Matthew 28:19–20, Jesus gave what is often called the Great Commission. He instructed and encouraged His disciples, directing, "Go therefore and make disciples of all the nations, baptizing them in the name of the Father and of the Son and of the Holy Spirit, teaching them to observe all things that I have commanded you; and lo, I am with you always, even to the end of the age."

With this sweeping statement, Jesus gives us the priority of the church. The priority of the church is not to get together as a social club to discuss our mutual faith, although fellowship is important. The priority of the church is not to get good, sound, doctrinal teaching, although that is essential—and, oh, how desperately it is needed today!

Jesus tells us that the priority of the church is to win the lost. Yes, we should gather together as a church for fellowship. Yes, we should gather together for the teaching of God's Word. However, those things are only for the express purpose of building up our most holy faith so that we can go out into the world.

We are to be, as Jesus said in Matthew 4:19, "fishers of men." God help us to see that our reason for living, our reason for remaining on this earth, is to share the gospel of Jesus Christ with those around us.

May the Spirit empower us to fulfill the Great Commission.

I want to be a fruitful Christian,
winning precious souls for Thee;
Telling them of how my Savior gave His life
to set them free.

Ozbun

Our Great High Priest

When the apostle John had his vision of Jesus Christ, he described Him in Revelation 1:12–13. He wrote that he saw Jesus walking in the midst of golden lampstands (which he says in verse 20 are the church) and wearing a garment down to His feet, with a golden band around His chest. The only biblical garment with golden bands on the chest is that of the high priest. John was describing Jesus walking in the midst of His church as our Great High Priest. What a comforting thought!

The high priest of the Old Testament was the one who made intercession for the people. He was the intermediary between man and God. Jesus is now our High Priest, and He lives to intercede for us (Hebrews 7:25). And Hebrews 4:15–16 comforts us and tells us: "For we do not have a High Priest who cannot sympathize with our weaknesses, but was in all points tempted as we are, yet without sin. Let us therefore come boldly to the throne of grace, that we may obtain mercy and find grace to help in time of need."

We can draw great security from the fact that when John saw Jesus Christ in His glory, He was walking in the midst of His church making intercession for us as our Great High Priest, just as He said He would do.

Let us give our Lord thanks for His ever-upholding arms.

What a fellowship, what a joy divine,
Leaning on the everlasting arms;
What a blessedness, what a peace is mine,
Leaning on the everlasting arms.
What have I to dread, what have I to fear,
Leaning on the everlasting arms?
I have blessed peace with my Lord so near,
Leaning on the everlasting arms.

Elisha A. Hoffman

Once Blind but Now Seeing

Read John 9:1–7 and meditate on it for a little while. Here we have the wonderful story of Jesus healing a blind man. The beautiful reality of this story is that it mirrors what takes place in the life of every believer when they recognize Jesus' touch. Did the blind man know that Jesus was going to heal his sight? No. He didn't even know that Jesus was there. Such is the blindness of the unredeemed soul.

In 2 Corinthians 4:4, we see that Satan blinds the minds of unbelievers so that they cannot see the light of the gospel. Ephesians 5:8 tells us that we were once in darkness. What does Jesus do? He comes and invades our darkness. Apart from Christ's intervening grace, we would be left in darkness. Detached from Christ, man has no capacity to see God. He is left blind and in his sin. He sees no God, no Christ, no truth, no love, no anything. We cannot come to salvation without the very grace of God reaching down and touching us as Jesus did this beggar. By His spiritually touching our blind hearts, we are able to see God.

Romans 3:11 says, "There is none who seeks after God." That is speaking of the true God. A lot of people seek after gods; they seek after religion. But no man on his own seeks after the true God without God's help. Why? Because we are blind without God. This lesson tells of the intervening grace of God for the sinner. We read in Romans 5:8, "But God demonstrates His own love toward us, in that while we were still sinners, Christ died for us." Jesus said in Luke 19:10 that "the Son of Man has come to seek and to save that which was lost."

We need to be grateful that Jesus came to rescue us and to be thankful that Jesus came to give us spiritual sight. God help us to walk in His light.

To live without God means to die without hope.

Anonymous

Birthing Ishmael

Psalm 27:14 says, "Wait on the Lord; Be of good courage, And He shall strengthen your heart; Wait, I say, on the Lord!" By nature, we rush ahead of God. We try to do things on our own and birth Ishmael.

God told Abraham in the book of Genesis that he and Sarah would have a son in their old age. They waited and they waited, but as the years went on, they felt that God needed some help. So at the age of eighty-six, Sarah said to Abraham, "Go in to my maidservant; surely this must be God's plan." The result was a son of the flesh—Ishmael.

Thirteen years later, God came to Abraham and told him He was going to give him a son. Abraham's response was, "There he is, Lord—Ishmael." God told him: "No. That's a son of the flesh. I'm going to give you a son in your old age." A year later, a son was born to Sarah and Abraham; she was ninety and he was hundred.

All too often we try to move ahead of God. We step outside the realm of the Spirit and by our actions tell God that He needs a little help. We need to take to heart what God told His servant Zerubbabel in Zechariah 4:6: "Not by might, nor by power, but by My Spirit."

May we be delivered from trusting in our own strength and birthing Ishmael. May we trust God's perfect timing and His perfect plan for us. May we wait on the Lord and rely on Him to do it right.

> *'Tis so sweet to trust in Jesus,*
> *Just to take Him at His word,*
> *Just to rest upon His promise,*
> *Just to know "Thus saith the Lord."*
> *Yes, 'tis sweet to trust in Jesus,*
> *Just from sin and self to cease,*
> *Just from Jesus simply taking*
> *Life and rest and joy and peace.*
>
> *Louisa M. Stead*

Dynamite Power

Jesus told His disciples in Acts 1:8, "You shall receive power when the Holy Spirit has come upon you." That word "power" is the Greek word dunimas, from where we get our English word dynamite. Jesus was telling His disciples that when they get filled with the Holy Spirit, they are going to have dynamite power. And that is exactly what happened. We read in Acts 17:6 that they "turned the world upside down."

Many Christians today say, "I wish I had that kind of dynamite power working in my life." You do! All born-again believers have the Spirit of God living within them (Romans 8:9). The problem is that many Christians fail to be filled with the Spirit.

When a person is filled with something, they are permeated and controlled by it. A person filled with sadness is controlled by grief. A person filled with bitterness is controlled by anger. And a person filled with the Spirit is controlled by the Spirit.

If you are a Christian, you have the Holy Spirit dwelling inside of you. The question is, are you filled with the Spirit? Are you controlled by the Spirit? God is in us. He is with us. The failure is not on His part; the failure is on our part, because we don't submit and yield to His guidance. The dynamite power of the Holy Spirit is manifested in the life of a believer who is controlled by the Spirit. Believers who are controlled by the Spirit have consciously nurtured their spiritual relationship through prayer, study of God's Word, and fellowship with other believers.

May we yield ourselves to the permeated power of the Holy Spirit and, in turn, experience His dunimas, power!

The Holy Spirit is always with us, no matter what is happening. We need Him all the time for everything. The great assurance is we can rely on Him to get the job done right.

B. R. S.

An Unsaved Spouse?

Living with an unsaved spouse is not easy. The question is, how does a Christian woman conduct her relationship with a non-Christian husband? Does she look down upon her husband because he is not saved? Does she stop submitting to his authority in the home? Does she leave him?

Peter gives us the answer in 1 Peter 3:1–2. He says, "Wives, likewise, be submissive to your own husbands, that even if some do not obey the word [meaning the unbelievers], they, without a word, may be won by the conduct of their wives, when they observe your chaste conduct . . ." He doesn't say to leave him. He doesn't say to harass him. He doesn't tell her to demand her Christian rights. What he does say is: submit to him and love him. God wants her to understand that when her husband sees her godly spirit, without even speaking a word, he'll be won by her godly life.

Peter doesn't give a time frame. It could be one year. It could be one month. It could be twenty years. There is a lady in our church who lived with her unsaved spouse for thirty years before he came to the Lord. That couple is a delight to see today.

So ladies, be faithful, consistent, and prayerful. Ask God to soften your spouse's heart and fill him with Christ's love. Maintain a closeness to the Savior. Find fellowship and support among the church family. Lead a life that glorifies and magnifies Christ.

Two simple guidelines for a marriage that pleases God: Admit wrong and keep quiet about being right. It's a good way to keep the relationship strong.

J. D. Branon

The Credentials of Christ

The Bible presents Jesus Christ as our King. As a king, He has royal credentials. His credentials are found in Matthew 4:23, which says, "And Jesus went about all Galilee, teaching in their synagogues, preaching the gospel of the kingdom, and healing all kinds of sickness and all kinds of disease among the people." Christ's words and works were His credentials.

When Jesus taught and preached, the Bible says, everyone was amazed because He taught with such authority—unlike anyone else. Jesus taught the Word with power because He was the Word!

Jesus works were His credentials. No one else could do the things Jesus did. He healed the sick with a word or by a touch. He healed the lame as well as the leper. If that weren't enough, He raised the dead. Everything that Jesus said, and everything that Jesus did—His words and His works—were His royal credentials. His credentials declared, This is Christ!

Great is the Lord, and most worthy of praise,
In the city of our God, the holy place,
The joy of the whole earth.
Great is the Lord in whom we have the victory,
He aids us against the enemy,
We bow down on our knees.
And Lord, we want to lift Your name on high,
And Lord, we want to thank You
For the works You've done in our lives,
And Lord, we trust in Your unfailing love,
For You alone are God eternal
Throughout earth and heaven above.

Steve McEwan

It's His Church

In Matthew 16:18, Jesus said, "I will build My church." This tells us that we are not to build the church. In fact, the Lord doesn't want us building the church. Jesus says, "I will build My church."

That doesn't mean we can't build the brick structure in which to worship. What it means is that we are not to build the church on men's schemes, men's gimmicks, men's teachings, men's techniques, men's programs, men's wisdom, or men's promotions. Jesus wants us to rely on His provision and His resources to build His church. It is His church!

As your pastor, I am not interested in building a church. I am, however, extremely interested in being involved in a church that Christ is building! Don't you think that God is grieved by all of the Madison Avenue techniques that many congregations are using today to build their churches? Why not stop the shifty, gimmicky programs, the constant pleading for money, and trust in God for His provision?

Lord, we ask for your wisdom and the courage to get out of Your way and to let You build Your church!

All you may need He will provide,
God will take care of you.

C. D. Martin

March on the Walls!

In Nehemiah 12, the Israelites had a dedication service to celebrate the rebuilding of the walls of Jerusalem. Nehemiah had appointed two thanksgiving choirs, and they marched throughout the city as well as on the walls, singing the wonderful praises of God. The most beautiful thing was that they marched on the walls. Why? Because during the construction of the walls, the enemies of God had continually mocked and discouraged them by saying, "You guys are so feeble and your work is so pitiful that even if a fox climbs up the wall, the wall will fall down." So it was especially wonderful to see that once the walls were completed, not only could a fox climb on them, but a multitude of people could walk on them, singing praises to God.

The enemy is always trying to wear us down. He mocks us, ridicules us, and discourages us. He lies to us and tells us that what we are doing for God will never amount to anything. He even tells us that we will never amount to anything. But the fact is, our labor of love is important to God.

Galatians 6:9 says, "And let us not grow weary while doing good, for in due season we shall reap if we do not lose heart." And when the enemy lies to us and tells us that we will never amount to anything, we need to remember Philippians 1:6, which says, "He who has begun a good work in you will complete it until the day of Jesus Christ."

Lord, when the enemy discourages us, help us to remember that the ultimate victory is ours!

God's guidance and help that we need day to day
Is given to all who believe;
The Spirit has sealed us—He's God's guarantee
That heaven we'll one day receive.

J. D. Branon

The Day of Pentecost

In Acts 2:1–4, we read:

> When the Day of Pentecost had fully come, they were all
> with one accord in one place. And suddenly there came a
> sound from heaven, as of a rushing mighty wind, and it filled
> the whole house where they were sitting. Then there ap-
> peared to them divided tongues, as of fire, and one sat upon
> each of them. And they were all filled with the Holy Spirit
> and began to speak with other tongues, as the Spirit gave
> them utterance.

Here we have the baptism of the Holy Spirit and the birth of the church. This
is one of the greatest transitions in the entire Bible. We have God bringing
man together in Christ through the giving of the Spirit and the birth of the
church.

What we actually have here is the reversal of the judgment at the Tower of
Babel. In Genesis chapter 11, God divided the single language of the people
into many languages, thus separating the people from one another. On the day
of Pentecost, God used many languages to bring all men together in Christ. At
the Tower of Babel, the people were unable to understand one another. On the
day of Pentecost, everyone understood. Acts 2:11 says that they were being
told of "the wonderful works of God." The Tower of Babel was actually con-
structed to bring praises to men. On the day of Pentecost, the disciples spoke
in many languages to bring praises to God.

Christ went to great lengths in birthing His church; He died for it. Through
His death and resurrection, He has sent the Holy Spirit to live inside of us. He
gave us this wonderful gift that we might be part of His body and filled with
the Spirit. Being filled with the Spirit gives us the capability to speak to many
people, praising God, just as the disciples did on the day of Pentecost.

Lord, we thank you for the incredible gift of the Holy Spirit.

We've a story to tell to the nations
that shall turn their hearts to the right:
A story of truth and mercy, a story of peace and light.

H. E. Nichol

223

Be Filled!

Ephesians 5:18 says, "And do not be drunk with wine, in which is dissipation; but be filled with the Spirit." The actual Greek translation is "keep on being filled with the Spirit." On the day of Pentecost, the disciples were baptized into the Holy Spirit; they were filled with the Holy Spirit. They are not exhorted to be born again over and over from that point on. They are not commanded to be baptized again and again into the body of Christ. They are, however, commanded to be filled with the Holy Spirit. Thus, throughout the book of Acts, after their conversions, after they have been baptized into Christ, after they have been converted, they are still being filled with the Holy Spirit.

In Acts 4:8, Peter was filled with the Spirit. In Acts 4:31, after the early church prayed, it was filled with the Spirit. In Acts 7:55, Stephen was filled with the Spirit. In Acts 9:17, many days after his conversion, Saul (soon to be the apostle Paul) was filled with the Spirit. And in Acts 13:52, we read about the disciples being filled with joy and the Holy Spirit.

We need to be filled with the Spirit! That which empowers us for service is the filling of the Spirit. That which gives us effectiveness in our witness is the filling of the Spirit. That which gives us victory over temptation and the devil is the filling of the Spirit. We are filled with the Spirit when we abandon our own agendas and yield completely to the control of the Holy Spirit of God in our lives.

Father, it is our desire to be continually filled with the Holy Spirit. We ask that You help us fulfill this yearning, so that we can tell others about the truth.

> *Spirit of God, descend upon my heart;*
> *Wean it from earth, through all its pulses move;*
> *Stoop to my weakness, mighty as Thou art,*
> *And make me love Thee as I ought to love.*
>
> *George Croly*

White as Light

In Mark 9, we read of Jesus' transfiguration. In front of a handful of His disciples, Jesus pulled back the veil of His humanity for a moment in time and revealed a portion of His glorified being. Mark 9:3 says, "His clothes became shining, exceedingly white, like snow, such as no launderer on earth can whiten them." Jesus became white as light.

When God portrays Himself in the Bible, He does so with light. This is called God's shekinah glory. When He appeared to Moses, it was in a bush of burning light. When He led the children of Israel across the desert, it was as a pillar of fire by night. When Ezekiel saw a vision of God (Ezekiel 1:28), there was brightness all around. Later, in Revelation 1:16, John had a vision in which Jesus' "countenance was like the sun shining in its strength."

Jesus was showing His disciples that He was God! In John 8:12, Jesus said: "I am the light of the world. He who follows Me shall not walk in darkness, but have the light of life." May we focus on Jesus, the one true light!

Shining like the morning sun, Jesus, the righteous One.
Clothed in majesty, splendor and glory,
Jesus, the righteous One.
Righteous One, Holy Son, flow through this vessel of mine.
Filled with You, shining through,
flow through this vessel of mine.

Bruce and Teresa Muller

Peter the Preacher

It is a joy to examine the fact that it was Peter who preached the church's first sermon on the day of Pentecost. This is surprising, and yet not so surprising. It is not surprising that Peter stood up on Pentecost with something to say, because Peter made a habit of standing up with something to say! Unfortunately, it was usually the wrong thing. However, to see Peter preach at this point is quite unexpected.

One of the last times we saw him was in Luke 22, warming his hands at the enemies' fire. A girl came over to the fire and said, "This man was also with Him." He denied it. Another girl came over and spoke to him regarding his association with Jesus, and he denied it again. Still a third person came over, and Peter denied His Lord. Think about it: the last time we saw Peter, he was confronted by a group of campfire girls, and he couldn't even preach to them.

However, when we come to the day of Pentecost, who is preaching in front of thousands? Peter! What a transformation!

Let us be reminded that this is exactly what God will do through us as we habitually yield our lives to the control of the Holy Spirit. We may not be called to be preachers, but God will do things through each of us as individuals that we never dreamed possible as we yield ourselves completely to Him.

> *Take my life, and let it be*
> *Consecrated, Lord, to Thee;*
> *Take my hands and let them move*
> *At the impulse of Thy love.*
> *Take my silver and my gold,*
> *Not a mite would I withhold;*
> *Take my moments and my days,*
> *Let them flow in ceaseless praise.*
> *Take my will, and make it Thine,*
> *It shall be no longer mine;*
> *Take my heart, it is Thine own,*
> *It shall be Thy royal throne.*
>
> *Frances Havergal*

Backed by Prayer

There are many reasons why Peter's sermon on the day of Pentecost was so effective. He was filled with the Spirit; he used the Scriptures to point people to Christ; his message centered on Jesus Christ; and it was the Lord's perfect timing. Another vital reason is in the fact that his message was backed with prayer. We can use the Scriptures and talk about Jesus all we want, but if the words are not backed with fervent prayer, those words are not going to be as effective as they need to be. Oh, that we might see the importance of uniting in prayer to pray for those who are God's mouthpieces!

C. H. Spurgeon once said, speaking about the effectiveness of Peter's sermon:

> There had been a long season of earnest, united, believing prayer on the part of the whole church. Peter was not alone. He was the voice of a praying community; and the believers had been with one accord in one place, crying for a blessing. Thus, not only was the Spirit resting upon the preacher, but on all who were there with him.

What a difference it makes to a preacher of the gospel when all of his congregation is as anointed with the Spirit as he himself. His power is enhanced a hundredfold. We will seldom see the greatest wonders brought about when the preacher stands by himself. When Peter is described as standing up with the eleven, there is a twelve-man ministry concentrated into one. When the inner circle is further sustained by a company of men and women who have entered into the same truth and are of one heart and soul, then the power is increased beyond measure. A lonely ministry may sometimes affect great things as Jonah did in Nineveh, but the greatest and most desirable results must come from one who is not alone but who is the mouthpiece of many.

> *The church's one foundation is Jesus Christ her Lord;*
> *She is His new creation, by Spirit and the Word;*
> *From heaven He came and sought her to be His holy bride,*
> *With His own blood He bought her, and for her life He died.*

Samuel J. Stone

Setting the Lord Before Us

David wrote in Psalm 16:8, "I have set the Lord always before me." This is actually a messianic Psalm through which we hear Jesus speaking. Jesus said in John 4:34, "My food is to do the will of Him who sent Me." In John 8:29, He said, "I always do those things that please Him." The secret of Jesus' success over temptation as a man was to set the Father's face always before Him. He kept His eyes on the Father. If we want victory in our lives, we also need to keep our eyes on the Father. We need to keep our eyes on the Master.

My family has a dog named Sampson. He is a 165-pound Great Dane. When he came to live with us, it was decreed from the beginning that I would be the one to wash, feed, and pick up after him. Consequently, I spend the most time with him. As a result, he sees me as his master. One thing I taught him from the beginning was that he must sit down and stay before I feed him. If he gets up at any time or jumps around, I'll take his bowl of food away. At first he did not obey, but once he learned that he had to sit before he got his food, he obeyed. The interesting thing I have noticed is that whenever I come out to feed him, he keeps his eyes fixed on me; he doesn't look at the food. You see, he knows himself well enough to realize that he cannot handle the temptation of looking at the food.

We can learn a lot from Sampson. Even a dog knows that, in order to overcome temptation, he must keep his eyes fixed on the master.

As long as we keep our eyes on the Lord, we are all right. But as soon as we take our eyes off of Him, we fall. David said, "I have set the Lord always before me" (Psalm 16:8). He trusted the Lord to help him through temptations—temptations that we all have. We can do the same.

> *Turn your eyes upon Jesus,*
> *Look full in His wonderful face,*
> *And the things of earth will grow strangely dim,*
> *In the light of His glory and grace.*
>
> *Helen Lemmel*

How is One Saved?

The question is often asked, "How is one saved?" Depending on who is answering, there can be a variety of responses. The legalist will say, "Keep the law." The moralist says, "Be a good person." The ritualistic will declare, "Follow the right liturgy." And the universalistic comment is, "Don't worry about it; everyone is going to heaven."

What is the right answer? The first thing we need to ask ourselves is, "What does the Bible say?" The best place to look is in the first sermon ever preached. When Peter gave the invitation to salvation on the day of Pentecost, he said, "Repent" (Acts 2:38). Later, in the second message ever preached to the church, he said, "Repent therefore and be converted" (Acts 3:19). Romans 10:9 says that "if you confess with your mouth the Lord Jesus and believe in your heart that God raised Him from the dead, you will be saved." Ephesians 2:8 says, "For by grace you have been saved through faith."

In light of what the Bible says then, the right answer is:

> We must confess with our mouths the Lord Jesus.
> We must believe in our hearts that Christ rose from the dead.
> We must recognize that salvation comes through faith.

Peter adds in Acts 3 that repentance is also necessary. There is no true conversion without true repentance. Repentance means to make a 180-degree turn and move in the other direction. It means giving up the things in our lives that are keeping us from the Lord. It means turning from the old ways to allow Christ to rule our life. How is one saved? Through repentance of sin and faith in Jesus Christ.

Lord, take my life, and make it wholly Thine;
Fill my poor heart with Thy great love divine.
Take all my will, my passion, self and pride;
I now surrender, Lord, in me abide.

J. Edwin Orr

229

Don't Skirt the Issue

We often put ourselves under pressure to present the gospel in a cool, subtle, disguised way. We like to skirt the issue of sin. As a result, a lot of so-called conversions are not conversions at all. We need to understand that if a person has not confronted the issue of his or her own personal sin, then there is no way that person can be saved.

Some preachers tell people that they can be saved simply by believing in Jesus. "Just believe," they say. Listen, the demons believe, and they definitely are not saved (James 2:19). The element that is often missing in preaching is repentance. Telling people about their sin and their rebellion against God is not an easy task. But we must tell them the truth. We must tell them that they need to turn from sin to be saved.

Telling people that they can go to heaven simply because they believe in Jesus, without telling that they need to turn from sin, is lying. It is like a doctor giving his cancer patient a pill and saying, "Just take this pill and you'll be fine. Just believe in this pill." All the while, that doctor knows that he needs to tell this patient the truth. His truthful comments might include statements about possible surgery or chemotherapy or both. He needs to tell the patient that this drastic change must be made or death will result.

God, help us to present the full counsel of God when presenting the gospel!

> *Who'll go and help this Shepherd kind,*
> *Help Him the wandering ones to find?*
> *Who'll bring the lost ones to the fold,*
> *Where they'll be sheltered from the cold?*
> *Out in the desert hear their cry,*
> *Out on the mountains wild and high;*
> *Hark! 'Tis the Master speaks to thee,*
> *"Go find My sheep where e're they be."*
> *Bring them in, bring them in,*
> *bring them in from the fields of sin;*
> *Bring them in, bring them in,*
> *bring the wandering ones to Jesus.*

Alex Thomas

A Spiritually Thriving Church (Part 1)

In Acts 2:42–47, we have the ten characteristics of a spiritually thriving church. The first characteristic is that the people within it are saved. Verse 42 says that the people in this fellowship "continued steadfastly." This means that they were saved. The basic identifying quality of a true convert is that he continues in the faith.

Many churches are controlled, managed, and filled with a majority of unsaved people. God blessed the early church because it was a church controlled and led by men who were saved and filled with the Holy Spirit. We want unbelievers coming in our doors, but we—and God—want them saved.

The second characteristic of a spiritually thriving church is that it studies God's Word. Acts 2:42 says that "they continued steadfastly in the apostles' doctrine," meaning that they faithfully participated in the teaching of God's Word. The church and the individuals within it grow only so far as they have a desire to be taught God's Word (1 Peter 2:2). The main assembly must first be saved, but after that they must be taught. We cannot function on principles that we do not know. God said in Hosea 4:6, "My people are destroyed for lack of knowledge." How important it is to go to a church that teaches God's Word! God grant us the ability to be those fair-minded Bereans of Acts 17:11.

> *Our week is not complete till we make it our goal*
> *To honor the Lord's Day and nourish our soul;*
> *The help that we need for the tasks that we face*
> *Will come as we worship and draw on God's grace.*

D. J. De Haan

A Spiritually Thriving Church (Part 2)

The third characteristic of a spiritually thriving church is that the congregation spends time in fellowship. In Acts 2:42, the first church "continued steadfastly in the apostles' doctrine and fellowship."

The word for fellowship is koinonia. It means more than a sentimental friendship. It means togetherness at the deepest level. When the early church believers got together, they encouraged one another in their mutual faith. They served one another with their spiritual gifts. They cared for one another.

We are commanded to fellowship regularly in a local assembly, "not forsaking the assembling of ourselves together" (Hebrews 10:25). We need one another. We need one another's accountability and encouragement. The fact is, a church that is full of people having true koinonia with one another is going to be a very healthy, stable church.

The fourth characteristic of a spiritually thriving church is that it prays. Acts 2:42 says, "And they continued steadfastly in the apostles' doctrine and fellowship, in the breaking of bread, and in prayers." Prayer is the key that unlocks the heavens. Prayer is the slender nerve that moves the muscle of omnipotence. Too often, the church talks a lot about prayer but does little in prayer itself. What works God can and will do through us if we will but get on our knees and request His will and His way through prayer!

Have Thine own way, Lord!
Have Thine own way!
Search me and try me,
Master, today!
Whiter than snow, Lord,
Wash me just now,
As in Thy presence
Humbly I bow.

Adelaide A. Pollard

A Spiritually Thriving Church (Part 3)

The fifth characteristic of a spiritually thriving church is that it is a God-fearing church. Acts 2:43 says, "Then fear came upon every soul." This is not terrified fear, but a holy, reverential awe of God. The early church had a holy reverence for God. The church was desirous of lifting high the standard of God. There was respect, honor, and love toward God.

This does not mean that God wants us to look like His frozen chosen. In reality, we should be expressive in our joy, and, within that, embody a holy reverence for God.

The sixth characteristic of a spiritually thriving church is that it is a miracle-working church. Acts 2:43 says, "And many wonders and signs were done through the apostles." God still moves in miracles through His church today! The greatest miracle of all occurs when we are born again. We were crippled in our sin, and Christ healed us. We were blind in our lost condition, and Jesus opened our eyes and gave us the faith to believe in Him.

God wants to do many miraculous things through His church; and, yet, because of its unbelief, He doesn't. We read in Matthew 13:58, "Now He did not do many mighty works there because of their unbelief." What a tragedy it is when, through our unbelief, we stop the hand of God! The early church was a church of miracles because it didn't put God into a box, and God was willing and able to do mighty works in its midst.

As we gather, may Your Spirit work within us.
As we gather, may we glorify Your name.
Knowing well that as our hearts begin to worship,
we'll be blessed because we came,
we'll be blessed because we came.

Tom Coomes and Mike Fay

A Spiritually Thriving Church (Part 4)

The seventh characteristic of a spiritually thriving church is that its members share. Acts 2:44–45 says, "Now all who believed were together, and had all things in common, and sold their possessions and goods, and divided them among all, as anyone had need." The church is to be a place of compassion, a place of caring, a place of helping those in need.

The apostle John wrote in 1 John 3:16–18, "By this we know love, because He laid down His life for us. And we also ought to lay down our lives for the brethren. But whoever has this world's goods, and sees his brother in need, and shuts up his heart from him, how does the love of God abide in him? My little children, let us not love in word or in tongue, but in deed and in truth." The natural byproduct of a healthy church is sharing.

The eighth characteristic of a spiritually thriving church is that it is joyful. Acts 2:46–47 says, "So continuing daily with one accord in the temple, and breaking bread from house to house, they ate their food with gladness and simplicity of heart, praising God." Their time together was one of gladness, and they praised God. Ivor Powell once said, "A miserable Christian broadcasts to the world that something is wrong with his Christianity." The Bible tells us that joy is a fruit of the Spirit. Joy is associated with the early church throughout the book of Acts. (Acts 8:8; 13:48, 52; 15:3; 16:34).

When the church is filled with saved people walking in the Spirit, it will be a joyful church. That joy-filled church is going to affect many. God help us to be those joyful believers!

> *Joyful, joyful, we adore Thee,*
> *God of glory, Lord of love;*
> *Hearts unfold like flowers before Thee,*
> *Opening to the sun above.*
> *Melt the clouds of sin and sadness;*
> *Drive the dark of doubt away.*
> *Giver of immortal gladness,*
> *Fill us with the light of day!*

Henry Van Dyke

A Spiritually Thriving Church (Part 5)

The ninth characteristic of a spiritually thriving church is that it is attractive. Acts 2:47 tells us that the early church was "having favor with all the people." They had such a wonderful testimony for those outside the church that even unbelievers couldn't help liking them. If only we would have that kind of testimony!

What kind of testimony do we have at work? What might people say about us when we're not around? Would they say that we complain all the time and never finish our work? Or would they say that we're the best worker they have and that they'd like to come to our church? The early church was attractive because its members were concerned about their testimony both within and outside the church.

The tenth characteristic of a spiritually thriving church is that it permeates its surroundings. Acts 2:47 says, "And the Lord added to the church daily those who were being saved." This church penetrated and won its community. This church permeated the world. Why? Because they had all of the right ingredients. Consequently, the Lord added to the church.

The church does not grow through high-pressure evangelistic programs. It does not grow by trying to be palatable to everyone. The church grows by the sovereign hand of God. When a church is faithful and follows the pattern set by the early church, it will be a church that thrives. When it follows that pattern as directed by the Lord, it will permeate its community and the world.

God builds His church and makes it strong
by using you and me;
And if we all will do our part,
the world Christ's love will see.

Spurgeon

235

Jesus Sees Potential

We often remember Peter's failure as he denied his Lord three times. However, we often forget that Jesus restored him and used Peter to birth the early church. What was the secret of Peter's restoration? Ultimately, the Lord's intervention.

Consider that even before Peter denied his Lord, Jesus had told Peter in the upper room while they were celebrating the Passover meal: "Simon, Simon! Indeed, Satan has asked for you, that he may sift you as wheat. But I have prayed for you" (Luke 22:31–32). The reason Peter came through his devastating failure and was restored to great usefulness was because Jesus was praying for him. If for one moment Jesus stopped interceding for us, we would fall away and never come back. Jesus knew that Peter was going to fail, but He also knew that Peter would return. Why? Because He prayed for him.

We should be thankful that Jesus ever lives to make intercession for us (Hebrews 7:25). We also should be thankful that when Jesus looks at us, He sees the end result. He sees potential. We see a blank canvas; He sees a portrait. We see a lump of coal; He sees a diamond in the rough. We see a Jacob; He sees an Israel. We see a Saul; He sees a Paul. We see a Simon; He sees a Peter.

It is an overwhelming reality that from morning through night, He pays personal attention to our circumstances and He prays for us! He actually prays for us!

B. R. S.

236

Not Knowing the Scriptures

In Matthew 22:29, Jesus blasted the unscriptural teachings of the Sadducees and said to them, "You are mistaken, not knowing the Scriptures." Many people are thoroughly mistaken simply because they do not know the Scriptures, having not read them. There are people who will spend eternity in hell simply because they will not take the time to read to see whether Scripture is true. What a tragedy it is to hear of a person who rejects Jesus Christ as God but when asked if they have ever read the Bible, say no. Only a fool makes a decision of destiny based on the opinion of others! If a person has never read the whole Bible to see who Christ is, he needs to begin immediately.

Likewise, Christians need to read through the entire Bible to be able to prove Scripture with Scripture. Christians are remiss in their calling to be witnesses for Christ if they are lax in this. It is amazing to note the number of Christians involved in unbiblical activity or attending churches that teach false doctrine. Why do they? Because they simply take what comes from the speaker's mouth as being truth and don't take the time to read or study it in the Bible.

Our personal motto should be taken from this verse: "These were more fair-minded than those in Thessalonica, in that they received the word with all readiness, and searched the Scriptures daily to find out whether these things were so" (Acts 17:11). May we be faithful to read and apply the Scriptures to our lives.

The Bible is God's Word to us,
Still fresh through all the ages;
And if we read it we will find
God's wisdom in its pages.

Spurgeon

The Blessing of Revelation

The book of Revelation opens in verse 3 by saying, "Blessed is he who reads and those who hear the words of this prophecy, and keep those things which are written in it; for the time is near." And then Jesus closes the book by saying: "Behold, I am coming quickly! Blessed is he who keeps the words of the prophecy of this book" (Revelation 22:7).

Revelation is the only book in the Bible that begins and ends with a promise of blessing to those who read it. And yet if there is one book in the New Testament that is often overlooked, it's this one. Many have sealed the book of Revelation, yet Revelation 22:10 says, "Do not seal the words of the prophecy of this book, for the time is at hand."

The devil wins a great victory when he can keep God's people from reading the book that describes his ultimate demise. The book of Revelation should be the believer's most-read book. Why? Because it shows us Jesus' ultimate victory and, in His victory, our ultimate victory. We should read it because the time is at hand. Jesus can come back at any time, and we need to be ready.

The question is, are we ready? Do we know enough about Christ's return to share about it with others? We should bless ourselves at least twice a year by reading and studying the book of Revelation.

Ready to suffer grief or pain, ready to stand the test;
Ready to stay at home and send others, if He sees best.
Ready to speak, ready to warn, ready o'er
souls to yearn;
Ready in life, ready in death. Ready for His return.
Ready to go, ready to stay, ready my place to fill;
Ready for service, lowly or great, ready to do His will.

Anonymous

Anything to Burn?

We read a beautiful passage of surrender in Acts 19:19: "Also, many of those who had practiced magic brought their books together and burned them in the sight of all. And they counted up the value of them, and it totaled fifty thousand pieces of silver." Some translations use "curious arts" instead of "magic"; both are terms for the occult and witchcraft.

When the believers in Ephesus were saved, those who had practiced witchcraft and sorcery came to the Lord with unhindered conviction and burned the very books they had previously consulted. Having found the true meaning of life, they burned their bridges behind them and surrendered their lives totally to Christ. Not only that, but they didn't hold a garage sale to make money off of their old ways of life. Theirs was a total departure. These people made a clean cut and abandoned their old lifestyle to follow after Christ with all of their hearts.

We would all be better witnesses for our Lord if we took our own spiritual inventory regularly and burned the irrelevant. We need to have the Holy Spirit point out the things in our lives that the Lord wants us to burn. Those things could be some old pictures, some old books, some old letters, or even the music we used to listen to.

Whatever it is, Jesus wants us to surrender it to Him in order that He might replace it with the satisfaction of Himself and His peace.

I want to live above the world,
Tho' Satan's darts at me are hurled;
For faith has caught the joyful sound,
The song of saints on higher ground.
Lord, lift me up and let me stand,
By faith, on heaven's tableland,
A higher plane than I have found;
Lord plant my feet on higher ground.

Johnson Oatman Jr.

God's Calling, Our Enablement

Before Jesus gave His disciples the commission to go and make disciples of all nations, He said this in Matthew 28:18: "All authority has been given to Me in heaven and on earth." Why did Jesus start off with that statement in giving His Great Commission? There are two reasons:

First, He was saying, "If I have all authority, then you need to line up in submission to that authority." He was teaching that failure to do all we can to fulfill the Great Commission is simply a failure to submit to the authority of Jesus Christ. When we say, "Oh, I can't share my faith," what we are saying is "I don't want to submit to Jesus' authority in fulfilling my mission."

Second, Jesus stated His divine authority as a comfort. Think about it! Jesus is giving these eleven men the inconceivable task of taking the gospel to all of the nations. They know themselves well enough to know that they don't have the resources, the know-how, or the ability to do something this grandiose. So Jesus is saying, "When you submit to My authority to do what I command you to do, I'll give you the ability to accomplish the task."

Another way to put it is that God's calling, and our submission to that calling, is God's enablement. May we all submit to our Lord's authority and realize that He enables us with all the resources needed to accomplish the task.

Be not dismayed what e're betide,
God will take care of you;
Beneath His wings of love abide,
God will take care of you.
No matter what may be the test,
God will take care of you.
Lean, weary one, upon His breast,
God will take care of you.

Civilla D. Martin

Don't Despise

In Matthew 18:10, Jesus said, "Take heed that you do not despise one of these little ones." The term "little ones" refers to other Christians. Jesus was speaking to His disciples and saying, "See that you don't mistreat God's people."

In what ways can Christians despise other Christians? One way is by looking down our noses at those who don't hold to the same exact theological system we do. Many Christians are taken over by spiritual pride. They look down at others because they are not Calvanist, Arminian, pretrib, posttrib, premillennial, or amillennial.

It is essential that we hold fast to the cardinal doctrines of the faith. We must agree on the non-negotiables, but there are minor issues within the faith on which we can agree to disagree. Therefore, it is a sin to look down our noses in spiritual pride at those who don't agree with us 100 percent.

We are also looking down on other Christians if we despise them when they have fallen into sin. We say things like: "What a pity. They should have known better. I always thought that they would fall." That is despising God's people. That is sin. Instead, we should be restoring them (Galatians 6:1–2).

Let us put our focus on the good of others instead of on despising them. God help us to be loving and concerned about recovering and restoring lost souls.

You can't help a person uphill without getting closer to the top yourself.

Anonymous

A Hot Prospect

In Matthew 19:16, we read about a young man who was probably one of the hottest prospects for salvation. He came running to Jesus and asked, "Good Teacher, what good thing shall I do that I may have eternal life?" Reflect on that: this man wanted to have eternal life! He wanted to know what to do to have salvation. Unfortunately, as hot a prospect as he was, verse 22 tells us that "he went away sorrowful." The question is, why? The answer is that

He wanted to know what good thing he could do to have eternal life. The Bible tells us in Ephesians 2:8–9, "For by grace you have been saved through faith, and that not of yourselves; it is the gift of God, not of works, lest anyone should boast." We don't work for salvation; it's a gift presented to us when we submit ourselves to the lordship of Jesus Christ.

We are told that went home sorrowful because he had great possessions, and Jesus had asked him to part with these. Although there is nothing wrong with having money and possessions, the problem was that money possessed him. Money was more important to him than eternal life.

Here is a very significant question we all need to ask ourselves—and ask often: What is the most important thing in my life?

As the deer panted for the water,
so my soul longeth after Thee.
You alone are my heart's desire,
and I long to worship Thee.
You're my friend and You're my brother
even though You are a King.
I love You more than any other,
so much more than anything.
I want You more than gold or silver,
only You can satisfy.
You alone are the real joy-giver
and the apple of my eye.
You alone are my strength, my shield;
To You alone may my spirit yield.
You alone are my heart's desire, and I long to worship Thee.

Martin Mystrom

Reverence toward God

In Revelation 1, the apostle John had a vision of our glorified Lord. Jesus Christ appeared to John robed in holiness, majesty, dignity, and glory. He came to John in a regal splendor of sovereignty, authority, and power such as no man had ever seen. We read of the vision's effect in verse 17, where John writes, "And when I saw Him, I fell at His feet as dead." John was completely overwhelmed!

It is interesting that throughout the Bible, this is always the response of those who come into the presence of God. Keep in mind the Old Testament instances of this as recorded in Genesis 17:1–3; Judges 13:15–22; Isaiah 6:1–5; Ezekiel 1:28, 3:23, 43:3, and 44:4; Daniel 10:5–9; and Habakkuk 3:16.

We might ask, why? Job best states it in Job 42:5–6: "I have heard of You by the hearing of the ear, But now my eye sees You. Therefore I abhor myself, And repent in dust and ashes." What Job is talking about, and John is displaying, is a reverential fear and awe of God.

When people recognize that they have come into the presence of God, they are immediately confronted with their own sinfulness. The only proper response is a sense of unworthiness and holy fear.

We may not have a visitation from God, but God is with us. And when we are in the Lord's presence, there should be a sense of worship and reverential awe of Him. May this adoration and reverence for our Lord be reflected in everything we do and say.

I see the Lord seated on the throne—exalted,
And the train of His robe fills the temple with glory;
And the whole earth is filled, a
nd the whole earth is filled,
And the whole earth is filled with His glory.
Holy, holy, holy, holy, holy is the Lord of lords.

Chris Falson

Surely I Am Coming Quickly

Revelation 22:20 records Jesus' last words in the Bible, where He says, "Surely I am coming quickly." We are living at the end of the age, anticipating the fulfillment of those very words. Let us walk with the Lord throughout the day, anticipating His return and believing that this may well be the day of our Lord's return.

Perhaps today our Lord will come
To bear us to our much loved home;
Before the evening shadows fall
May sound the longed-for clarion call;
Then out of sorrow, tears and strife,
We'll rise to realms of joy and life.

Perhaps today will be the last,
And time shall be forever past.
Our light affliction will be o'er,
The glory! Glory! Evermore!
These days of toil and pain will cease
And faithful workers rest in peace.

Perhaps today mine eyes shall see
The Lamb of God who died for me;
Oh, nothing else will matter then,
If unto Him I've faithful been.
Live for that day, O soul of mine,
And joy eternal shall then be thine.

Unknown

Godliness Brings on Persecution

In 2 Timothy 3:12, we read, "Yes, and all who desire to live godly in Christ Jesus will suffer persecution." That is a promise! Godly lives automatically go against the grain of a society that is hostile to Christ and His church. When a person says, "I'm not suffering persecution at all, and I never have," it should tell you something very clear: they are not living a godly life.

Now when the apostle Paul wrote to Timothy that all who desire to live godly lives will suffer persecution, he didn't mean to say that our lives will just be one long series of persecutions, one after another. However, he did mean that there will be times when our faith will get us into trouble in the world.

If a person has never experienced any resistance from the world, it means one of three things:

1) They have purposely hidden their faith so well that nobody knows about it.

2) They have fallen so far into sin that they have become just like the world, and no one can tell the difference.

3) They are not saved.

None of those three scenarios is beneficial. Jesus said in Matthew 5:14–16 to let our light shine before men in the world. The truth is, if we are obedient to that, there will be times when the world will hate us. What do we do when that happens? We must trust God and use any persecution, or semblance thereof, as an opportunity to proclaim God's truth.

Stand up, stand up for Jesus,
Stand in His strength alone;
The arm of flesh will fail you,
Ye dare not trust your own.
Put on the gospel armor,
Each piece put on with prayer;
Where duty calls or danger,
Be never wanting there.
Stand up, stand up for Jesus,
The strife will not be long,
This day the noise of battle,
The next the victor's song;
To him that overcometh
A crown of life shall be;
He, with the King of glory,
Shall reign eternally.

George Duffield Jr.

245

Dealing with Persecution (Part 1)

In Acts 4:1–31, we have the first wave of persecution brought against the church. Peter and John had healed a lame man in the temple area. As a result, they were thrown in jail and stood before the Sanhedrin. Peter had only preached two sermons, and hostility had already broken out. Make note of the church's response in the midst of this persecution.

First, they were submissive to the situation. They didn't resist arrest, go limp, or complain. They didn't try to argue their way out of the situation. Rather, they went right along with the arrest and allowed themselves to stand before these men in trial. Why? Because they had an underlying trust in God. In the midst of persecution, if our obedience to God gets us in trouble, then understand that the trouble has been sent by God. When we submit to the situation, trusting Him, watch out! God is going to open up some wonderful opportunities to share the gospel. That is exactly what happened with Peter and John in this situation.

Second, these men were bold. They didn't roll over and play dead. They used the opportunity to preach the Word of God. When under pressure, we are often tempted to silence ourselves. These men did just the opposite. When the pressure was turned up, they turned up their volume and used the occasion to proclaim God's truth.

When persecution confronts us, we need to submit to it, trust God in it, and use it as an opportunity to proclaim the Word of God with boldness.

> *Open my mouth, and let it bear,*
> *Gladly the warm truth everywhere;*
> *Open my heart, and let me prepare,*
> *Love with Thy children thus to share.*
> *Silently now I wait for Thee,*
> *Ready, my God, Thy will to see;*
> *Open my heart, illumine me,*
> *Spirit divine!*
>
> *Clara H. Scott*

Dealing with Persecution (Part 2)

The believer's third response to persecution is obedience. It would have been easy for Peter and John to buckle under in front of the Sanhedrin. Compared to the Sanhedrin, they were a couple of hayseeds from Galilee facing the noblest, ablest, richest, and most powerful men of Judaism. However, when the Sanhedrin tried to silence them, they responded with great clarity: "Whether it is right in the sight of God to listen to you more than to God, you judge. For we cannot but speak the things which we have seen and heard" (Acts 4:19–20).

Peter and John essentially said, "Threaten us all you want, but we're going to keep preaching and teaching the Word of God!" When faced with persecution, we must be more concerned about what God thinks than what men think.

The fourth response to persecution should be one of praise. In Acts 5:41, when the disciples were actually scourged for Christ, we read that they were "rejoicing that they were counted worthy to suffer shame for His name." We never see the early church murmuring, regretting, grumbling, bemoaning, or pouting. It was always praising! When its people were under attack, their response was, "Lord, you are in control of our circumstances, so we praise you for what you have allowed, and we submit to your wisdom regarding this persecution, and we praise You in the midst of it."

The fifth response to persecution is that of prayer. We read in Acts 4:31, "And when they had prayed, the place where they were assembled together was shaken; and they were all filled with the Holy Spirit, and they spoke the word of God with boldness."

What should we do when put under pressure? Pray! How should we react in the midst of persecution? Pray!

Pray for great things, expect great things, work for great things, but above all, pray!

R. A. Torry

September 1

Leaving Your First Love

In Revelation 2:1–7, we read about the church that had left its first love—the church of Ephesus. Here was a church that at one time was the most spiritually influential and Holy Spirit–empowered church in Asia Minor. Yet by the turn of the century, it had become known to our Lord as a church that had left its first love.

As we read about this church, we see that it was doctrinally sound. The congregants were concerned for righteousness, and they were hard workers. Through the course of time, however, they had become mechanical. They were just going through the motions, and their love for God had grown cold.

We must all be on our guard against spiritual apathy and indifference. These are things that polarize us from our first love relationship with Jesus Christ. In God's economy, the church's most valuable commodity is love (1 Corinthians 13:1–3).

We need to take our spiritual temperature regularly to see where we are. Are we as on fire for God as we once were when we first gave our life to Jesus Christ? Or are we comfortably warm in our relationship with Christ? Or have we left our first love altogether and are spiritually frigid?

If we are anything but on fire for Christ, the Holy Spirit would have us return to our first love. And when being on fire is our deep desire, the Holy Spirit will prick our hearts to do what God would want.

> *Come, Holy Spirit, fall afresh on me.*
> *Fill me with Your power, satisfy my needs.*
> *Only You can make me whole,*
> *Give me strength to make me grow.*
> *Come, Holy Spirit, fall afresh on me.*
>
> *Malcolm Fletcher*

Truth Is Truth

If a person drives a car down the road and comes across a sign that reads Dangerous Curve Ahead, a choice must be made. The driver can 1) observe the sign and slow down, 2) choose to ignore the sign and proceed at the present speed, or 3) defy the sign and speed up. No matter the choice, the truth of the sign will not be changed. The curve ahead remains dangerous whether the truth of the sign is acknowledged or not.

Winston Churchill once said: "The truth is incontrovertible. Panic may resent it; ignorance may deride it; malice may distort it; but there it is."

Jesus said in John 14:6, "I am the way, the truth, and the life." The greatest fact on earth is that Jesus Christ was crucified, died, and was buried, and on the third day rose again—all for the sins of man.

Have we responded to that truth? Did we defy it? Did we ignore it and proceed as if we had never heard it? Or did we observe and respond to it the way God intended? Jesus said in John 8:32, speaking of those who were true disciples, "And you shall know the truth, and the truth shall make you free."

I believe in Jesus, I believe He is the Son of God.
I believe He died and rose again,
I believe He paid for us all.
Here with the power to heal now,
and the grace to forgive.
And I believe that He's here now, standing in our midst.
Here with the power to heal now,
and the grace to forgive.
I believe in You, Lord, I believe You are the Son of God.
I believe You died and rose again,
I believe You paid for us all.
And I believe that You're here now,
standing in our midst.
Here with the power to heal now,
and the grace to forgive.

Marc Nelson

Keep the Bride Pure

In Acts 5, God took the lives of Ananias and Sapphira because they lied to the Holy Spirit. God purged out the sin. Then we read in verse 11, "So great fear came upon the church and upon all who heard these things," and in verse 13, "Yet none of the rest dared join them." But in verse 14, we read, "And believers were increasingly added to the Lord."

Because God was faithful to purge the sin out of the church, fear came upon those who were only idly curious and wanted the fringe benefits of Christianity. They stayed away for fear of their lives. On the other hand, adoration was kindled in the hearts of those who truly had enthroned Jesus in their hearts, and they were added daily to the church.

When a church of believers is concerned for the righteousness of God and willing to confront sin, then the mixed multitude won't join themselves to it and the church is kept pure. However, when a church ceases to deal with sin and allows anything and everything to go unchallenged and unchecked, then the church looks just like the world. And, instead of making an impact on society, they are ignored by society.

O God, help us to keep Your bride pure. Help us to be continually alert to unrighteousness among our assembly, and give us the courage and boldness to deal with it.

Father in heaven, who loves all,
O help Thy children when they call,
That they may build from age to age
An undefiled heritage.
Teach us to rule ourselves always,
Controlled and cleanly night and day;
That we may bring, if need arise,
No maimed or worthless sacrifice.

Rudyard Kipling

Comfort in Suffering

Jesus wrote to the suffering church of Smyrna (Revelation 2:9) and comforted them by saying in verse 9, "I know your works, tribulation, and poverty (but you are rich)." Jesus encouraged them in three ways:

First, "I know your works." He is saying that He sees everything that they are doing for His name's sake and it wouldn't go unrewarded.

Second, "I know your tribulation." The word tribulation in Greek describes a crushing pressure. Jesus is saying that He knows the crushing pressure they feel, and that He will relieve the pressure when the time is right.

Third, "I know your poverty." This word poverty in Greek means "absolute nothingness." Jesus says, "I know that you have nothing physically." However, He adds, "But you are rich."

How could they be rich when they literally had nothing but the clothes on their backs? He wanted them to realize they were rich in Him! Second Corinthians 8:9 tells us Paul says of Jesus, "Though He was rich, yet for your sakes He became poor, that you through His poverty might become rich." When we have Jesus Christ in us, we are rich!

Let us ask ourselves, Am I in the midst of an overwhelming trial? Am I under crushing pressure? Perhaps it's the threat of losing a job. Maybe it's a wayward spouse or even the worry of never having a spouse. Whatever it is, Jesus knows. He says, "I know your works, tribulation, and poverty (but you are rich)." Turn to the rich source of your salvation. Draw near to God, and He will draw near to you.

There is a place of quiet rest, Near to the heart of God.
A place where sin cannot molest, Near to the heart of God.
There is a place of full release, Near to the heart of God.
A place where all is joy and peace,
Near to the heart of God.

C. B. McAfee

Suffering Presses Us Closer to God

Often we wonder why God allows suffering in the life of the believer. Sure, we understand why the ungodly suffer—they have rejected Christ. But often believers don't understand why God allows dear saints to suffer.

There are many reasons. Sometimes it's for disciplinary reasons. Hebrews 12:6 says, "Whom the Lord loves He chastens." Sometimes God allows suffering as a preventative. For example, the apostle Paul was given "a thorn in the flesh," lest he become too proud and, in the process, be of no use for the kingdom of God (2 Corinthians 12:7). Sometimes God allows suffering to teach us. There are certain things He knows that we can learn only through trials. Perseverance is one of them (Romans 5:3–5). Still another reason God allows suffering in the life of the believer is because it tests one's faith and draws that person closer to Him. In the midst of suffering, the unbeliever will abandon ship, whereas the true believer will be drawn closer to God. In that sense, then, suffering also becomes an assurance of true faith.

So, as believers, we should never be frustrated with God in the midst of suffering, but rather be thankful to Him that He is pressing us to know only Him as our Helper.

Pressed out of measure, pressed to all length,
Pressed so intently, it seems beyond strength.
Pressed in body and pressed in soul,
Pressed in mind till the dark surges roll.
Pressure by foes and pressure by friends,
Pressure on pressure till life nearly ends.
Pressed into loving the staff and the rod,
Pressed into knowing no helper but God.

Annie Johnson Flint

Men of Leadership

The church today is in desperate need of men in leadership like the men of the early church. When the apostles were faced with the overwhelming task of managing the church, it was obvious that they needed help in dealing with the mass of people. That being the case, they looked among themselves and selected seven men. These were men whom they could appoint over the daily distribution of feeding the poor and taking care of the widows. The qualifications of these men serves as great example of what we need to see today in the church. Acts 6:3 says that they were "Men of good reputation, full of the Holy Spirit and wisdom"—three significant traits.

Men of good reputation. Men of unblemished character. Men of integrity. Men who avoid evil at all cost. Men who have a testimony not only within the church, but from without the church as well.

Men full of the Holy Spirit. Men who are not drunk with wine, but continuously filled with the Holy Spirit (Ephesians 5:18). Men whose lives are not their own but lost in the will of God. Men filled with the Holy Spirit will exhibit the fruit of the Spirit. Galatians 5:22–23 says this is "love, joy, peace, longsuffering, kindness, goodness, faithfulness, gentleness, self-control."

Men full of wisdom. Men who apply knowledge correctly. Men who make the right decisions at the right time.

May the church in these last days strive to put these kinds of men in leadership positions. Let us do this so the true church may be a pure church with an untainted testimony!

Being filled with the Holy Spirit is everything. He rules me with the utmost authority. I am grateful for His presence and tolerance.

B. R. S.

An Effective Church

When we look at the early church in the book of Acts, we see a vibrant and effective fellowship. What made them so effective? Here are five observations:

They were unified. In the early chapters of Acts, we read that they were with one accord; they were of the same heart and the same mind. A unified church will impact a nation.

They were courageous. They boldly proclaimed the truth when the truth wasn't popular. The truth isn't popular today; but no church is ever going to make an impact on its community unless it courageously and boldly proclaims the truth.

There was total involvement. Everyone was so on fire for the Lord that they all got involved. No one had "spectator-itis." There was total involvement because there was total commitment.

They preached a pure message. They taught the pure milk of God's Word. Today, a lot of churches teach pabulum, if not heresy. God wants us to teach and proclaim His unadulterated word.

They backed their pure message with a pure life. The early church dealt with sin. They didn't allow ungodliness to go unchecked in their midst. As a result, they stood out from the rest of the world. Those who wanted to embrace Christianity knew the clear, high standards. Those who were around just for the perks didn't hang around too long.

The church that is unified, courageous, totally involved, preaching the pure milk of God's Word, and backing it up with a pure life will be a church that makes an impact on society.

Hallelujah! Thine glory,
Hallelujah! Amen;
Hallelujah! Thine glory,
Revive us again.

William P. MacKay

A Whole Life

I have heard it said when someone died at a ripe old age that "they lived a whole life." It isn't necessarily true that just because someone lived to old age, they lived a whole life. The effect of a person's life is not measured by how long they lived but how they lived. If they lived a long, unproductive, carnal life as a believer, what did they accomplish? Conversely, if their life was short but holy, they lived a whole life. A holy life is a whole life.

Robert Murray McCheyne was a young Scottish preacher in the early 1800s. He died at the age of twenty-nine, and yet his impact has continued to be felt. One of his favorite sayings was "Live so as to be missed." He did just that!

Consider Stephen in the book of Acts. Christianity had just gotten started when he died as the church's first martyr. Yet the impact of his life is still being felt. It was his death that catapulted the gospel from the Jews in Jerusalem to the Gentiles at the ends of the earth.

Again, the effect of one's life is not measured by how long they live, but how they live. A whole life is a holy life. God help us to live so as to be missed!

Living for Jesus a life that is true,
Striving to please Him in all that I do.
Yielding allegiance, glad-hearted and free,
This is the pathway of blessing for me.

O Jesus, Lord and Savior, I give myself to Thee,
For Thou, in Thine atonement,
didst give Thyself for me.
I own no other Master, my heart shall be Thy throne.
My life I give, henceforth to live, O Christ
for Thee alone.

Thomas O. Chisholm

Godly Influence

Andrew Murray was a pastor in the late 1800s. He lived such a godly life that it permeated those who were closest to him, which, by the way, is where it should begin.

Those to whom his influence was greatest were his children and his grandchildren. He had eleven children. Five of his sons became ministers of the gospel. Four of his daughters became pastors' wives. Even the third generation did well. Ten of his grandsons became pastors, and thirteen of his grandchildren became missionaries. That speaks of the powerful influence of a godly life!

Jesus said in Matthew 5:13–14: "You are the salt of the earth . . . You are the light of the world." We are to permeate and influence the world!

Do our coworkers see an obvious distinction in our lives? What do our friends see in us that is different from everything else they see promoted by the world? If they don't see anything different, then we are not being salt and light.

God grant us to be that salt and light to a dark and thirsty world!

Come to the Light, 'tis shining for thee;
Sweetly the Light has dawned upon me.
Once I was blind, but now I can see:
The Light of the world is Jesus.

Philip P. Bliss

No Fear of Death

Shakespeare wrote in Othello, "The weariest and most loathed worldly life that age, ache, penury, and imprisonment can lay on nature—is a paradise to what we fear of death." In other words, the worst that life has to offer is a paradise as compared to death. That is not so for the believer! This world is the closest a believer in Christ will ever get to hell. However, to an unbeliever this world is the closest they will ever get to heaven.

The world fears death and rightly so. A life without Christ will result in an eternity without Christ. But for the believer there is great confidence. For the believer, death is not an obstacle; it is a passage—a passage that leads us to Christ.

The apostle Paul said in 2 Corinthians 5:8, "We are confident, yes, well pleased rather to be absent from the body and to be present with the Lord." When we die in Christ, we go immediately to be with Him and death has no sting.

Paul wrote in 1 Corinthians 15:54–57: "Death is swallowed up in victory. O Death, where is your sting? O Hades, where is your victory? . . . But thanks be to God, who gives us the victory through our Lord Jesus Christ."

We Christians need not fear death! As our life is filled with Christ, so our death will be filled with Christ; and thus we will live with Christ forever!

Face to face with Christ, my Savior,
Face to face—what will it be,
When with rapture I behold Him,
Jesus Christ who died for me.
Face to face, O blissful moment!
Face to face—to see and know;
Face to face with my Redeemer,
Jesus Christ who loves me so.

Mrs. Frank A. Breck

Spiritual Dynamos

As Christians we often look at people in the Bible, as well as those today who are spiritual dynamos, and say, "That is what I want to be. Lord, make me that spiritual stick of dynamite." Understand though, those who are spiritual dynamos for the kingdom are always going to come up against opposition. When God's people say, "Let us arise and build!" the enemy says, "Let us arise and oppose!"

Being a spiritual dynamo is going to cost you. There will be spiritual battles to fight—daily battles. But is there any better place to be? Absolutely not! Better to fight in the front ranks for God and be wounded from time to time than to sit in the rear flanks licking your wounds saying: "I could have done that. I could have said that. I could have served in that capacity." Listen, don't be content to dwell in the plains of mediocrity. Instead, keep fighting and clawing your way to God's mountaintop—for His glory!

The apostle Paul said in Philippians 3:14, "I press toward the goal for the prize of the upward call of God in Christ Jesus." May it be so of us!

My heart has no desire to stay
Where doubts arise and fears dismay;
Tho' some may swell where these abound,
My prayer, my aim is higher ground.
I want to live above the world,
Tho' Satan's darts at me are hurled;
For faith has caught the joyful sound,
The song of saints on higher ground.
Lord, lift me up and let me stand,
By faith, on heaven's tableland,
A higher plane than I have found;
Lord, plant my feet on higher ground.

Johnson Oatman Jr.

When Jesus Stood Up

We read in Hebrews 1:3 that when Jesus ascended into heaven, He "sat down at the right hand of the Majesty on high." Jesus also told Caiaphas at His trial in Matthew 26:64, "Hereafter you will see the Son of Man sitting at the right hand of the Power." The "right hand of the Power" (God) represents the highest place of honor.

In light of that, it is interesting that when Stephen was being stoned to death for his faith, Acts 7:55 tells us, "But he, being full of the Holy Spirit, gazed into heaven and saw the glory of God, and Jesus standing at the right hand of God." Why in other passages is Jesus sitting at the right hand of God, but at Stephen's death Jesus is standing at the right hand of God?

I believe that Jesus stood up to greet the church's first martyr into the kingdom. It is as if Jesus was saying to Stephen, "Well done, good and faithful servant; you were faithful over a few things, I will make you ruler over many things. Enter into the joy of your lord" (Matthew 25:21). Think about it! Stephen only lived a few months as a believer, but was he ever a powerhouse for the kingdom.

This is the only New Testament account we have of what is going on in heaven at the time of a believer's death. Could it be that Christ stands up to greet all of His saints into the kingdom?

We can't be dogmatic, but one thing we can do: live so as to hear our Savior say, "Well done, good and faithful servant."

I will love You Lord
With all my heart
I will praise Your name
With every thought
And with all my soul
I will bless You O Lord
And with all my strength
I will run the race
Until that final day when I hear You say
Enter in, Enter in, Enter in
Thou good and faithful child
Enter in, Enter in, Enter in
To the joy of Your Lord

Dan Loaiza

Crisis Grace

We read in Acts 7:60 that while Stephen was being stoned to death for his faith in Christ, "he knelt down and cried out with a loud voice, 'Lord, do not charge them with this sin.' And when he had said this, he fell asleep." He learned that from the Lord himself.

Remember, when Jesus was dying on the cross, He said, "Father, forgive them, for they do not know what they do" (Luke 23:34). Stephen lived and died what he saw in the life of his Lord. At the end of his life, Stephen was given an extra measure of grace to endure this time and pray for those who were murdering him.

This is what we could call "crisis grace." When we are faithful to obey the call of God, and that places us in a crisis situation, God is faithful to give us an extra measure of His grace to bear the situation so that even though we are weak, He will be strong on our behalf and work through us.

That is why the apostle Paul was able to say in 2 Corinthians 12:10: "Therefore I take pleasure in infirmities, in reproaches, in needs, in persecutions, in distresses, for Christ's sake. For when I am weak, then I am strong."

As Christians, we can be confident that if God does allow a crisis to occur when we are obeying His call, He will be strong on our behalf and give us the grace to bear it.

He will deliver me, my God will set me free,
From all my enemies. He will deliver me.
My God and Savior, Savior, He will deliver me.
My God and Savior, Savior, He will deliver me.

Bill Batstone

Compromise

A Russian parable tells of a hunter who once raised his rifle and took careful aim at a large bear. When the man was about to pull the trigger, the bear spoke in a soft, soothing voice: "Isn't it better to talk than to shoot? What do you want? Let us negotiate the matter." Lowering his rifle, the hunter replied, "I want a fur coat."

"Good," said the bear, "that is a negotiable question. I only want a full stomach, so let's negotiate a compromise." They sat down to negotiate and, after a time, the bear walked away alone. The negotiations had been successful. The bear had his full stomach, and the hunter had his fur coat.

The moral of the parable is that compromise never satisfies both parties in equal measure.

Relating that to the Christian walk, we could say this: the Christian who compromises his or her Christian values always ends up on the losing end. James 4:4 says, "Do you not know that friendship with the world is enmity with God?" When we compromise with the world, we set ourselves against God's best guidance and end up getting swallowed by something foolish in the world.

Compromise short-circuits the believer. How do we avoid the pitfalls of compromise? Ephesians 5:15–16 says, "See then that you walk circumspectly, not as fools but as wise, redeeming the time, because the days are evil." Be wise, believer! Walk circumspectly, walk carefully, and don't compromise with those things in the world that can easily cause you, as an individual, to fall.

Lord, You are my refuge, my life is in Your hand.
I know that I can trust You, and with Your help I'll stand.
I will not be shaken if Your favor I can see.
I'll stand strong like a mountain if
You just shine Your light on me.

Rick Founds

What If Christ Came to Visit?

If Jesus came to your house to spend a day or two,
If He came unexpectedly, I wondered what you'd do.
Oh, I know you'd give your nicest room to such an honored guest.
And all the food you'd serve to Him would be your very best.
And would you keep assuring Him you're glad to have Him there?
But when you saw Him coming, would you meet Him at the door
With arms outstretched to welcome your heavenly visitor?
Or would you maybe change your clothes before you let Him in?
Or hide some magazines and put the Bible where they'd been?
Would you turn off the radio and hope He hadn't heard?
And wish you hadn't uttered that last loud, hasty word?
Would you hide your worldly music and put some hymn books out?
Could you let Jesus walk right in or would you rush about?
And I wonder if the Savior spent a day of two with you,
Would you go right on doing the things you always do?
Would you go right on saying the things you always say?
Would life for you continue as it does from day to day?
Would your family conversation keep up its usual pace?
Or would you find it hard each meal to say a table grace?
Or would you sing the songs you always sing, read the book you read?
And let Him know the things on which your mind and spirit feed?
Would you take Jesus with you everywhere you plan to go?
Or would you maybe change your plans for just a day or so?
Would you be glad to have Him meet your very closest friends?
Or would you hope they'd stay away until His visiting ends?
Would you be glad to have Him stay forever on?
Or would you sigh with great relief "At last!" when He was gone?
It might be interesting to know the things that you would do
If Jesus came in person to spend some time with you.

Anonymous

Truth and Love

In the book of Revelation, we find an interesting contrast between the church of Ephesus and the church of Thyatira. The church of Ephesus had begun to leave its first love, but they were very faithful to keep false doctrine out. On the other hand, the church of Thyatira was continuing to grow in their love, but they had allowed false doctrine to infiltrate their fellowship.

We must avoid both extremes. Mainly, we need to display the love of God. However, in wanting to show God's love, we cannot implement sloppy agape and water down the truth to get someone into the church. On the other hand, we don't want be cold, calculating Bible bashers that act like God's frozen chosen. We don't want to be doctrinally correct but then show no love.

We need to do what the apostle Paul said in Ephesians 4:15: "But, speaking the truth in love, may grow up in all things into Him who is the head—Christ."

May we display the love of Christ without deviating from the truth. May we pursue a balanced walk through the guidance of the Holy Spirit.

O Jesus, Master, when today,
I meet, along the crowded way,
My burdened brothers—mine and Thine,
May then through me Thy Spirit shine.
To cheer them in their onward way,
Till evening ends the varied day,
To kindle so a growing light,
Where else might be but gloom and night.

Charles S. Newhall

Revival

An article in the paper stated that our society needs to be shocked with crisis—that our nation needs a rebirth. We probably all agree; it is what the church calls revival. We hear a lot about revival. Some churches have a week-long meeting every year and call it revival. But that is not a revival.

A true revival is a sovereign work of God. It is when God supernaturally tears open the heavens and comes to visit His people in a very special way. There are two significant keys to inviting God to bring this visitation. They are sincere prayer and the preaching of God's Word.

First, let's look at prayer. Jonathan Edwards said, "When God is about to do a great work, he pours out a spirit of supplication." Leonard Ravenhill said, "If the church today had as many agonizers as she has advisors, we would have a revival in a year." God brings revival when we have a bent knee, a wet eye, and a broken heart.

Second, revival is always centered on God's Word. There are always new winds of doctrine blowing through the church. There is always someone manufacturing something new in the flesh and packaging it to make it seem that it is a move of God. But all true revivals in the Bible are centered on the preaching and expositional teaching of God's Word.

Listen, it doesn't matter how high you jump in church. It matters how straight you walk when you get out. The only way to bring about true revival in our churches is by getting down on our knees in prayer—fueling that prayer with God's Word.

Stretch out Your hand and heal this nation.
Stretch out Your hand and bring restoration.
Let Your mercy overflow us like a never-failing stream,
By the blood of Jesus cleanse us, Oh, Lord, it's You we seek.
Cause your face to shine upon us again.

Scott V. Smith and Malcolm du Plessis

One Life—Many People

Throughout the Bible, we see that God often uses one individual to impact many lives for the gospel. God needs only one sold-out individual. When Jesus went to the city of Sychar in Samaria, He met a woman at a well. Through the course of the conversation, she received the living water that Jesus spoke of and she gave her life to Christ. John 4 tells us that she then left her water pot and went back in to the city, telling everyone about Jesus. As a result, many Samaritans gave their lives to Him. One life impacted many.

There was the man possessed with a legion of demons (Mark 5). Jesus cast the demons out of him, and the man gave his life to Christ. The Bible tells us that he was "clothed and in his right mind." At that point Jesus proceeded to leave, and the man wanted to come with Him. But Jesus said in Mark 5:19, "Go home to your friends, and tell them what great things the Lord has done for you, and how He has had compassion on you." The healed and changed man did just that and more. In fact, he shared the gospel with the surrounding ten cities. The next time Jesus came to that region, multitudes of people came to Him and were saved. Again, one life impacted many.

Each of us needs to ask himself these questions: Am I willing to be that one? Am I willing to stand up for Christ wherever He has placed me and be willing to be His voice? Do I love Him enough and feel grateful enough to tell others what He's done for me?

There is but one question of the hour:
How to bring the truth of God's Word
Into vital contact with the minds and hearts
Of all classes of people.

William Ewart Gladstone

Using Every Opportunity

While the apostle Paul was imprisoned in Rome, he wrote a letter to the Colossian church with an interesting request. In Colossians 4:3, he asked them to be "praying also for us, that God would open to us a door for the word."

It is not shocking that Paul asked for prayer, but it is important to note what he didn't ask for in his prayer. He didn't ask them to pray for his release. He didn't ask them to pray for a successful trial or for better living quarters. He didn't ask them to pray for release from his hard task. What he did ask for, though, was that God would open up another opportunity to preach the Word of God.

Think about it! Paul saw his imprisonment as God's divine appointment. He was always desirous of using every opportunity to present the gospel.

Instead of praying that God take us out of our circumstances, we need to pray that God would use us in those circumstances. We need to see them as divine appointments to present the gospel. God doesn't send us trials to make us bitter, but to make us better. Instead of grumbling, we should be grateful that God would use us to present His good news. When we make ourselves available to Him to be used for His redemptive purposes, He gladly enriches and applies what we are to impact lives.

I press on toward the goal to win the prize for which God has called me.
Philippians 3:14 NIV

The important thing in this world is not where we stand, but in what direction we move.

Johann Wolfgang von Goethe

Fiery Trials

We read in 1 Peter 4:12, "Beloved, do not think it strange concerning the fiery trial which is to try you, as though some strange thing happened to you." Peter is telling Christians to not be surprised when trials come. Yet there are those within the body of Christ who will say that we are going through a trial because we are in sin. That is nothing short of a lie! In fact, Peter tells us here to expect trials! They are inevitable! Why? Because God sends them. He sends them to work some very beautiful things in our lives.

Trials are given to purge us of sin. They get us back on track with God if we have departed. They draw us closer to God. Trials prove the genuineness of our faith. When the smoke clears from the fiery trial of someone you know, you will see who God's redeemed are, because they will be clinging to God even more.

Trials cause us to flex our spiritual muscles. And, frankly, unless those muscles are stretched, we won't grow and mature. So in reality, trials are a blessing from God. That is why James said in James 1:2, "My brethren, count it all joy when you fall into various trials."

The next time we find ourselves in the middle of a trial, instead of feeling grated, let's be grateful.

He giveth more grace when the burdens grow greater,
He sendeth more strength when the labors increase;
To added affliction He addeth His mercy,
To multiplied trials, His multiplied peace.

Annie Johnson Flint

A Light to the World

In Matthew 5:14, Jesus said that "you are the light of the world." Let us look at three things He was teaching with this little statement:

First, Jesus was saying that you are someone who is purposely seen. You don't put a light underneath a basket or in the closet, but you put a light in the middle of the room so it will be exposed to everyone.

Jesus was also saying that you are to be a guide to the world. We live in a world that has been blinded by the darkness of sin. As Christians, we are the only true light in a dark world. We are the only true spiritual guides leading a darkened world to Christ.

Additionally, Jesus was saying that you are to expose darkness. When a person walks into a pitch-black room and strikes a match, that light immediately pierces the darkness and exposes everything in that darkness. As Christians living godly lives, we will very naturally expose the darkness in the people we touch. In a sense, we are the warning lights of eternity.

God, grant us the ability to be that light in a dark world!

I do not ask for mighty words
To leave the crowd impressed;
Lord, grant my life may ring so true
My neighbor may be blessed.

Anonymous

Washed in the Blood of the Lamb

Have you ever had a blood stain on one of your garments? It is very hard to get off. In fact, if it isn't gotten out quickly, it can leave its mark permanently. Revelation 7:14 gives us an interesting statement concerning the redeemed believers who come out of the tribulation. We read that they "washed their robes and made them white in the blood of the Lamb."

How do you wash a robe in blood and have it come out white? In a worldly, physical sense, you cannot. However, spiritually it happens all the time. Every individual who takes his or her soiled life garment and places it in Jesus Christ's blood will have that garment made pure white. The garment is made completely and perfectly clean by the work accomplished by Jesus' blood that was shed on the cross.

There is only one perfect cleansing agent in the entire universe for the sin of man, and that is the blood of Jesus Christ. It is through Christ's shed blood that we are made as white as snow. His blood is our propitiation (Romans 3:25).

In Romans 5:9, Jesus' blood is also our justification. In Ephesians 1:7, it is our redemption. In Colossians 1:20, it is our peace and our reconciliation. And in Hebrews 9:14, His blood is that which cleanses our consciences from serving dead works to serving the living God. There is nothing in all of life like having your life washed in the blood of the Lamb.

Have you been to Jesus for the cleansing power?
Are you washed in the blood of the Lamb?
Are you fully trusting in His grace this hour?
Are you washed in the blood of the Lamb?
Are you washed in the blood,
In the soul-cleansing blood of the Lamb?
Are your garments spotless? Are they white as snow?
Are you washed in the blood of the Lamb?

Elisha A. Hoffman

The Bittersweet Truth

In Revelation 10, an angel gave the apostle John a book and asked him to eat it. We read in verse 10: "Then I took the little book out of the angel's hand and ate it, and it was as sweet as honey in my mouth. But when I had eaten it, my stomach became bitter." What is this book that John ate and found both bitter and sweet?

The book represents the second coming of Christ. It consisted of all of the seals, the trumpet, and bowls of judgments in the book of Revelation. The point is that Christ's second coming is both bitter and sweet. It is sweet in the fact that when Christ returns, we believers will reign with Him in His kingdom and on into eternity. However, it is bitter because right at this very moment millions of people don't have a personal relationship with Christ. If He were to return today, they would go into a timeless eternity without Him.

How should this move us? The angel says to John in the next verse, "You must prophesy again about many peoples, nations, tongues, and kings." Prodding and encouraging John, the angel tells him not to keep this revelation bottled up but to get out there and tell everyone!

We need to do the same! In light of the truth that we know, we need to tell people about Christ's return so that that great day might be a sweet one for them as well.

If, at the dawn of the early morning,
He shall call us one by one,
When to the Lord we restore our talents,
Will He answer us, "Well done"?
Oh, can we say we are ready, brethren?
Ready for the soul's bright home?
Say, will He find you and me still watching.
Waiting, watching when the Lord shall come?

Fanny Crosby

Free from the Weight of Sin

An old Arabian story tells of how a royal prince once seized the land of a poor widow and made it part of his garden. The destitute woman complained to the chief judge of the country and asked for justice. The judge was sympathetic and fair, but he faced a very difficult situation; confronting the rich and powerful prince who ruled the land would not be easy. Mustering the courage, the staunch champion for justice decided to take a daring step and challenge the prince. He came to the palace with a large sack in hand and, to the amazement of the prince, asked if he could fill his sack with earth from the palace garden. Deeply mystified, the prince agreed, and the judge laboriously filled the huge sack to the rim. When he was done, he asked the prince to lift the sack to his shoulder. The prince understandably protested and said that the sack was too heavy for any one man to lift. "This sack," firmly replied the honest judge, "which you thought too heavy to bear, contains only a small portion of the land which you took from the rightful owner. How then, at the day of judgment, will you be able to support the weight of the whole?"

This story gives a good picture of the weight of our sin. Without Christ to bear our sins for us, we would never, throughout all eternity, be able to bear the entire burden. Nor would we be able to pay back to God what we owe Him in compensation for our rebellion. The good news, though, is that Christ did for us what we could not do for ourselves and that He bore all of our sin in order that we might be set free throughout eternity.

I must tell Jesus all of my troubles;
He is a kind, compassionate friend;
If I but ask Him, He will deliver,
Make of my troubles quickly an end.
I must tell Jesus, I must tell Jesus!
I cannot bear my burdens alone;
I must tell Jesus! I must tell Jesus!
Jesus can help me, Jesus alone.

Elisha A. Hoffman

271

Satan Is a Liar

Speaking about the devil, Jesus said in John 8:44: "He was a murderer from the beginning, and does not stand in the truth, because there is no truth in him. When he speaks a lie, he speaks from his own resources, for he is a liar and the father of it."

Satan is the Father of Lies, and he will come to us in various ways. He will promise power and success and friends and popularity. He will even seemingly bless people in their evil for a short period of time. However, when he has finished using a person for his purposes, he will discard them only to leave them in ruin and marked by their habitual sin. Satan is not a rewarder but a heavy taskmaster. He promises life, but he rewards with death. He promises success, but his type of success leads to sin. He promises power, but it leads to poverty. He even promises heaven, but he leads men to hell.

As Christians, we must be prayerfully concerned and on guard. Although Satan cannot undo our eternal destination, he can certainly mess up our present situation. He will lie to us and tell us that our walk with the Lord is fine and that we don't need to be so diligent. He will tell us that we don't need to go to church so often. He will put thoughts into our heads trying to convince us to stay home and read our Bibles instead. We need to understand why Satan would do these things. He persists because he knows that if he can get us isolated from our church, our church family, and our Christian friends, he has already won half the battle.

God help us to be constantly on guard, lest Satan's lies cause us to sin against our Lord. Peter warns us, "Be sober, be vigilant; because your adversary the devil walks about like a roaring lion, seeking whom he may devour" (1 Peter 5:8).

When we know what is true,
we can discern what is false.

Unknown

Things, Things, Things

Mr. and Mrs. Thing were a very pleasant, successful couple—at least to those who measure success with a thing-o-meter. When a thing-o-meter is applied to the life of Mr. and Mrs. Thing, the result is startling. They sit down on very expensive, luxurious things, almost hidden by a large number of other things. Things to sit on, things to sit at, things to cook on, things to eat from—all shiny and new. Things, things, things. Things to clean with, things to wash with, things to clean and wash. Things to amuse, things to give pleasure; things to watch, things for play. Things for the long hot summer; things for the short, cold winter. Things for the big things in which they live, things for the garden, things for the lounge, things for the kitchen, things for the bedroom. Things on four wheels, things on two wheels, things to put on top of the four wheels and things to pull behind the four wheels. Things for the interior of the thing with four wheels. Things, things, things. There in the middle are Mr. and Mrs. Thing—smiling, pleased pink with things, thinking of more things to add to their things. Secure in their castle of things.

Unfortunately, things can't last but always come to an end. They may come to an end in an error in judgment, a temporary loss of concentration. They may be passed to a second-hand things dealer or maybe end up a mass of twisted metal to be towed to the thing yard.

Jesus said in Matthew 6:19–21: "Do not lay up for yourselves treasures on earth, where moth and rust destroy and where thieves break in and steal; but lay up for yourselves treasures in heaven where neither moth nor rust destroys and where thieves do not break in and steal. For where your treasure is, there your heart will be also."

Godliness with contentment is great gain.

1 Timothy 6:6

The Right Vessel for the Right Occasion

I was reminiscing not long ago about a few comical incidents that happened to my wife and me on our wedding day. For one thing, we got married outside and placed a paper white runner on the grass for an aisle. The problem was, as the bridesmaids came down the aisle, their heels plunged through the paper and into the grass, leaving the runner filled with holes before my bride ever appeared. It would have actually been better had the bridesmaids worn Nikes! Another laughable event was when my wife and I left the wedding to go to our reception. We went in my father's 1928 Model A Ford. Unfortunately, the gas tank had problems, and we broke down. Hindsight tells me that I would have been better off renting a limousine.

In both cases, it was a matter of using the wrong equipment for the right occasion. The women should have worn tennis shoes, and I should have rented a limo!

All of this reminds me that God never uses the wrong equipment. He always uses the right tool, the right vessel at the right time. Paul said in 2 Timothy 2:20, "But in a great house there are not only vessels of gold and silver, but also of wood and clay, some for honor and some for dishonor." God wants to use us as His vessels of honor. He wants to use us for the right occasion at the right time. We become those vessels fit for the Master's use as we keep ourselves pure from this world. Paul says in the next verse, "Therefore if anyone cleanses himself from the latter [dishonor], he will be a vessel for honor."

God help us to be the kind of vessels He would want to use.

If I'm to be whom You desire all throughout my life
A vessel unto honor Lord, to Thee
And before Your throne to hear You say
that I have done my part
Lord I need an undivided heart

That I might know You
That I might serve You
That I might worship You as King
To see the morning star
To know how great You are
Lord I need an undivided heart

Dan Marks

A Compliant Tool

I grew up in a family of artists. In fact, over the years my parents developed a national wholesale ceramics company specializing in one-of-a-kind, handmade, whimsical creations, ranging from the very small to the very large. As a result, I grew up knowing my way around a sculptor's table and made a lot of my own unique creations. When working with clay for a long time, you learn to know your tools well. I even made several of my own tools to meet my specific needs. After a while, you begin to learn which tools are more compliant and which ones do the best job with ease.

The Lord has fashioned each one of us, and He has created us with a uniqueness all our own. It is that special uniqueness that He desires to use. However, it is only as we are obedient to His Word and compliant with His desires that He can use us to accomplish His redemptive purposes. Often, the reason we don't sense the Lord's using us is because we have shelved ourselves from use through our disobedience.

How do we get back on track? "Humble yourselves in the sight of the Lord, and He will lift you up" (James 4:10).

Hear ye the Master's call, "Give Me thy best!"
For, be it great or small, that is His test.
Do then the best you can, not for reward,
Not for the praise of men, but for the Lord.
Wait not for men to laud, heed not their slight;
Winning the smile of God brings its delight!
Aiding the good and true ne'er goes unblessed,
All that we think or do, be it the best.
Every work for Jesus will be blest,
But He asks from everyone His best.
Our talents may be few, these may be small,
But unto Him is due our best, our all.

S. C. Kirk

Drastic Changes
Call for Drastic Measures

When we give our life to the Lord, there should be such a transformation that our former life appears to be like night as compared to day. In 1 John 3:14, we read that when we are born again, "We know that we have passed from death to life." When God makes that great transformation a reality, it ought to affect our lives in a drastic way.

It is written of Augustine, one of the early church fathers, that before he was converted, he had indulged in many vulgar and heinous sins. One day, after his conversion, a woman who had been one of his partners in sin approached him winningly and said to him, "Augustine." But he ran away from her with all the strength he had. She called after him again, "Augustine, Augustine, it is I." As Augustine was running out the door, he turned about and said to her, "Ah, but it is not I. The old Augustine is dead and I am a new creature in Christ Jesus!"

In 2 Corinthians 5:17, the apostle Paul says, "Therefore, if anyone is in Christ, he is a new creation; old things have passed away; behold, all things have become new."

Praise God for His faithfulness in taking us where we are at a particular moment and accepting our desire to yield our life unconditionally to Him. He then removes our desire to sin and replenishes us with His Spirit.

Jesus will save you just as you are,
Jesus will welcome you from afar,
Jesus will heal sin's pitiful scar;
Just as you are, come home.

Runyan

A Total Transformation

We live in a day and age when everyone is trying to transform themselves. People try to transform their exterior appearance. They try to push it in, push it out, place it here, and place it all about. We can take the conventional way of working out or go under the knife and cut it out. The problem is that these fixes only last for a little while. Other people try to transform their financial status. Some think, "If I could just win the lottery—if I could just win the sweepstakes, my worries would be over; no more problems." We bamboozle ourselves into believing that our life will be transformed from poverty to riches. The problem is, those who have money only have more problems. Still other people try to transform their psyche. They spend thousands of dollars on therapists, analysts, psychiatrists, and sociologists. Thousands of dollars are spent attempting to transform behavior.

Although things can be altered a little and can be suppressed for a short while, we can't change the real problem. None of these fixes can transform the real you. The problem is man's heart; it is sick. Jeremiah 17:9 says, "The heart is deceitful above all things, And desperately wicked; Who can know it?" We need someone to change our heart, and that is exactly what Jesus came to do. As Paul wrote in 2 Corinthians 5:17, "Therefore if anyone is in Christ, he is a new creation; old things have passed away; behold, all things have become new." That speaks of total transformation.

Breathe on me, breathe on me,
Holy Spirit, breathe on me;
Take Thou my heart, cleanse every part,
Holy Spirit, breathe on me.

Edwin Hatch (Alt. by B. B. McKinney)

Get Into the Game

In the parable of Matthew 25:21, the master of the household says, "Well done, good and faithful servant; you were faithful over a few things, I will make you ruler over many things." God uses faithful vessels that are already serving Him, and He gives them more ways to serve. When God has a job to be done, He doesn't go to a dusty shelf where the nonfunctioning sit and say to Himself, Hey, I have an important task to do; I think I'll dust off Pew Potato Pete and give him the job.

God uses people who are already in the flow of His work and who have been faithful in doing it. That is why you will see someone with an abundance of ministry being blessed by the Lord. They have been faithful, and God is giving them more responsibility.

On the other hand, there are those believers who sit on the sidelines saying, "Gee, I wonder when God is going to make me the next Billy Graham?" If you want to be used greatly, you first have to get into the ball game. It's like the boy who says, "One day I'm going to be a great baseball player. One day I'm going to be in the Baseball Hall of Fame" —but never even signs up to play Little League.

Start faithfully serving the Lord where you are. Be faithful in the little things, and He will put you in charge of many things. When the Holy Spirit nudges us about a particular task God needs done, we had better step forward and apply for the job. Always remember that He never gives us a job to do for which He doesn't also give us the ability to get it done.

O use me, Lord, use even me,
Just as Thou wilt, and when, and where,
Until Thy blessed face I see
Thy rest, Thy joy, Thy glory share.

Havergal

Turn Up the Heat

Many years ago, five young Christian men were in London. They thought it would be wonderful to visit the church of the great Charles Haddon Spurgeon. They arrived early to get a good seat, but the doors were still locked. As they sat on the steps in the front of the church, a man approached and said to them, "Gentlemen, would you like to see the heating apparatus of the church?" The young men looked at each other thinking, "Heating apparatus? Who wants to see the heating apparatus of a church? Perhaps this gentleman has a screw loose." But with nothing else to do, and wanting to please the man, they said, "All right, show us the heating apparatus of this facility." The man then proceeded to lead them through a door and down a long series of steps to the end of a hallway; he then opened the final door. On the other side of that door was a large room filled with 700 people on their knees in prayer. The man turned around and said, "That is the heating apparatus of this church! And by the way, I haven't properly introduced myself. My name is Charles Haddon Spurgeon."

Is it any wonder that God blessed that fellowship? Is it any wonder that God used that church in a mighty way? Spurgeon recognized that his effectiveness and his church's effectiveness didn't lie in his or in anyone else's abilities, but in God. If we want God to use us greatly, it will happen only when we realize that the ability does not lie within us, but in God alone. Consequently, it behooves us to turn up the heat and go to our knees in prayer.

No greater help and care is given
To others in their need
Than when we bear them up in prayer
And for them intercede.

D. J. De Haan

A Special Place in Eternity

In Hebrews 1:2, we read of creation through Christ, "through whom also He made the worlds." The Greek word for world here means "ages." Understand, not only did Jesus create the physical worlds that exist, but He created the very ages or concepts in which they exist. In other words, He created time, space, energy, and matter. He created the things that allow the worlds to exist. What an awesome thought to ponder! Yet the evolutionist will tell us that it all just somehow came into being.

Scientist A. K. Morison said this: "The conditions for life on earth demand so many billions of minute, inter-related circumstances appearing simultaneously in the same infinitesimal moment that such a prospect becomes beyond belief and beyond possibility." Meaning, it takes more faith to believe in evolution than in Christianity!

We should thank the Lord that He created the worlds using a design that also created a special place for us in eternity.

> *All things bright and beautiful,*
> *all creatures great and small,*
> *All things wise and wonderful;*
> *the Lord God made them all.*
> *Each little flower that opens, each little bird that sings;*
> *He made their glowing colors,*
> *He made their tiny wings.*
> *Cold wind in the winter, pleasant summer sun,*
> *Ripe fruits in the garden; He made them every one.*
> *He gave us eyes to see them, and lips that we might tell*
> *How good is God our Father who doeth all things well.*
>
> *Cecil F. Alexander*

His Handiwork

Psalm 19:1 says, "The heavens declare the glory of God; And the firmament shows His handiwork." When I was a youth pastor, my wife Kym and I used to take our high-school group to Yosemite Valley, California. Every evening we would take all of the kids into an open meadow, turn out all of our flashlights, and worship the Lord while staring into the galaxy. Invariably, we would witness at least four shooting stars every evening. Those times are probably some of the greatest spiritual highs I have ever experienced—just being out in the open field worshiping the Lord while gazing into His handiwork.

How foolish to think that our planet, as well as our whole galaxy, as well as other galaxies, just spontaneously came into being! The fact is, Jesus Christ created it all. Colossians 1:16 says, "For by Him all things were created." Then Paul adds in Ephesians 1:10 "that in the dispensation of the fullness of the times He might gather together in one all things in Christ, both which are in heaven and which are on earth— in Him." All things are His workmanship. What a fantastic truth to ponder! All of us would feel encouraged if we set aside time to take a walk, or to go sit in a quiet place in the openness of God's creation and contemplate His handiwork and worship Him!

Slow me down, Lord. Ease the pounding of my heart by the quieting of my mind. Steady my hurried pace with a vision of the eternal reach of time. Give me, amid the confusion of the day, the calmness of the everlasting hills. Break the tensions of my nerves and muscles with the soothing music of the singing streams that live in my memory. Help me to know the magical, restoring power of sleep. Teach me the art of taking minute vacations of slowing down to look at a flower, to chat with a friend, to pat a dog, to read a few lines from a book. Slow me down, Lord, and inspire me to send my roots deep into the soil of life's enduring values that I may grow toward the stars of my greater destiny.

Author Unknown

Filled in Completeness

In Colossians 1:9, the apostle Paul says, "For this reason we also, since the day we heard it, do not cease to pray for you, and to ask that you may be filled with the knowledge of His will in all wisdom and spiritual understanding." That word filled means to be filled up to completeness.

An analogy of Paul's message would be people filling the gas tank in their car so full that they can't get another drop in it or it would overflow. That is Paul's prayer for the church: that we, as God's people, would be filled to completeness in Christ.

When we are filled thoroughly with one thing, that one thing will control and dominate us. It is God's loving desire that we be controlled, dominated, and filled totally with the knowledge of His will in all wisdom and spiritual understanding.

Taking a regular inventory and asking the following questions will help keep us on track:

1. What am I filled with?

2. What dominates my thoughts?

3. What controls my life?

4. What do I need to do to be sure that God is pleased?

May the Lord grant us the steadfastness to be dominated and permeated by His will and His Spirit!

More like Jesus would I be, let my Savior dwell in me;
Fill my soul with peace and love, make me gentle as a dove.
More like Jesus, while I go, pilgrim in this world below;
Poor in spirit would I be; let my Savior dwell in me.
More like Jesus when I pray, more like Jesus day by day;
May I rest me by His side, where the tranquil waters glide;
Born of Him, through grace renewed,
by His love my will subdued,
Rich in faith I still would be; let my Savior dwell in me."

Fanny Crosby

Pray Without Ceasing

The apostle Paul writes in 1 Thessalonians 5:17 to "pray without ceasing." Prayer is one of the greatest gifts God ever gave to the church. Unfortunately, it is talked about more than it is performed, despite the fact that the Bible exhorts us to be in a constant attitude of prayer. As Christians, we need to wake up to the reality that prayer gives strength to our fellowship with God.

Let's look at some of the ways this occurs:

Prayer is the source of power against Satan and his demons. Ephesians 6:10–18 tells us to put on the "whole armor of God" in order to be strong in Him. We are instructed to always be in prayer and supplication in the Spirit.

Prayer is the vehicle by which we confess our sins and pour out our hearts to God, and in turn receive forgiveness.

Prayer is an awesome privilege in which we come as a spiritual child to our heavenly Father. (Matthew 6:9)

Prayer lines us up with the will of God. (Luke 22:42)

By praying, we bring glory to the Father. (John 14:13)

Don't put prayer off! Make a commitment to pray without ceasing throughout the day!

I would be prayerful through each busy moment;
I would be constantly in touch with God;
I would be tuned to hear His slightest whisper;
I would have faith to keep the path Christ trod.

Walter

A Good Pattern for Prayer (pt. 1)

In Acts 12, we read about Herod's harassment of those in the first church. He had killed James and imprisoned Peter because his actions appeared to please the Jews. However, we read in verse 5, "But constant prayer was offered to God for him by the church." Here we have good insight concerning powerful prayer:

First, prayer must be offered to God. The church offered up their prayers to God. You say, "Isn't that elementary?" Yes, it is, and yet there are many Christians who treat God as if He is their heavenly butler instead of their heavenly Father. With their mouths, they act as though they can command our omnipotent Father to do what they want Him to do. God doesn't hear those kinds of prayers; in essence, they are praying with themselves. God wants us to pray to Him, and that comes through a humble and contrite spirit.

Second, prayer should be constant. The church offered up constant prayer to God. We often stop praying when we don't get immediate results. The instant gratification of today's society rubs off on us, and we cease to pray when we don't get quick answers. God wants us to stretch our spiritual muscles through prayer, and so often He allows the answers to come later. We must always remember that God is sovereign and has a perfect time for everything. In light of that, we should not faint, but we should be constantly in prayer. One person said this: "Real prayer grasps the hand of God and never lets go!"

God help us to offer up prayer continually. Let us not give up just because our prayer is not answered right away. May God help us remember that He has an answer and it will be good, right, and just.

Lord, thank You for inviting me
To come and talk with You;
Now help me to revere this time
And pray my whole life through.

K. De Haan

A Good Pattern for Prayer (pt. 2)

Today, we continue to explore Acts 12:5.

Our next point is that prayer should be specific. We read that the people prayed for Peter. Often, we pray in general terms, and that is not bad. But consider this: When we pray specifically, our prayers are answered specifically. It is all right to pray for all of the missionaries in the world, but it is better yet to pray for those missionaries whom we know and see God work through.

Finally, prayer should be offered up by the church. We read that prayer for Peter was offered up by the church. Certainly, all of us should be praying as individuals; but one of the lost arts of the twenty-first-century church is revealed by the fact that it is often called the church of programs instead of the church of prayer. God help us to be those individuals who encourage our churches to pray. God help us to offer our schedules and our homes for prayer meetings to lift up our pastor and the fellowship of believers.

Look at the result of the early church's prayer. As we read in the next few verses, God sent an angel to Peter's prison cell, and Peter was set free. Prayer is powerful! Prayer works, and it shouldn't surprise us when God answers our prayers.

Forgive us, Lord, when we're surprised
By answers to our prayer;
Increase our faith and teach us how
To trust Your loving care.

Spurgeon

Gird up the Loins of Your Mind

How much time do you spend thinking about godly things instead of the tainted things of this world? How much time does your mind soak up God's Word rather than the newspaper or People magazine? Think about it: whatever occupies your mind the most is going to be the side that wins. That is why Peter said in 1 Peter 1:13 to "gird up the loins of your mind."

The ancient Jews wore robes, and it wasn't very easy to run in a robe. So what they did was cinch the robe up and tuck it under their belt so that their legs would be free to run. It would be like saying today, "Roll up the sleeves of your mind," or, "Put some gym shorts on so you can run the race without any hindrance." And Peter says, "Gird up." In other words, cinch up, brace up, prepare, concentrate, tie up your mind, have your mind bolted down, have your priorities right, have your mind set on God!

We must tie up our thoughts (gird up our mind) in Christ in order to be able to run the race without hindrance!

Give of your best to the Master,
give of the strength of your youth;
Throw your soul's fresh, glowing ardor
into the battle for truth;
Jesus has set the example,
dauntless was He, young and brave;
Give Him your loyal devotion,
give Him the best that you have.
Give of your best to the Master,
give Him first place in your heart;
Give Him first place in your service, consecrate every part;
Give, and to you shall be given, God His beloved Son gave;
Gratefully seeking to serve Him,
give Him the best that you have.
Give of your best to the Master,
give of the strength of your youth;
Clad in salvation's full armor, join in the battle for truth.

Howard B. Grose

Your Mission Field

In Matthew 5:14, Jesus said: "You are the light of the world. A city that is set on a hill cannot be hidden." Notice the emphasis. You are light! You cannot help being what you are, so you cannot be hidden. As Christians, we are light and we should not be able to be hidden. In fact, we have been commissioned to let our lights shine.

Henry Martyn, that great missionary to India and Persia, once said, "The spirit of Christ is the spirit of missions and the nearer we get to Him, the more intensely missionary we must become."

You say, "I don't have the gift of evangelism!" You are still called to let your light shine. You say, "I don't feel called to go out into the mission field." You are still called to be a missionary. You say, "How so?" Being a missionary doesn't mean you have to travel halfway around the world to tell about God's redemptive purpose. For many of us, our place of employment is our mission field. For others, it can be your home if you are married to an unbelieving spouse.

The focus needs to be letting our light shine as Christians; when we do, God is honored. Jesus said in Matthew 5:16, "Let your light so shine before men, that they may see your good works and glorify your Father in heaven." May that be our directive today and always!

While passing through this world of sin,
And others your life shall view,
Be clean and pure without, within,
Let others see Jesus in you.
Let others see Jesus in you,
Let others see Jesus in you;
Keep telling the story, be faithful and true,
Let others see Jesus in you.

B. B. McKinney

The Birthmarks of Christianity

In Matthew 5:3–11, we have what are commonly called the Beatitudes. I call them the birthmarks of Christianity. Christians should find these qualities in themselves to one degree or another.

Blessed are the poor in spirit [means you acknowledge your need for God] . . .
Blessed are those who mourn [means seeing yourself as a sinner and mourning over the sin] . . .
Blessed are the meek [humility should be part of your new life in Christ] . . .
Blessed are those who hunger and thirst for righteousness [you continue to hunger and thirst for God] . . .
Blessed are the merciful [you display compassion] . . .
Blessed are the pure in heart [you desire to walk a holy life]
Blessed are the peacemakers [you hold up God's standard, no matter what the cost] . . .
Blessed are those who are persecuted for righteousness' sake [living a godly life may lead to persecution] . . .

Are these parts of your character? This is why they are called the Beatitudes. They are to Be-the-Attitudes of God's people.

More like the Master I would ever be,
More of His meekness, more humility;
More zeal to labor, more courage to be true,
More consecration for work He bids me do.
Take Thou my heart, I would be Thine alone;
Take Thou my heart and make it all Thine own;
Purge me from sin, O Lord, I now implore,
Wash me and keep me Thine forever more.

Charles H. Gabriel

The Basic Four

As we look at the early church's operation, we see that the believers had these four basic activities:

1) The early church was a *praying* church. In the first chapter of Acts, 120 people went into the upper room to pray. As a result of their prayer, the church was birthed, and they never ceased to pray.

2) The early church was a *teaching* church. The first thing Peter did on the day of Pentecost was to preach a sermon, and 3,000 people were added to the church. As the church grew, they ceased not to teach.

3) The early church was a *fellowshipping* church. In the second chapter of, we read that its members went from house to house, breaking bread and eating with gladness and simplicity of heart. There was accountability and encouragement.

4) The early church was a *witnessing* church. In Acts 1:8, Jesus said, "But you shall receive power when the Holy Spirit has come upon you; and you shall be witnesses to Me in Jerusalem, in all Judea and Samaria, and to the end of the earth."

The call and operation of the corporate church, as well as the individuals within the church, should be no different. God calls us to pray, teach, fellowship, and witness. God, help us to constantly maintain these basic four.

Blest be the tie that binds our hearts in Christian love!
The fellowship of kindred minds is like to that above.
Before our Father's throne we pour our ardent prayers;
Our fears, our hopes, our aims are one,
our comforts and our cares.
We share our mutual woes, our mutual burdens bear;
And often for each other flows the sympathizing tear.

John Fawcett

Deadly and Healing

The Bible tells us in Hebrews 4:12, "For the word of God is living and powerful, and sharper than any two-edged sword, piercing even to the division of soul and spirit, and of joints and marrow, and is a discerner of the thoughts and intents of the heart."

There is a story about a Wycliffe translator working with a remote tribal group in the Philippines. The translator came to Hebrews 4:12 and needed a word for "powerful." His national helper suggested that he use the word magadat. The translator asked, "What does that mean?" His helper responded, "We use it to describe what happens when a person is bitten by a poisonous snake. We also use it to describe the medicine. Many of our medicines are made from the extract of the snake's venom."

The translator responded, "How will the reader know whether the Bible is saying that the Word of God is living and poisonous or that the Word of God is living and medicinal?"

The translator's helper then said, with great insight, "It won't matter. If you ignore the Word, it will bite you. If you submit to the Word, it will heal you. Either way it will affect you."

God's Word is, indeed, like that. To ignore it is to make the biggest mistake we can ever make, but to embrace it is to find healing for our souls.

Sing them over again to me, wonderful words of life;
Let me more of their beauty see, wonderful words of life;
Words of life and beauty, teach me faith and duty,
Beautiful words, wonderful words, wonderful words of life.
Christ, the blessed One, gives to all, wonderful words of life;
Sinner, listen to the loving call, wonderful words of life;
All so freely given, wooing us to heaven,
Beautiful words, wonderful words, wonderful words of life.

Philip P. Bliss

Bold for Christ

When Paul and Barnabas were in Antioch preaching the gospel, we read in Acts 13:45, the Jews "were filled with envy" and "opposed the things spoken by Paul." What they wanted to do was to intimidate Paul and Barnabas right out of town. However, verse 46 tell us, "Then Paul and Barnabas grew bold." I love that! Instead of cowering their way out of town, they kept their composure. When things look bad in a crisis, God's people get bold for Christ!

When Daniel was told not to pray, what did he do? He got bold for God. He opened his window, as he always did, and prayed. So what happened? They threw him into a lions' den. Then what happened? God preserved him. That is a good example of what happens when we get bold for God: God gets bold for us.

When the three Jewish youths were told to bow down before the golden image of a pagan king, what did they do? They told the king that they would do no such thing. So what happened? They were thrown into the fiery furnace. Then what happened? Nothing! God protected them.

Again, when we get bold for God, God gets bold for us. When things get bad in a crisis, Christians get bold in Christ. When we stand up for Christ, Christ stands up for us! "In all these things we are more than conquerors through Him who loved us" (Romans 8:37).

> *We will stand for the Lord, we will carry our cross,*
> *Like the ones who've gone before us,*
> *we've counted the cost.*
> *And the union Christ purchased is now reality,*
> *As we stand up together, the world will believe.*
> *So stand up for the Savior, stand up for the King,*
> *In unison together, let His anthem ring.*
> *The Rock of all ages is living in our heart,*
> *Now arm in arm we take the light and stand*
> *against the dark.*
>
> *Milton Carroll*

October 15

Born to Serve

Charles Haddon Spurgeon once said: "As an arrow which falls short of the mark, as a fig tree which yields no figs, as a candle which smokes but yields no light, as a cloud without rain and a well without water, is a man who has not served the Lord. He has led a wasted life—a life to which the flower and glory of existence are lacking. Call it not a life at all, but write it down as animated death."

Think about it: idleness and slothfulness are unequivocally opposed to all that is Christian. From the moment we are born again, it should be our newly born natural desire to serve the Lord and serve His people. In truth, we have been born to serve.

Matthew 8:14–15 says: "Now when Jesus had come into Peter's house, He saw his wife's mother lying sick with a fever. So He touched her hand, and the fever left her. And she arose and served them."

The moment our lives are touched by Christ, we naturally want to serve Him. Christianity and servanthood are used synonymously in the New Testament. Moreover, we are not called to serve out of a sense of duty. Our service is not intended to be compulsive or mediocre. We should be serving out of love and gratitude if we expect to be effective, faithful servants.

Galatians 5:13 says, "For you, brethren, have been called to liberty; only do not use liberty as an opportunity for the flesh, but through love serve one another." God help us to be those willing servants today.

No man ever lost anything by serving God with a whole heart or gained anything by serving Him with a half one.

Thomas V. Moore

Humility Keeps the Lid On

Each one of us within the body of Christ has been blessed with spiritual giftedness, and as Christians, we love to be used by the Lord. However, one of the inherent problems of being used by the Lord is the tendency toward pride. We can be operating with all of the giftedness that the Holy Spirit has given us, but, as the saying goes, "He who has other graces without humility is like one who carried a bowl of precious powder without a cover on a windy day."

Humility is of the utmost importance. Humility is that which keeps us on our toes for the Lord. Peter said, "All of you be submissive to one another, and be clothed with humility, for 'God resists the proud, But gives grace to the humble.' Therefore humble yourselves under the mighty hand of God, that He may exalt you in due time" (1 Peter 5:5–6).

As God begins to use us, Satan comes to us and whispers in our ears: "You are wonderful! You are the greatest! Nobody prays like you do! Nobody reads their Bible like you do! You are so faithful! You are such a great Christian!"

Watch out! If you are not careful, you will begin to walk in the flesh; and if you are walking in the flesh when Satan comes around lying to you, you'll be sure to take a fall. Proverbs 16:18 says, "Pride goes before destruction, And a haughty spirit before a fall."

God help us to walk today in humility. Why? Because humility keeps the lid on! Humility allows us to have a right perspective on ourselves and a right perspective on God, thus allowing us to be used by God.

Forbid it, Lord, that I should boast,
Save in the death of Christ, my God.
All the vain things that charm me most,
I sacrifice them to His blood.

Isaac Watts

293

No Compromise

In Acts 14:11, we are told that God did such incredible miracles through Paul and Barnabas when they were in Lystra that the people said, "The gods have come down to us in the likeness of men!" The people began to worship them.

Consider the opportunity that Paul and Barnabas had to compromise. Paul could have looked over at Barnabas and said, "Are you thinking what I'm thinking?" In other words, "Let's go along with this for a while and enjoy ourselves." A little bit of special treatment must have looked very good. Moreover, they could have even reasoned with themselves, saying, "If we become popular first, then we'll have an opportunity to preach the gospel."

Nevertheless, Paul and Barnabas did not compromise. Because they were spiritual men, they were able to resist the temptation of Satan and turn away the praises of men.

Satan is clever and subtle; it is important for us to stay on guard and keep ourselves clear of compromise. It was compromise that caused Samson to lose his eyes and his life. It was compromise that caused Saul to lose his kingdom. It was compromise that led David to commit adultery and murder a man. And it is compromise that has robbed many Christians of their joy.

As we go about our daily activities—at home, at work, or wherever we find ourselves—may we keep ourselves clear of compromise and close to Jesus.

> *The Lord is with me no matter where I roam,*
> *And if I stumble, He'll take my hand I know,*
> *When the snares of Satan tempt me,*
> *When my earthly friends are gone,*
> *I'll walk in sweet assurance,*
> *For I'll never walk alone, I'll never walk alone.*
>
> *W. F. Lakey and V. B. Ellis*

Dead to Sin, Alive to God

In Romans 6:11, the apostle Paul tells us, "Likewise you also, reckon yourselves to be dead indeed to sin, but alive to God in Christ Jesus our Lord." The secret of success over sin in the Christian life is to regard ourselves as dead to sin. How much sin can you tempt a dead man to commit? As we walk in the Spirit and die to ourselves, Satan's temptations to sin have no power over us.

James Calvert was a missionary to the cannibals of the Fiji Islands many years ago. When he arrived in the islands and prepared to leave the ship to begin work, the ship's captain tried to dissuade him from his plan, crying out, "You'll lose your life and the lives of those with you if you go to live among such savages!" Calvert turned and replied, "We died before we came here!"

Jesus said in Luke 9:23, "If anyone desires to come after Me, let him deny himself, and take up his cross daily, and follow Me." The secret of a successful Christian life is death to self, which in turn causes death to sin. Paul explained in 1 Corinthians 15:31, "I die daily."

Through the power of the Holy Spirit and through the strength of God, may we die to ourselves today; may we reckon ourselves dead to sin and alive to God!

You have longed for sweet peace, and for faith to increase,
And have earnestly, fervently prayed;
But you cannot have rest, or be perfectly blest
Until all on the altar is laid.
Is your all on the altar of sacrifice laid?
Your heart, does the Spirit control?
You can only be blest and have peace and sweet rest,
As you yield Him your body and soul.

E. A. Hoffman

October 19

Grace Alone

Ephesians 2:8–9 says, "For by grace you have been saved through faith, and that not of yourselves; it is the gift of God, not of works, lest anyone should boast."

Salvation is all of grace. The word grace means "gift." We do nothing to earn our salvation. It is God's free, unmerited gift to us. Unfortunately, there are those who always try to add to God's grace through legalistic systems.

For example, some say that one must obey the Ten Commandments in order to be saved. That would mean that faith plus the Ten Commandments equals salvation. Some say a person must obey the Sabbath and eat the dietary foods of the Old Testament in order to be saved. That would mean that faith plus obeying the Sabbath and eating the dietary foods of the Old Testament equals salvation. Others teach that one must be baptized in order to be saved. Furthermore, they teach that if you have not been baptized before dying, you will go to hell at the time of death. (Of course, they don't have a biblical answer for the thief on the cross.) Still others claim that salvation is by grace through faith, but that grace is mediated through the sacraments; therefore, one has to partake of the Lord's Supper to be saved.

Man is always trying to add to his salvation. Consequently, we must constantly be careful never to add to the message of salvation. The danger we must watch for when witnessing for Jesus is telling people that they have to clean up their act before they get saved. In Matthew 4:19, Jesus said, "Follow Me, and I will make you fishers of men." Many Christians try to clean up the fish before they are caught. It is only after men are hooked by Christ that Christ cleans them up.

Praise the Lord that we are saved by grace, and by grace alone!

> *His work is sufficient, on Him I believe;*
> *I have life eternal when Him I receive.*
>
> *Anonymous*

Spiritual Discernment

On a blizzard-filled January day at the turn of the century, a crowded passenger train steamed its way from Chicago to St. Louis. At one of the many stops along the way, a passenger observed a young mother board the train with two small children in tow. "Please, sir, I need to get off at the city of Beaumont," he heard her say to the conductor before looking for a seat on the crowded train.

The passenger, taking note of the overworked conductor, approached the young woman and said: "The conductor is busy. No doubt he'll forget you want to get off at Beaumont. I've been on this train a hundred times. I'll make sure you get off at the right place."

Several hours later, as the train decelerated, the man made his way to the young mother and said: "This is the spot. Here is where you want to get off." Thanking him, she gathered her children and went out into the blizzard.

Half an hour passed before the conductor called out, "Where is the woman who wanted to get off at Beaumont? It's coming up in five minutes." Horrified at what he heard, the man said, "What do you mean? Beaumont was the last stop we made."

"No, sir," replied the conductor. "The last stop we made was to pick up water at a tank in the middle of nowhere." And both men instantly realized that the woman and children had been sent off the train to a certain death.

Many people are being led to a spiritual death through false teachers. Those teachers speak of leading folks to the truth, but in reality, they lead men to an eternal death. Jesus said that in the last days "many false prophets will rise up and deceive many" (Matthew 24:11). As Christians living in the last days, it is important that we exercise spiritual discernment. We need to go to the Bible when we hear something to see if it lines up with God's Word. If it lines up, receive it; if it doesn't, reject it!

> *Holy Bible, book divine,*
> *Precious treasure, thou art mine;*
> *Mine to tell me whence I came,*
> *Mine to teach me what I am.*

Burton

Grace

The work of salvation is described this way in Ephesians 2:1 by the apostle Paul: "And you He made alive, who were dead in trespasses and sins." We were spiritually dead, but now we are alive through Christ. Furthermore, since we were dead, this tells us that we did nothing to make ourselves alive.

Salvation is all of grace. Salvation is not based on what you have done, can do, or will do. Salvation is based solely upon what Jesus Christ has done for us. By His grace, He has made us alive who were once dead in trespasses and sin.

It has been said that Henry Wadsworth Longfellow could take a worthless sheet of paper, write a poem on it, and make it worth about six thousand dollars. Some call that genius. Ross Perot can sign his name on a check and make it worth millions. That's called capital. Uncle Sam can take a piece of paper, put some numbers on it, and make it worth twenty dollars. That's called money. A computer whiz can crunch a bunch of numbers into a code, stick them onto a disk worth pennies, and sell the disk as software worth thousands. That's called ingenuity. A mechanic can take a material that's worth only fifty dollars and make it worth five hundred. That's called skill. An artist can take a canvas worth about ten dollars, paint a picture on it, and make it worth a million dollars. That's called art.

However, only God can take a wretched, worthless life that is dead in trespasses and sin, wash it in the blood of Jesus Christ, put His Spirit into it, and give that life eternal salvation. Moreover, that salvation is based on absolutely nothing the person alone has done. And you know what that is called? Grace.

> 'Twas grace that taught my heart to fear,
> And grace my fears relieved;
> How precious did that grace appear
> The hour I first believed!
>
> *John Newton*

Don't Lock It Up

Herbert Carson once said, "The gospel is not to be preserved like the crown jewels, locked in our ecclesiastical strong room. It is to be spread locally and to the ends of the earth."

I remember once going camping with my family and some other people, one of whom had one of those bright safari lights. He turned it on but immediately took it into his tent. One moment the light was exposed to the whole campsite, and the next it was kept to himself in the comfort of his private tent.

That is how many believers are. They have the light of Christ, they have been transported from the kingdom of darkness into the kingdom of light, yet they keep that light to themselves. They keep the crown jewels of the gospel locked away in their ecclesiastical strong room.

God help us to let the light of our lives, the light of the gospel, shine through our lives to others. Hudson Taylor, that great missionary to China, once said: "The great commission is not an option to be considered, but a command to be obeyed." May we be faithful to our mission field today.

Every Christian is a postmaster for God. His duty is to pass out good news from above.

Vincent Havner

Your Spiritual Temperature

In Acts 16, we read about Paul and Silas being thrown into jail for preaching the gospel—and this wasn't the first time Paul had run into trouble for being a Christian. Trials are part and parcel of life for every believer.

Often, God allows trials in our lives so we may take our spiritual temperature. They don't make or break us; they simply reveal what's going on inside. They provide an opportunity to see just how far we've come in our maturation process in Christ. As one person said, "Christians are like tea bags. We don't know what our flavor is until we're in hot water."

What happened when Paul and Silas were thrown in jail? Were they frustrated or thankful? Were they going to be tarnished by the trial, or would they triumph through the trial? Acts 16:25 says that "at midnight Paul and Silas were praying and singing hymns to God." As a result, Paul and Silas were set free, and the jailer, along with his family, was saved.

Trials come to every believer to show where we are with the Lord. We need to ask ourselves daily, Where am I today? What would be my reaction if God put me in the prison of a major trial? When the trials come, may we lean on the Lord, our Steadfast Rock.

> *O sometimes the shadows are deep,*
> *And rough seems the path to the goal,*
> *And sorrows, sometimes how they sweep*
> *Like tempests down over the soul!*
> *O sometimes how long seems the day,*
> *And sometimes how weary my feet;*
> *But toiling in life's dusty way,*
> *The Rock's blessed shadow, how sweet!*
> *O then to the Rock let me fly,*
> *To the Rock that is higher than I;*
> *O then to the Rock let me fly,*
> *To the Rock that is higher than I.*
>
> *Erastus Johnson*

Little Is Much

The apostle John tells us in chapter 6 of his Gospel that when Jesus fed the multitude of five thousand, He did it with five barley loaves and two small fish that Andrew had borrowed from a young boy. When Andrew presented these to Jesus, he had no idea what the Lord was going to do. He said to Jesus, "But what are they among so many?" When the boy's mother had packed his lunch that morning, he certainly had no idea either that Jesus was to miraculously multiply it among thousands. He probably thought about his loaves and fishes, as Andrew did, What are they among so many?

We often feel that way about ourselves: Lord, how can you use me, since I have so little to offer? Who am I among so many? However, just as the disciples learned, just as this young boy learned, and just as the whole multitude learned, little is much in the Master's hands.

God is not looking for our perfection. He is not looking for great talents and abilities. He is looking for submissive servants who are willing to give the little they are so He can take it and multiply it. May God bless us as we consciously surrender all we are into the Master's hand.

> *Just as I am, without one plea*
> *But that Thy blood was shed for me,*
> *And that Thou bid'st me come to Thee,*
> *O Lamb of God, I come! I come!*
> *Just as I am, and waiting not*
> *To rid my soul of one dark blot,*
> *To Thee whose blood can cleanse each spot,*
> *O Lamb of God, I come! I come!*
> *Just as I am, Thou wilt receive,*
> *Wilt welcome, pardon, cleanse, relieve.*
> *Because Thy promise I believe,*
> *O Lamb of God, I come! I come!*
>
> *Charlotte Elliott*

The Fragrance of Christ

On a scale of one to ten, how would you rate the effect you have for Christ on the people around you? Would you say you are a ten—that everyone knows you are a Christian and you've had the opportunity to lead many to Christ? Or are you an undercover Christian and no one knows about your faith, so you have zero spiritual influence?

There once was a woman by the name of Helen Ewing. She was saved as a young girl in Scotland and gave her life completely to the lordship of Christ. It is said that when she died at the age of twenty-two, all of Scotland wept. She had expected to serve God as a missionary in Europe and had become fluent in the Russian language, but she was never able to fulfill that dream. She had no obvious gifts such as speaking or writing, and she never traveled far from home. Yet, by the time she died, she had won hundreds to Jesus Christ.

Countless missionaries mourned her death because they knew that a great channel of their spiritual strength was gone. She had risen every morning at five o'clock to study God's Word and pray. Her diary revealed that she regularly prayed for more than three hundred missionaries by name. Everywhere she went, the atmosphere changed. If someone was telling a dirty story, they would stop when they saw Helen coming. If people were complaining, they would become ashamed of it in her presence. One acquaintance reported that while she was at Glasgow University, Helen Ewing left the fragrance of Jesus Christ everywhere she went.

God help us to leave the fragrance of Christ everywhere we go!

You are writing a gospel, a chapter each day,
By the deeds that you do, by the words that you say;
People read what you write, whether faithless or true;
Say, what is the gospel according to you?

Anonymous

The Number Seven

In the book of Revelation, we have more numbers than in any other book of the Bible. However, the number seven is the one most often used. There are seven churches, seven spirits, seven candlesticks, seven stars, and seven lamps. There are seven horns, seven eyes, and the seven thousand. We read of seven angels, seven trumpets, seven bowls, seven seals, seven plagues, and seven thunders. There are seven doxologies in heaven. The question is, why seven?

The first seven is found in the book of Genesis. When God finished His creation, He rested on the seventh day. From that moment on, the number seven was significant. The law required man to rest on the seventh day, no child could be circumcised until after the seventh day, the land was to rest each seventh year, Elisha told Naaman to dip in the Jordan seven times, King Nebuchadnezzar was insane for seven years, and so on. The number seven is used over and over in the Old Testament.

The New Testament also has seven beatitudes, seven petitions in the Lord's Prayer, and the seven kingdom parables of Matthew 13. In the Gospel of John, we have the seven "I am" statements of Jesus. Jesus spoke from the cross seven times.

The number seven signifies completion. It is over. It is done. So the reason the book of Revelation has the number seven used more than any other book is because, if anything, God wants us to know that this is it. There is no more. The book of Revelation is the capstone of God's redemptive purpose. Guess what? He could come for His church at any moment!

He surely is coming, I do not know when;
But this I am sure of, He's coming again;
So you'd better get ready, no time for delay,
For Jesus is coming, it may be today!

Smith

God's Protection

In Psalm 34:7, we read that "the angel of the Lord encamps all around those who fear Him, And delivers them." God has a way of faithfully protecting His children.

I read once of a family serving the Lord in one of the most remote parts of the world. The people they were trying to reach were a hostile people. One evening, the village chief decided that he and the other villagers needed to do away with these foreigners. All night long they made preparations. They sharpened their spears and beat the tribal drums in preparation for the kill. That night, in their tent, the missionaries knew full well what those tribal drums meant: death to them and their family. They got down on their knees and prayed all night for God's protection. Early the next morning, having fallen asleep in exhaustion, they awoke to find themselves alive, looking outside. They were surprised to find no warriors. Nothing came of this situation.

A year later, however, these missionaries had the opportunity to lead this village to the Lord. In the course of their conversation, they asked the chief why he and his men hadn't attacked them a year earlier. The chief responded, "We had intended to kill you that night and had come to the edge of your camp armed to the hilt; however, we stopped dead in our tracks when we saw all of the warriors you had surrounding your tent."

What a blessed truth it is to know that God's protection is ever with us and that the angels of the Lord encamp around us. May we go forth each day in peace, knowing that "if God is for us, who can be against us?" (Romans 8:31).

> *A mighty fortress is our God,*
> *A bulwark never failing;*
> *Our helper He amid the flood*
> *Of mortal ills prevailing.*
>
> *Martin Luther*

Cut It Out!

In Matthew 5:29–30, Jesus said: "If your right eye causes you to sin, pluck it out and cast it from you; for it is more profitable for you that one of your members perish, than for your whole body to be cast into hell. And if your right hand causes you to sin, cut it off and cast it from you; for it is more profitable for you that one of your members perish, than for your whole body to cast into hell." Was Jesus advocating mutilation? Was He speaking literally?

No! He was not saying, "Be like a lizard; better your tail than your whole body." Had Jesus meant those instructions literally, we would all be blind and limbless. Beyond that, if we did pluck out one eye and cut off one hand, our other eye and our other hand would work twice as hard to sin.

The key to overcoming sin is not to mutilate ourselves. Rather, Jesus was saying, "Be willing to give up, cut out, and throw away whatever causes you to sin." God wants our lives to be pleasing to Him. May we be honest with ourselves today and deal with our sin forthrightly.

Have Thine own way, Lord! Have Thine own way!
Thou art the potter, I am the clay;
Mold me and make me after Thy will,
While I am waiting, yielded and still.
Have Thine own way, Lord! Have Thine own way!
Search me and try me, Master, today!
Whiter than snow, Lord, wash me just now,
As in Thy presence humbly I bow.
Have Thine own way, Lord! Have Thine own way!
Wounded and weary, help me, I pray!
Power, all power surely is Thine!
Touch me and heal me, Savior divine.
Have Thine own way, Lord! Have Thine own way!
Hold o'er my being absolute sway!
Fill with Thy Spirit till all shall see
Christ only, always, living in me.

Adelaide A. Pollard

Run the Race

In 1 Corinthians 9:24, the apostle Paul wrote: "Do you not know that those who run in a race all run, but one receives the prize? Run in such a way that you may obtain it." Paul often referred to the Christian life as a race. In Philippians 2:16, he wrote about "holding fast the word of life, so that I may rejoice in the day of Christ that I have not run or labored in vain."

If the Christian life is a race, then we need to understand that it is not a sprint. What a tragedy it is to see so many casualties in the faith! Some people seem to start out so well but, somewhere down the line, fizzle out.

Concerning our faith, God wants us to be long-distance runners. God is not interested in short-term commitments; He is interested in life-long commitments demonstrated through endurance. Hebrews 12:1 says, "Let us lay aside every weight, and the sin which so easily ensnares us, and let us run with endurance the race that is set before us."

May we prepare and train ourselves to run with faithfulness and endurance for the glory of Christ.

"Are ye able," said the Master,
"To be crucified with Me?"
"Yea," the sturdy dreamers answered,
"To the death we follow Thee."
"Are ye able?" still the Master whispers down eternity,
And heroic spirits answer, now, as then in Galilee.
Lord, we are able, our spirits are Thine.
Remold them, make us, like Thee, divine.
Thy guiding radiance above us shall be
A beacon to God, to love and loyalty.

Earl Marlatt

The Conscience

We are encouraged in 1 Timothy 1:19 to hold on to "faith and a good conscience." The conscience is an important tool for the believer. Yet without the constant strengthening of God's Word, at least four harmful things can happen to it:

1) The conscience can be weakened. (1 Corinthians 8:12)

2) The conscience can be defiled. (Titus 1:15)

3) The conscience can be overcome with evil. (Hebrews 10:22)

4) The conscience can be seared. (1 Timothy 4:2)

The fourth point is worst of all. I remember how back when I was dating my wife, I accidentally cut my hand all the way through my nerves. Even with surgery, one part of my hand is still numb today. Scar tissue has built up and anesthetized the feeling in that part of my hand. That is exactly what happens to a conscience that is constantly allowed to go against God's will. It is like a rubber band that is stretched and stretched so many times that it doesn't snap back anymore.

What is the cure for a worn-down conscience? How does a person get his or her conscience back again? The answer in both cases is the Word of God! Ephesians 5:26 tells us that the Word of God is that which can wash us clean again and purify us. God can renew and wash our consciences and our minds through the power of His Word.

A good conscience is the palace of Christ, the temple of the Holy Spirit, the paradise of delight, the standing Sabbath of the saints.

Augustine

307

Be the Hope of Heaven

Today, people around the world will be celebrating what is commonly called Halloween. It is a time that countless people see as an innocent time of fun and games. However, there are many others who see this day as the highest of all satanic days of the year.

The word Halloween comes from the term for the druidic New Year known as Samhain or Sowein. The ancient Druids were involved in satanic rituals including both animal and human sacrifice. Contemporary Druids as well as self-professed Satanists will be celebrating today as the highest day in their religious calendar.

What should we do as believers? The best thing Christians can do on this day is to pray for the lost. We also need to pray for opportunities to share Christ. This is one of the only days we will have people knocking on our door asking us to give them something. In our home, we pass out Christian tracts and look for opportunities to share Christ. May we be the hope of heaven to those who are deceived by the hype of hell.

Great is the Lord, He is holy and just.
By His power we trust in His love.
Great is the Lord, He is faithful and true.
By His mercy He proves He is love.
Great is the Lord and worthy of glory!
Great is the Lord and worthy of praise!
Great is the Lord, now lift up your voice.
Now lift up your voice, great is the Lord;
Great is the Lord.

Michael W. Smith and Deborah D. Smith

Discouraged

Sometimes Christians are tempted to be discouraged. Perhaps it is the loss of a loved one or maybe the loss of a job. It could be the loss of vision and purpose in life. There was a time when even the great apostle Paul could have been tempted to feel discouraged. In Acts 23, he was tried in Jerusalem for simply standing up for truth and doing what the Lord had called him to do. Sitting in the prison cell, Paul could easily have had a pity party.

We read, however, in verse 11: "But the following night the Lord stood by him and said, 'Be of good cheer, Paul; for as you have testified for Me in Jerusalem, so you must also bear witness at Rome.'" When Paul was in need, Jesus came to him. First, He comforted him and said, "Be of good cheer." Second, He commended him with the words "You have testified for Me in Jerusalem." He is saying, "You have done a great job, Paul!" Third, Jesus gave him confidence by telling him, "So you must also bear witness at Rome."

Although the Lord may not appear to us individually, He wants to comfort, commend, and give each of us confidence when we get discouraged. As the Psalmist wrote in Psalm 94:19, "In the multitude of my anxieties within me, Your comforts delight my soul." Every time we come to God's Word in humility and need, we will find comfort, commendation, and confidence to face the day with a greater trust in our Savior's ability to meet our needs.

> *There is One who can comfort when all else fails,*
> *Jesus, blessed Jesus;*
> *A Savior who saves though the foe assails,*
> *Jesus, blessed Jesus;*
> *Once He traveled the way we go,*
> *Felt the pangs of deceit and woe;*
> *Who more perfectly then can know,*
> *Than Jesus, blessed Jesus.*
>
> *Charles H. Gabriel*

Seeking Those Things

In Colossians 3:1, the apostle Paul wrote, "If then you were raised with Christ, seek those things which are above, where Christ is, sitting at the right hand of God."

What did Paul mean? He wasn't talking about the physical things of heaven. He wasn't saying, "Think what it will be like to stroll down the golden sidewalks of heaven," or, "Think what it will be like to defy gravity and fly from place to place," or, "Just imagine what it will be like to do a swan dive from a cloud." No, not at all! We are not to seek heavenly geography or the material things of heaven. We are not to seek the things that make up the city. Rather, we are to seek the one who reigns there—Jesus Christ.

We are also to seek the qualities that characterize Christ's sovereign rule in heaven: righteousness, joy, peace, kindness, meekness, longsuffering, patience, truth, love, and so forth. As we spend our time seeking these things, we will find them becoming part of our lives.

If you should ask me how the blood of Jesus Christ can
cleanse, And how His Spirit in the heart can dwell;
If you should ask me to explain how God His blessing sends,
I'm sure that I could never tell.
If you should ask me how the Spirit, witnessing within,
Can give assurance that I'm born again;
Can tell me that the precious blood has washed away my sin,
I'm sure that I could never make it plain.
I don't know how He does it, I only know He does it,
He just comes in and cleanses every stain,
For sorrow and for sadness, He gives me joy and gladness.
I don't know how He does it, but He does it. Praise His
name!

Mrs. H. S. Lehman

The Separate Life

In Leviticus 11:44, God tells us, "You shall be holy; for I am holy." Then Peter exhorts us to live up to the same truth in 1 Peter 1:16. What is holiness, and how do we live it? Holiness simply means separation. When we talk about living a holy life, we are talking about living a separate life to God.

We often think of a holy life as a gloomy life of separation from all things. However, as T. Edwards puts it, "a holy life is not an ascetic, or gloomy, or solitary life; but a life regulated by divine truth and faithful Christian duty. It is living above the world while we are still in it." Leonard Ravenhill put it this way: "The greatest miracle that God can do today is to take an unholy man out of an unholy world and make that man holy and put him back into that unholy world and keep him holy in it."

The truth is that we cannot do it on our own. We need to walk in the Spirit to have the ability and the strength to live holy unto God. As we seek to live that separate life for His glory in His strength, we will see Him do great things in us, as well as through us for those around us.

The Scottish preacher Robert Murray McCheyne put it this way: "A holy man is an awesome weapon in the hand of God, and it is our likeness to Christ that makes us powerful." God help us to be those instruments in the hand of God today. God help us to live the separate life—the holy life, a life consecrated to Him.

If I'm to be whom You desire all throughout my life,
A vessel unto honor, Lord, to Thee.
And before Your throne to hear You say
that I have done my part,
Lord, I need an undivided heart.
That I might know you, that I might serve You
That I might worship You as King,
To see the Morning Star, to know how great You are,
Lord, I need an undivided heart.

Dan Marks

The Great Physician's Assistant

We read in 2 Corinthians 5:18, "Now all things are of God, who has reconciled us to Himself through Jesus Christ." The New Testament Greek word for reconciled was a medical term used to describe a bone that had been broken and reset. It meant to take that which was out of alignment and adjust it back into its proper position. Through faith in Jesus Christ, we have been reconciled to God. We were once enemies of God but are now the sons of God.

In light of that, Paul continues that God "has given us the ministry of reconciliation." In other words, once we have been realigned, God calls us to go into the world seeking to realign others to Christ. That is why Paul adds in verse 20, "Now then, we are ambassadors for Christ, as though God were pleading through us: we implore you on Christ's behalf, be reconciled to God." An ambassador represents his country's government in a foreign land. As Christians, we are in a foreign land representing the government of God.

What is our message? Reconciliation. Our heart's cry should be to see those around us, who are broken down and out of joint, put back into alignment by the Great Physician, Jesus Christ. All of us have been given the ministry of reconciliation.

May we be willing to be the Great Physician's assistants.

Throw out the lifeline across the dark wave,
There is a brother whom someone should save;
Somebody's brother! Oh, who then will dare,
To throw out the lifeline, his peril to share.
Throw out the lifeline with hand quick and strong;
Why do you tarry, why linger so long?
See! he is sinking; Oh, hasten today,
And out with the lifeboat! Away, then, away!

Edward S. Ufford

312

Make Me That Person

Leadership has always been a commodity in great demand. Leadership is in high demand in our society in such places as the work force, where trained leaders are needed instead of self-appointed authoritarians; the home, where children need to be raised by the standards of God's Word instead of the standards of the world; and in the nation's capitol, where decisions are made every day that affect many lives.

Yet there is no greater need for leadership than in the church. Godly leadership is always in high demand, and God is always on the lookout for vessels He can use to advance His kingdom. We see scriptural proof of this in 2 Chronicles 16:9, which says, "For the eyes of the Lord run to and fro throughout the whole earth, to show Himself strong on behalf of those whose heart is loyal to Him."

One young man was talking to his friend one day, who said to him, "You know, the world has yet to see what God can do with a man who is totally committed to Him." Such a simple statement, and yet this young man was never able to shake those words which struck deep into his heart. After some time he got on his knees and prayed, "God make me that man!" That young man's name was D. L. Moody. As a result of that prayer, along with unrestrained commitment to God, he was used by God in a profound way in the late 1800s.

We need to ask ourselves, Am I willing to be that kind of man or woman? Am I willing to be the person to whom the Lord shows Himself strong? It can begin today with a commitment just like D. L. Moody's "God, make me that person!"

Faith can be summed in the willingness to serve God whether or not there is a reward.

B. R. S.

Stirred up to Remembrance

Peter wrote in 2 Peter 1:12–13: "For this reason I will not be negligent to remind you always of these things, though you know and are established in the present truth. Yes, I think it is right, as long as I am in this tent, to stir you up by reminding you." Peter was saying, "As long as I have breath to breathe, I'm going to remind you concerning the essential truths that make you a believer in Jesus Christ." It is important that we remind ourselves of these truths regularly. Why? Lest we fall away from the central truths that make us believers. Lest we fall prey to false truths.

This was the reason why, before the Israelites went into the Promised Land, Moses reminded them to follow the Lord. This was also why Joshua reminded the people to follow the Lord just before he died. Again, this was why David reminded Solomon to follow the Lord at the end of his life. And this was why Nehemiah reminded the people to look to God's faithfulness as they attempted to rebuild the walls of Jerusalem.

We need to be reminded regularly of God's goodness in our lives and of the central truths which make us believers. Otherwise, we might forget where we have come from and fall prey to false truths or to our own desires. May we be continually reminded of where we have come from and what God has done for us!

> *I was sinking deep in sin, far from the peaceful shore,*
> *Very deeply stained within, sinking to rise no more;*
> *But the Master of the sea heard my despairing cry,*
> *From the waters lifted me, now safe am I.*
> *All my heart to Him I give, ever to Him I'll cling,*
> *In His blessed presence live, ever His praises sing;*
> *Love so mighty and so true merits my soul's best songs;*
> *Faithful, loving service, too, to Him belongs.*
> *Love lifted me! Love lifted me!*
> *When nothing else could help, Love lifted me.*
>
> *James Rowe*

The Middle of the Road

Compromise is a sin by which we are all tempted. Perhaps it's to compromise the quality of work we do on our job. Maybe it's to compromise the amount of time we know we should be spending with our family. Or we might compromise our witness to those around us because we think we'll be ridiculed otherwise. Compromise does not happen overnight; it usually is a gradual process. It can be like "the little foxes that spoil the vines" (Song of Solomon 2:15).

Think about compromise as the little allowances, the tiny sins. Every day we are faced with decisions that will side with our Lord or side with the world. We can ask ourselves, Do I follow through with what I know is right? Or do I allow certain issues to slide by?

Jesus said in Matthew 6:24, "No man can serve two masters; for either he will hate the one and love the other, or else he will be loyal to the one and despise the other." As Christians, we can't ride the fence concerning salvation, nor can we ride the fence concerning our daily walks. When faced with decisions regarding faith, family, work, witnessing, or whatever we do, either our actions please the Lord or they don't.

Compromise tries to talk us into living somewhere in the middle. However, as any modern-day motorist can tell you, most accidents take place in the middle of the road. When believers try to live their lives in the middle of the road, attempting to serve two masters, it usually ends in disaster.

God help us to make a commitment to get out of the middle of the road, to rise above mediocrity and compromise, and to live a life of excellence for one Master—Jesus Christ.

Temptation is the devil looking through the keyhole. Yielding is opening the door and inviting him in.

Billy Sunday

Justification

We read in Galatians 2:16 about "knowing that a man is not justified by the works of the law but by faith in Jesus Christ." Justification is the act of God where He declares the believing sinner righteous in Jesus Christ.

Justification is an act, not a process. When we give our life to Christ, we are not in the process of being saved; we are saved. It is an act of God. We cannot save ourselves; we are saved purely by the grace of God. At birth, we were sentenced to death as a result of sin. But through faith in Christ, God declares us not guilty. It is an act of God declaring the believing sinner righteous. God doesn't justify good people; He justifies believing sinners.

This was the issue the Pharisees couldn't understand. We read in Mark 2:16–17: "And when the scribes and Pharisees saw him eating with tax collectors and sinners, they said to His disciples, 'How is it that He eats and drinks with tax collectors and sinners?' When Jesus heard it, He said to them, 'Those who are well have no need of a physician, but those who are sick. I did not come to call the righteous, but sinners, to repentance.'"

Jesus justifies people who see themselves as sinners and who place their faith in Him. In the story of the Pharisee and the tax collector, Jesus said in Luke 18:13–14: "And the tax collector, standing afar off, would not so much as raise his eyes to heaven, but beat his breast, saying, 'God be merciful to me a sinner!' I tell you, this man went down to his house justified rather than the other."

Justification is the act of God declaring the believing sinner righteous in Jesus Christ. Praise the Lord today for His justifying power as the Great Physician to heal those who come to Him by faith!

Justification is the very hinge and pillar of Christianity.

Thomas Watson

A Spiritual Dress Code

You know, you can tell a lot about a person by the clothes they wear. Certain professions require that certain clothes be worn. By just looking at the clothes of a policeman, a postal worker, a security guard, or a person enlisted in the army, you can tell what their line of work is. You can tell by a person's clothes who is going to work on the construction site and who is going to work at the bank. We live in a society that requires certain people to wear certain clothes according to their profession.

Christians have their own special clothing. We have a spiritual dress code to be worn in accordance with our new identity in Christ. The apostle Paul describes it this way in Colossians 3:12–14: "Put on tender mercies, kindness, humility, meekness, longsuffering; bearing with one another, and forgiving one another, if anyone has a complaint against another; even as Christ forgave you, so you also must do. But above all these things put on love, which is the bond of perfection."

The uniforms or other identifying clothing people wear to their jobs may change in their lifetime. However, the spiritual clothing which becomes a part of us through the Holy Spirit dwelling within us should never leave our being. Those items of special clothing that the apostle Paul described should only expand and grow in us. May we walk in the spiritual clothing of Christ!

A believer who has yielded to Christ and donned His spiritual clothing will smile with His eyes; listen with His ears; speak with His lips; touch with His hands; and love with His heart.

B. R. S.

Foolish

Paul says in Galatians 3:1: "O foolish Galatians! Who has bewitched you?" The word foolish here does not refer to mental deficiency but to mental laziness. The believers in Galatia had been duped by false teachers into embracing the lie that we are saved by works. Paul is not reproving them because they couldn't understand the truth; he is prodding them because they knew the truth but failed to use their spiritual intelligence to discern it.

Many believers today get sucked into false teaching simply because they check their brains at the door. The fact that God wants us to use our minds, however, is clear in Scripture. Consider these verses:

"For God has not given us a spirit of fear, but of power and of love and of a sound mind." (2 Timothy 1:7)

"Put on the new man, who is renewed in knowledge according to the image of Him who created him." (Colossians 3:10)

"And be renewed in the spirit of your mind." (Ephesians 4:23)

"Be transformed by the renewing of your mind." (Romans 12:2)

The point is that as we renew our minds in God's Word, we will be wise unto salvation and wise to the lies of false doctrine. Lack of discernment leads to theological inconsistency; yet the believer who is renewed in the knowledge of God is theologically sound. As Paul said in Ephesians 5:15, "See then that you walk circumspectly, not as fools but as wise."

A man is what he thinks about all day long.

R. W. Emerson

Labor for the Unlikable

Let us honestly ask ourselves how much we truly love our fellow believers. All of us may easily respond with a quick "Of course I love my brothers and sisters in Christ!" However, if we think about it long enough, how far are we willing to go to demonstrate that love?

The apostle Paul writes to the Galatian believers as "my little children, for whom I labor in birth again until Christ is formed in you" (Galatians 4:19). The Galatian believers were the fruit of his labors. They were his children in the faith. Nevertheless, in his absence they spurned his love and started following the self-righteous ways of the Judaizers. Paul's response to them was both loving and firmly honest. He told them that although he had to go through all of the work to remind and teach them again, he would gladly do it. He wanted them to know that he would do it because he cared for them as a friend and as their pastor.

We need to ask ourselves often, How much do I love my brother and sister in Christ? How far does my love extend to them? What if they fall into sin? What if they fall away from church? What if they don't want to speak to me anymore? What if they say false things about me? How much do I love them?

In the Christian walk, we are going to come into contact with believers whom we rub the wrong way (for some unknown reason). Do we ignore them? Do we get back at them? Do we throw up our hands and say, "Well, I tried"? No! We labor in love with them.

God help us to pray for those who don't pray for us, to love those who don't particularly like us. May we be a source of blessing to them and seek to labor in love for them until Christ be formed in them.

The people we like the least
may need our love the most.

Unknown

Liberated to Love

We hear talk of freedom, liberty, and rights echoed throughout America almost every day. We hear it in the home, on the job, on the radio; we read it in the newspaper and see it on TV. People are always talking about their freedoms and liberties and how no one has the right to tell them what they can or cannot do.

In the news, a constant parade of people state that either their rights have been violated or that they are pushing for some new right. There is a constant battle cry of "Freedom! Freedom! Freedom!" Men, women, and even children today are demanding more freedom to do as they please. In the name of personal rights, authority is being disregarded and restrictions are being resisted.

As believers, where do we stand? What are our rights? Don't we have a newfound freedom? Don't we have a newfound liberty? Absolutely! What, however, does the Lord command us to do in light of our liberty? In Galatians 5:13–14, Paul writes: "For you, brethren, have been called to liberty; only do not use liberty as an opportunity for the flesh, but through love serve one another. For all the law is fulfilled in one word, even in this: 'You shall love your neighbor as yourself.'"

What does our liberty give us the right to do? It gives us the right to love our neighbor. Holy Spirit, help us to walk in the strength of our liberty—the liberty to love.

Lord, lay some soul upon my heart,
and love that soul through me;
And may I bravely do my part to win that soul for Thee.
Lord, lead me to some soul in sin, and grant that I may be
Endued with power and love to win that soul,
dear Lord, for Thee.
To win that soul for Thee alone will be my constant prayer;
That when I've reached the great white throne
I'll meet that dear one there.

Mack Weaver and B. B. McKinney

Blessed

In the greatest of all sermons, the Sermon on the Mount, Jesus begins by saying the word blessed and repeats it no fewer than eight times. The Greek word for this means happy, fortunate, joyful, and blissful. As Jesus begins His sermon, it is His desire that all of His children be blessed.

Being blessed is not a superficial happiness but a happiness that is in the heart of a person, something independent of his outward, physical, temporary, or positive circumstances. Biblical blessedness is not superficial feelings of well-being based on our circumstances. Biblical blessedness is based on deep spiritual contentedness that our life and soul are right with God! The world offers happiness based on what we can do. Jesus offers deep-down blessedness based on what He has already done for us!

We should ask ourselves, Am I content? Am I happy? Am I blessed? If you are reading this and are saying no to these questions, be assured that there is a way to answer yes. By surrendering your life to Jesus Christ as Lord and Savior, you can experience the blessedness that He talked about so often. David said in Psalm 34:8, "Blessed is the man who trusts in Him!"

Why should I feel discouraged,
Why should the shadows come,
Why should my heart be lonely,
And long for heaven and home,
When Jesus is my portion?
My constant friend is He;
His eye is on the sparrow, and I know He watches me.
"Let not your heart be troubled." His tender word I hear,
And resting on His goodness, I lose my doubts and fears;
Tho' by the path He leadeth, But one step I may see;
His eye is on the sparrow, and I know He watches me.
His eye is on the sparrow, and I know He watches me.
I sing because I'm happy, I sing because I'm free,
For His eye is on the sparrow, and I know He watches me.

Mrs. C. D. Martin

Bearing Witness of the Light

In John 1:7 we read, "This man came for a witness, to bear witness of the Light, that all through him might believe." This text is talking about John the Baptist. He came to bear witness of the Light, Jesus Christ. He pointed men to Jesus, saying: "Behold! The Lamb of God who takes away the sin of the world!" (John 1:29).

Believers are to bear witness of the Light as well. However, we cannot bear witness of the Light unless we are spending time in the Light. How can we be a witness of what we do not personally possess? A lot of Christians want to be used by God, want to be witnesses of and for God, yet don't want to spend any time with God.

It is important that we spend time with the Lord each and every day. We need to spend time soaking up the light of Christ's love if we are to give it to others. It is also important that we spend time soaking up the light of Christ's wisdom and knowledge to equip us for the day and whatever situation we may encounter.

We are all called to bear witness of the Light, but in order to bear that witness, we need to spend quality time with Him who is the Light—Jesus Christ.

> *How lovely is Your dwelling place, Almighty Lord;*
> *There's a hunger deep inside my soul.*
> *Only in Your presence are my heart and flesh restored,*
> *How lovely is Your dwelling place.*
> *In Your courts there's shelter*
> *for the greatest and the small,*
> *The sparrow has a place to build her nest.*
> *The pilgrim finds refreshment in the rains that fall,*
> *And each one has the strength to meet the test.*
> *How lovely is Your dwelling place, Almighty Lord.*
>
> *Tom Howard*

A God of Personal Pronouns

When speaking to His disciples, Jesus said in Matthew 10:30, "But the very hairs of your head are all numbered." Here we have Jesus expressing the intimate detail of His love for those who are His children. Psalm 56:8 tells us that the Lord numbers our wandering and keeps all of our tears in a bottle. In other words, our loving and omniscient Savior notices everything that happens in our lives. He is a personal God. A personal Savior.

Paul writes in 1 Timothy 1:2, "Grace, mercy, and peace from God the Father and Jesus Christ our Lord." Notice the pronoun our. When Jesus taught His disciples to pray, He said in Matthew 6:9, "In this manner, therefore, pray: Our Father in heaven."

Someone has rightly said that we serve a God of personal pronouns. We don't serve a distant deity. We don't serve an impersonal God who doesn't know us intimately. We serve a God who knows us better than we know ourselves. Nonetheless, with everything He knows about us, He still desires to commune with us.

A spiritually healthy question to ask ourselves is, How is my communion time with God? We need to recognize that if it isn't what it ought to be, Jesus misses us and wants to spend more time with us. Just as parents are thrilled when their children love to be with them, so God loves it when we simply come to spend some time with Him.

> *I come to the garden alone,*
> *while the dew is still on the roses,*
> *And the voice I hear, falling on my ear,*
> *the Son of God discloses.*
> *He speaks, and the sound of His voice, is so sweet the birds*
> *hush their singing,*
> *And the melody that He gives to me,*
> *within my heart is ringing.*
> *And He walks with me, and He talks with me,*
> *And He tells me I am His own;*
> *And the joy we share as we tarry there,*
> *None other has ever known.*
>
> *C. Austin Miles*

323

Wage a Good Warfare

In 1 Timothy 1:18, Paul told Timothy to "wage the good warfare." Then, in 1 Timothy 6:12, Paul encouraged him to "fight the good fight of faith." Timothy was called to arms because he, like all of us, was in a spiritual battle. We war against the flesh (Romans 7:15–25) and we war against the world (1 John 3:13). But ultimately, we war against Satan and his demons. It is Satan, through deception, who brought sin into the world; and it is Satan who, at this time, is the ruler of the world. Therefore, Paul encouraged Timothy, as well as us, to "wage the good warfare."

Satan attacks the church today in four predominant ways:

He attacks by tempting believers to sin as a means of destroying the credibility of our testimony. If he can tarnish our testimony, he can render our witness ineffective.

He attacks by seeking to diminish our faith and trust in God. This is why Paul instructs Christians to take up the shield of faith (Ephesians 6:16). The devil wants us to diminish our faith in God, thus diminishing our effectiveness in the battle.

He attacks the church by attacking its leaders. The devil is not witless. He knows that if he can get the shepherd to fall, he can get the sheep to scatter (Zechariah 13:7).

He attacks the church through false doctrine. This is his favorite and most effective weapon. False doctrine not only keeps unbelievers from getting saved but engages true believers in unproductive tangents that have no eternal value, putting them out of the battle for truth.

God help us in these last days to be wise—to be on guard against our enemy (1 Peter 5:8) and to "wage the good warfare," a noble warfare for the King of Glory.

You will not get leave to steal quietly to heaven in Christ's company without a conflict and a cross.

Samuel Rutherford

The Priority of Prayer

Prayer is to be a priority in the life of the believer. Yet prayer is often put at the bottom of our spiritual list. Why is it that when we make an announcement at church concerning a special speaker or a special event, there is a large turnout? Why is it we can announce a special picnic and have a massive crowd yet hold prayer meetings throughout the week which are sparsely attended?

First, prayer is simply hard work! It takes spiritual exertion and commitment. Often that spiritual exertion doesn't have immediate or external benefits. Sometimes God does not answer our prayers right away, for often He is working on our spiritual rather than external well-being. Because prayer doesn't always bring immediate results, many Christians view prayer as a lackluster exercise.

Second, Christians often abandon prayer because it elicits spiritual warfare. The reason it elicits spiritual warfare is because Satan knows that habitual, continual prayer spells his defeat. Consequently, he will attack us and even distract us with seemingly good things to keep us from the priority of prayer. Paul wrote in 1 Timothy 2:1, "Therefore I exhort first of all that supplication, prayers, intercessions, and giving of thanks be made for all men." Paul is teaching us to make it a priority to pray.

God help us to do just that. Once spending quality time with our Lord is made a habit, then prayer with Him becomes automatic. Ask God to help us remember to pray now, then, and throughout the day.

No time is so well spent in every day
as that which we spend upon our knees.

J. C. Ryle

Keep Your Eyes on the Giver

The Bible says in 1 Corinthians 12:7, "But the manifestation of the Spirit is given to each one for the profit of all." That term, "for the profit of all," could be translated, "for the mutual benefit of others." Spiritual gifts are given for the benefit of God's people, for the mutual benefit of the church. It becomes extremely important that we keep our eyes on the Giver and not the giftedness.

Why? Because God may gift us in a tremendous way, but if we take our eyes off the Lord and the purpose of the gifts, we can become very proud. At that point, neither we nor the gifts are useful for the Lord's work. The gifts are given to the believer so that God's people can be blessed.

There was a Christian performer in the 1970s whose singing and playing of the guitar could easily fill a high-school stadium with eager teenagers and their parents. At the end of each song, as the crowd applauded, he would raise his arm as high as he could with his index finger pointing toward heaven. He gave God the credit! What a terrific example he set for the young people in the audience!

It is a tragedy when we see a man of God take the glory for something that God has supernaturally enabled him to do. May we never take the credit for God's work. Let us keep our eyes on the Giver of the gifts and, in so doing, bless God's people and give all the glory to God!

I'm singing, I'm singing
Because He gave a song to me;
His presence fills my heart with joy and victory.
I praise Him, I praise Him
For tokens of his wondrous grace;
And tho' I love Him dearly now,
Someday I'll see Him face to face.

Homer W. Grimes

Spiritual Leaders (Part 1)

There is a great need within the church for godly leaders. Often when a church begins losing members, it looks at its bulletin and says, "Maybe we ought to change our programs," or, "If we only had more talented people. If we only had more gifted people. If we only had more committed people." More often than not, however, the reason is substandard holiness within the leadership.

An inseparable link exists between the character of the church and the character of its leaders. This is why the qualifications of an elder in the church are so stringent (1 Timothy 3:1–7, Titus 1:5–9). God is looking for spiritual leaders. God does not look at human ability or talent. He looks for spiritual commitment and holiness.

S. L. Brengle, one of the early leaders of the Salvation Army, once said:

> Spiritual leadership is not won by promotion, but by many prayers and tears. It is attained by confession of sin, and much heart-searching and humbling before God; by self-surrender, a courageous sacrificing of every idol, a bold deathless, uncompromising and uncomplaining embracing of the cross, and by an eternal, unfaltering looking to Jesus crucified. It is not gained by seeking great things for ourselves, but rather, like Paul, by counting those things that are gain to us as loss for Christ. That is a great price, but it must be unflinchingly paid by him who would not be merely a nominal, but a real spiritual leader of men, a leader whose power is recognized and felt in heaven, on earth, and in hell.

May that be our personal prayer. May we each die to ourselves and live for Christ. May we commit to pray for those in spiritual leadership in our own church, as well as those who are spiritual leaders throughout the body of Christ.

It is very rare for the spirituality of a group of Christians to exceed that of its leaders.

John Benton

327

Spiritual Leaders (Part 2)

Oswald Sanders wrote:

> The church has always prospered most when it has been
> blessed with strong spiritual leaders who experienced the
> touch of the supernatural in their service. The lack of such
> men is a symptom of the malaise that has gripped the body
> of Christ. The clarion voices that used to make the pulpit
> the paramount influence in the land are tragically few. In a
> world aflame, the voice of the church has sunk to a pathetic
> whisper.

How needful is spiritual leadership? The church in the United States is falling
prey to every wind of doctrine. Pulpits are giving way to ploys, exhortation
is giving place to entertainment, and so-called holy laughter is exchanged for
holy living. As a result, we are in desperate need of spiritual leadership! The
church needs to wake up! It needs godly men, holy men, men of integrity,
men of truth, and men with a loyal heart toward God.

In 2 Chronicles 16:9, we read: "For the eyes of the Lord run to and fro
throughout the whole earth, to show Himself strong on behalf of those whose
heart is loyal to Him." God is looking for spiritual leaders who cannot be
bought by sin, and cannot be bought by the world, and cannot be bought by
the devil. God is looking for leaders of no compromise who will stand in the
gap, no matter what the cost.

God said to the prophet Ezekiel in Ezekiel 22:30, "So I sought for a man
among them who would make a wall, and stand in the gap before Me on behalf of the land, that I should not destroy it; but I found no one." We are living
in a day and age where godly men are desperately needed to stand in the gap
for God and His people.

Let us commit ourselves once again to pray for our churches and our spiritual
leaders.

> *We will recognize our spiritual leaders by their humility,*
> *kindness, gratitude, forgiveness, compassion, and uncondi-*
> *tional love; not just one or two days a week, but all the time.*

B. R. S.

328

Flies in the Ointment

We have all heard the expression, "Practice what you preach." That is a good tenet to live by. It's been said that people who don't practice what they preach destroy what they build. If we as Christians do not live out what we proclaim, then our witnessing loses its effectiveness.

C. H. Spurgeon put it this way: "Take heed therefore to yourself first that you be that which you persuade others to be, and believe that which you persuade others to believe, and have heartily entertained that Christ and Spirit which you offer to others."

It is important that we examine our lives daily to make sure that our house is in order before we start asking others to rearrange theirs. Solomon said in Ecclesiastes 10:1, "Dead flies putrefy the perfumer's ointment, And cause it to give off a foul odor." Do you see this vivid picture? Here you have this beautifully aromatic perfume, carefully prepared to bless all who take in its beguiling qualities. However, because a few flies have fallen into the mixture, their composition has spoiled the entire substance, causing it to emit a foul stench.

If we as believers fail to deal with sin daily, we give opportunity for flies to spoil our testimony. Instead of our lives being an aid to God's message, they become a hindrance. That great Puritan Richard Baxter said this: "Take heed to yourselves, lest your example contradict your doctrine, and lest you lay such stumbling blocks before the blind, as may be the occasion of their ruin; lest you unsay with your lives, what you say with your tongues."

May our manners match our message, and our testimony match our tongues.

Example is more forceful than precept. People look at me six days a week to see what I mean on the seventh day.

Richard Cecil

The Living God

The psalmist prayed in Psalm 42:2, "My soul thirsts for God, for the living God." Why did he say "the living God"? This is a phrase used throughout the Bible to distinguish our God, the one true God, from those the pagans worship, which are dead gods. This is why Joshua said to the children of Israel in Joshua 3:10, "By this you shall know that the living God is among you, and that He will without fail drive out from before you the Canaanites and the Hittites and the Hivites and the Perizzites and the Girgashites, and the Amorites and the Jebusites." In other words, God will demonstrate that He is the one true, living God by wiping out those who follow dead gods.

Paul called the church in 1 Timothy 3:15 "the church of the living God, the pillar and ground of the truth." That was very significant. Paul was writing to Timothy, who was the pastor of the church in Ephesus. This city was the headquarters for the worship of the goddess Diana. Paul was reiterating that God alone is the true and living God. People came from all over the world to worship the goddess Diana; however, she was a dead god like all other gods.

"Therefore You are great, O Lord God. For there is none like You, nor is there any God besides You" (2 Samuel 7:22).

Let's praise the Lord today that we serve the true and living God. May we, as the psalmist did, thirst for God—for the living God.

When a man makes alliance with the Almighty, giants looks like grasshoppers.

Vance Havner

Hands Off!

There was a summer camp once where the counselor would gather all the kids together and explain to them how God had a purpose for everything He had created. There was a purpose for the rocks, the trees, the rivers, and so forth. The group would go down the list and discuss things in nature and their purpose. All the kids could understand with no problem how there was a purpose for the trees, the animals, and the rivers. But then one kid raised his hand and asked, "If God has a purpose for everything, why did He create poison ivy?" The counselor couldn't think of an answer.

Then another little boy sitting next to the one who had asked the question said: "I can answer that. God created poison ivy because He wanted us to learn that there are certain things we should keep our cotton-pickin' hands off of!" That's good theology! God has told us to keep our hands off certain things. We could sum them up as "the things of this world."

The apostle John put it this way in 1 John 2:15: "Do not love the world or the things in the world." The temptation to put our hands on the things of this world, which God has commanded us not to touch, begins in the heart. If we can tackle the temptation inside, we will keep our hands off on the outside as well.

May we keep our hands off the things of this world and our hearts on God's Word.

Be alert! Look at everything in the light of God's Holy Word.

B. R. S.

Empty or Full?

The book of Ruth begins with a woman by the name of Naomi returning to her homeland, Bethlehem of Judah. She brings along her daughter-in-law Ruth. They had just spent ten years in the idolatrous nation of Moab. Consequently, she says in Ruth 1:21, "I went out full, and the Lord has brought me home again empty." What an important principle to mark in our Bibles as well as in our minds! Whenever we depart from the presence of God, we will always leave full and return empty.

I'm reminded of the Prodigal Son in Luke 15. He left his father's presence with a full inheritance and returned with nothing in hand. To put it plainly, sin never pays. It always produces a harvest of sorrow and sadness and, in the end, leaves us empty.

Look at the mathematics of sin: Sin adds to our sorrow, subtracts from our energy, multiplies our troubles, and divides our loyalty. No matter how we add, subtract, multiply, or divide, sin never adds up to an acceptable quantity. When we seek the Lord, we will find true what the psalmist said of the Lord: "You anoint my head with oil; My cup runs over" (Psalm 23:5). However, to leave His presence, to leave His goodness and love, is to be left empty.

Pray to cling to Jesus who sticks closer than a brother (Proverbs 18:24). Pray for those who have left and have retuned empty, that they will face their sin and be refilled. Praise the Lord that we serve a God who can restore what sin has destroyed (Joel 2:25). Jesus said in Matthew 5:6, "Blessed are those who hunger and thirst for righteousness, For they shall be filled." May that be our hearts' desire today!

Our sinful ways can sap our joy and isolate us from the Lord;
Confession and repentance, though, provide the way
to be restored.

Spurgeon

Thinking Little of Self

If we are honest with ourselves, we will admit to struggling with pride. Some of us may not struggle with blatant pride, but we still don't mind if someone mentions our name in a positive light or speaks highly of us to someone else when we're around. In other words, it never hurts to get a little recognition.

Jesus called John the Baptist the greatest of men (Matthew 11:11), and yet when John spoke of himself he said, "I am 'the voice of one crying in the wilderness'" (John 1:23). He was saying, in effect, When you think of me, you need only listen to what I'm saying to you about the Christ. I don't need to talk about myself. I don't need any recognition. I'm just a voice. The motto of his life and career was, "He [Christ] must increase, but I must decrease" (John 3:30).

If we profess any true Christianity, let us strive to be as John the Baptist. Let us study his humility. John the Baptist was clothed in humility. He said in John 1:27, "It is He [Christ] who, coming after me, is preferred before me, whose sandal strap I am not worthy to loose." John could not have stated a more menial task. There was a rabbinic saying that "a disciple might do for his master anything that a servant does, except untie his sandals." In other words, it was the lowest of the low. Yet John the Baptist was not beyond doing the lowliest task. He was a man who was willing to obliterate himself so that Christ might shine alone.

Dr. Martyn Lloyd-Jones once said, "I sometimes think that the very essence of the Christian position and the secret of a successful spiritual life is just to realize two things: I must have complete, absolute confidence in God and no confidence in myself."

May we be willing to obliterate and think little of self today and live in absolute surrender and obedience to Christ.

O Heavenly Father, for Thy dear Son's sake,
keep me from climbing.

George Whitefield

A Kingdom of Joy

In Matthew 13:44, Jesus said, "Again, the kingdom of heaven is like a treasure hidden in a field, which a man found and hid; and for joy over it he goes and sells all that he has and buys that field."

Here, and throughout the Bible, the kingdom of God is characterized by joy. Jesus said in John 15:11, "These things I have spoken to you, that My joy may remain in you, and that your joy may be full." In John 16:24, He said, "Ask and you will receive, that your joy may be full." John wrote in 1 John 1:4, "And these things we write to you, that your joy may be full." And the apostle Paul clearly defines the nature of God's kingdom in Romans 14:17, saying, "For the kingdom of God is not eating and drinking, but righteousness and peace and joy in the Holy Spirit." Therefore, true joy, lasting joy, eternal joy, is only found in the kingdom of God.

Praise God for the deep joy we have in our hearts when we know we are eternally saved. Then let us display that joy to everyone we come in contact with!

Laughter adds richness, texture and color to otherwise ordinary days. It is a choice, a discipline and an art.

Tim Hansel

The Last Days

The apostle Paul writes in 1 Timothy 4:1, "Now the Spirit expressly says that in latter times some will depart from the faith, giving heed to deceiving spirits, and doctrines of demons." We live in a time where anything and everything is promoted and taught as truth. Tragically, most of these promotions are either dancing with deception or have married into it completely. Deviant doctrines and practices abound, even within the church. Many are leaving the essential truths of Christianity for the deceitful doctrines of demons.

Jesus said, "For many will come in my name, saying, 'I am the Christ,' and will deceive many" (Matthew 24:5). In Matthew 24:11–12, He said, "Then many false prophets will rise up and deceive many. And because lawlessness will abound, the love of many will grow cold."

Consider the words of General William Booth, founder of the Salvation Army, who said toward the end of the nineteenth century, "I consider the chief dangers that will confront the twentieth century will be: religion without the Holy Spirit, Christianity without Christ, forgiveness without repentance, morality without God and heaven without hell." Though General Booth would never have considered himself a prophet, his words were prophetic.

We are saddened by this insidious work of the enemy. On the other hand, we are excited because Jesus said in Luke 21:28, "Now when these things begin to happen, look up and lift up your heads, because your redemption draws near." Christ could return for His bride any day!

May we be those available and useful servants ready to rescue any lost soul that is perishing without Christ. And may we be ready to receive our returning Savior.

Be ready for the last moment
by being ready at every moment.

Unknown

God's Word and Prayer

In Ephesians 6, we are given seven pieces of armor, five defensive and two offensive. Our offensive weapons are found in verses 17 and 18: "And take the helmet of salvation, and the sword of the Spirit, which is the word of God; praying always with all prayer and supplication in the Spirit." The Word of God and prayer are the dynamic duo that cut through the enemy's attacks.

Our first weapon is the Word of God. The apostle Paul is not saying to hold up your Bible against the enemy and he will flee. No! It is the idea of knowing God's Word, then using specific verses, in specific situations, to ward off specific attacks. The only way we will be able to do that is by knowing God's Word.

The second offensive weapon we have is prayer. Think of the many exhortations we have in the Bible to pray; yet the angels of heaven must be frustrated to no end when they see us struggling in areas of our lives and yet not praying! Prayer is such an awesome weapon that the devil would rather see us do anything but pray.

Being familiar with God's Word allows us to comfortably answer the questions posed by the lost. Knowing His Word gives us the ability to prove Scripture with Scripture. Prayer helps us have an intimate relationship with our Savior. We express all of our concerns and joys to Him through prayer. Our relationship with Him can be so intimate, in fact, that we continually sense His presence in us and become more like Him.

May we learn how to use these offensive weapons—God's Word and communication with Him through prayer!

Restraining prayer we cease to fight;
Prayer makes the Christian's armor bright;
And Satan trembles when he sees
The weakest saint upon his knees.

William Cowper

A Complete and Sufficient Savior

In John 1:29, John the Baptist said of Jesus: "Behold! The Lamb of God, who takes away the sin of the world!" Here we have the Messiah formally introduced to the world. Notice what John doesn't say. He doesn't say, "Behold the Holy One of God," or, "Behold the Word of God," though those statements would have been true. Why? Because in this one statement, John goes right to the heart of the people's need. The nation of Israel wanted a king; however, God gave them a Lamb. They wanted a powerful potentate; yet God gave them a Sacrifice. Why? Because you can't reign with God until you are related to God, and you can't be related to God until your sin has been taken out of the way.

Jesus Christ is the perfect sacrificial Lamb who takes our sin out of the way. Jesus did not come to earth to be a militant conqueror, a mystical philosopher, or a teacher of high morality. He came to earth to be a Savior (1 Timothy 1:15). Jesus didn't come to earth to hand out a few pardons, nor did He come to take care of "most" sin. Our Savior came to take all sin away.

We read in Colossians 2:13–14: "And you, being dead in your trespasses and the uncircumcision of your flesh, He has made alive together with Him, having forgiven you all trespasses, having wiped out the handwriting of requirements that was against us, which was contrary to us. And He has taken it out of the way, having nailed it to the cross."

Jesus is a complete Savior, and He is a sufficient Savior. Although He died on the cross for all men's sins, that does not mean that all men's sins are forgiven. There must be repentance for sin and application of faith. Theologically, Christ's atonement was sufficient for all mankind; however, His atonement is only efficacious for those who come to Him in repentance and faith in His name.

May we praise the Lamb of God for His atoning sacrifice on the cross—a sacrifice that was both complete and sufficient to all that will come to Him (John 6:37).

You can never praise God too much.

Unknown

337

Love in Action

Jesus was always the perfect example of love in action! Even when he cleansed the temple, He acted out of sincere love. When He arrived in Jerusalem for the first time in His earthly ministry, he went right to the temple area and ran out all of those who had turned it into a flea market. They were using this area for selling sacrifices to make a profit. He literally made a whip and drove them out.

How is that an act of love? Before Jesus ever preached a sermon in Jerusalem, He needed to show the people the seriousness of sin. Until a person confronts his or her sin, that person cannot be saved. And so as Jesus arrives in Jerusalem for the first time, His main concern is not the people's social injustices, deprivations, poverty, sickness, or oppressions; His main concern is that He deal with sin.

The first place Jesus must work in our lives is the area of sin. Without the issue of sin dealt with, nothing else matters. Through faith in Jesus Christ, our sin is judicially eradicated. Nonetheless, we still sin. That is why John tells us that we need to come to the Lord daily, confessing our sins (1 John 1:9). What if we don't? Christ's love comes into action. In His love for us, Jesus will start overturning tables in our lives and driving out those things that defile us. Jesus is concerned with our holiness, and so in His love for us, He'll do whatever needs to be done to "fetch out" the sin. (See quotation below.)

May we yield today to His love in action.

God would not rub so hard if it were not to fetch out the dirt that is ingrained in our natures. God loves purity so well, he had rather see a hole than a spot in his children's garments.

William Gurnall

Walk in the Light!

In John 12:35, Jesus said: "A little while longer the light is with you. Walk while you have the light, lest darkness overtake you." The word walk is used throughout the Bible as a metaphor of a person's manner of living. The way you walk is the way you live your life. As an example, Paul says in Ephesians 4:1, "Walk worthy of the calling with which you were called." In other words, let your practice match your profession. Then he says in Ephesians 5:2, "Walk in love," and in verse 8, "Walk as children of the light," and verse 15, "Walk circumspectly."

Jesus teaches us in John's gospel to live our life in the light and place our life in Him. Why? "Lest darkness overtake you." Some translations say, "Lest darkness come upon you!" The inherent truth Jesus is teaching here is that if we don't walk in the light, if we are not proactively placing our faith in Christ, darkness will just naturally overtake us. You see, the darkness itself is proactive. Therefore, if we don't walk in the light, that darkness will catch up and overtake us.

In context, Jesus is talking about saving faith. Without faith in Jesus Christ, a person will succumb to the darkness of this world and, in the end, dwell in eternal darkness. However, this passage of Scripture is also applicable to us as believers. We are either going forward in the kingdom or backward. As Christians, we are children of the Light, and nothing can take that essential truth or our ultimate destiny away. Consequently, it is exceedingly important that we be proactive in our walk with Christ lest we aid the darkness by doing nothing.

May we be that light today that Jesus calls us to be (Matthew 5:16).

When we focus on God and His love, we see life more clearly and witness more effectively.

B. R. S.

339

December 2

Setting Your Mind

The Bible says in Colossians 3:2, "Set your mind on things above, not on things on the earth." We will all agree that as Christians we can easily fall into the trap of being preoccupied with the things on the earth. That is why the apostle said, "Set your mind on things above." Setting our mind is a deliberate act of the will. We often set our minds to take a vacation. We set our minds to purchase an object. We set our minds to finish a project.

As Christians, we need to set our minds to make a deliberate act of our wills to seek God daily. We do that by:

Reading His Word.

Communicating with Him through prayer.

Seeking with all of our heart to do His will daily.

Every day we have a choice of whether or not to deliberately preoccupy and set our minds on the things of this world or on the things that are above. It's been said that in the company of others we need to guard our tongues and in solitude we need to guard our thoughts. God help us to set our minds on that which is pleasing to Him.

As the image on the seal is stamped upon the wax, so the thoughts of the heart are printed upon the actions.

Stephen Charnock

Praise the Lord

What's the first thing that comes to mind when we hear "Praise the Lord"? We may think of it as a catchy phrase that is thrown out when nothing else comes to mind, or perhaps it holds little or no meaning at all. In spite of all the misuses of this phrase, praising the Lord is one of the believer's greatest expressions of love and gratitude to their God! And consider this: When we bless Him, it is with words of praise. When He blesses us, it is with deeds of kindness (1 Peter 1:3, James 1:17).

Praising God shows humility, since we understand it is from His gracious hand that all of our needs are provided (Philippians 4:19). Praise acknowledges God's rightful place it our hearts and minds as Sovereign Lord. From a heart of praise flows inexpressible joy and thanksgiving (1 Thessalonians 5:16–18).

May we recognize that everything touching our life is a gracious gift from God (James 1:17). As a result of that enlightenment, let us be generous in our praise and thanksgiving to Him! Set aside some time today, simply to thank Him for all the undeserved blessings He has so freely given. Pray for opportunities to share His goodness with others. May we acknowledge His blessings even in the simplest things! May we continually remind ourselves that God created us and redeemed us because He loves us and wants to be an intimate part of our lives. Therefore, one of the best ways to praise Him is by giving Him our thoughts throughout the day.

Praise to the Lord,
who o'er all things so wondrously reigneth,
Shelters thee under His wings, yea, so gently sustaineth!
Hast thou not seen how thy desires e'er have been
Granted in what He ordaineth?
Praise to the Lord, O let all that is in me adore Him!
All that has life and breath,
come now with praises before Him.
Let the Amen sound from His people again,
Gladly for aye we adore Him.

Joachim Neander (Trans. by Catherine Winkworth)

Grow in Grace

The last request we have of the apostle Peter is found at the end of his second epistle when he tenderly wrote: "But grow in the grace and knowledge of our Lord and Savior Jesus Christ. To Him be the glory both now and forever. Amen" (2 Peter 3:18).

Growing "in the grace and knowledge of our Lord" is not a growth upward but a growth downward. The more we understand the great grace we have been given and the more we understand all that Christ has done for us, the lower we are brought, and the more humbled we find ourselves. Grace is the favor God gives to us when He forgives us. It is the ability He gives us to live the way He desires for us. Acknowledging God's grace in our lives produces Christlike qualities that work to accomplish His redemptive purpose for all mankind. Growing in the grace and knowledge of our Lord is a growth that causes Christ to increase and us to decrease.

Each day to grow more humble,
Yet stronger in Thy might,
More valiant, Lord, to carry,
Thy standard for the right.
Each day to grow more gracious,
More sweet and gentle too;
Yet braver, more courageous,
More firm, more pure, more true.
That I may grow like Thee,
In me Thy Spirit shine;
Transformed from grace to glory,
Touched by Thy power divine.

Anonymous

Fervent Love

Over and over again, the Bible exhorts us to love one another. 1 Peter 4:8 says, "And above all things have fervent love for one another." The word fervent is very expressive. It describes activity that strains at, that strives for, and that reaches to the furthest extent possible.

Fitness experts tell us that if we want our muscles to grow, we must constantly change our routine and strain the muscles to the point of exhaustion. This practice needs to be followed to get the best results. Peter is saying the same thing: when it comes to loving your brother, you need to take it to the limit!

Fervent love is described in 1 Corinthians 13:4–8, which tells us it "suffers long and is kind . . . does not envy . . . does not parade itself, is not puffed up; does not behave rudely, does not seek its own, is not provoked, thinks no evil; does not rejoice in iniquity, but rejoices in the truth; bears all things, believes all things, hopes all things, endures all things. Love never fails."

When we realize that God loves us no matter what mistakes we have made, He fills us with the kind of love we are taught about in 1 Corinthians 13, the "love chapter." This filling of the Holy Spirit turns us into the kind of person He wants us to be—for Him. This action becomes the foundation from which we are able to express "fervent love" to our brethren.

God help us to strain for this kind of love!

Unfailing is God's matchless love—
So kind, so pure, so true;
And those who draw upon that love
Show love in all they do.

D. J. De Haan

The Need for Spiritual Unity

Paul said in Philippians 1:27 to "stand fast in one spirit, with one mind striving together for the faith of the gospel." A.W. Tozer once said, "Unity in Christ is not something to be achieved; it is something to be recognized."

How true! A church that is unified in spirit and purpose can accomplish great things for the kingdom of God. However, a church that is broken apart by strife and criticism will be weak and crippled in its witness. Unity of spirit is a key element to a church's influence and effectiveness for Christ.

Sadly, disunity in the body of Christ is often the result of petty differences, personality clashes, or just plain pride. Within every church, there are various personalities and backgrounds, as well as differing spiritual abilities to edify the body of Christ. These variances are meant for our benefit and for God's glory. However, if we are not walking in the Spirit, they may be perceived as a bother rather than a blessing.

Look at the disciples: Peter, an impetuous fisherman; Matthew, a hated tax collector; James and John, the "Sons of Thunder"; Philip, a pessimist; Bartholomew, a prejudiced Jew; and Simon, a political fanatic, just to mention a few! All of them were brought together to preach the gospel of Jesus Christ! Do you see the potential for catastrophe? Yet, through the grace of God and the surrender of these men to the Spirit of God, they were able to turn the world upside down! That is the fruit of spiritual unity! As Christians, we are part of a spiritual team. Because of this, Satan will try to sow seeds of discord among us. Pray for spiritual harmony, and live out that attitude every day.

Blest be the tie that binds our hearts in Christian love;
The fellowship of kindred minds is like to that above.
We share our mutual woes, our mutual burdens bear;
And often for each other flows the sympathizing tear.
When we asunder part, it gives us inward pain;
But we shall still be joined in heart, and hope to meet again.

John Fawcett

What's Your Preoccupation?

What are the three things I am currently seeking with utmost exertion? What things do I love the most? What things do I think about the most?

These are good questions to ask ourselves, because they let us know whether our preoccupation is heavenly or earthly, directed toward God or toward self. These questions really get to the core of our being.

Jesus put it this way in Matthew 6:21: "For where your treasure is, there your heart will be also." He was saying that a man's true character is shown by his mind's preoccupation. What we think reveals where our treasure is.

We need to continually ask ourselves where our heart is in relation to Jesus. What is the preoccupation of our mind? Who is our priority? With the help and prompting of the Holy Spirit, we can answer all of these by calling out, Jesus!

There have been names that I have loved to hear,
But never has there been a name so dear
To this heart of mine, as the name divine,
The precious, precious name of Jesus.
There is no name in earth or heaven above,
That we should give such honor and such love,
As the blessed name, let us all acclaim,
That wondrous, glorious name of Jesus.
And someday I shall see Him face to face
To thank and praise Him for His wondrous grace,
Which He gave to me, when He made me free,
The blessed Son of God called Jesus.
Jesus is the sweetest name I know,
And He's just the same as His lovely name,
And that's the reason why I love Him so;
Oh, Jesus is the sweetest name I know.

Lela Long

Fighting Our Foe

The apostle Paul wrote in 2 Corinthians 10:4, "For the weapons of our warfare are not carnal but mighty in God for pulling down strongholds."

The topic of spiritual warfare is becoming more and more popular in the church these days. Yet at the same time, it is somewhat misunderstood. In Ephesians 6:12, Paul reminds us that our struggle is not against people but against supernatural forces, which influence and dictate the mindset of the world. Satan uses the world and the flesh to accuse and condemn believers in an effort to render them useless to God.

How do we fight against such a formidable foe? As Christians, we must understand that our success in spiritual warfare is directly related to our readiness for the battle. Our defense is to rely on Christ's strength (1 John 4:4) and to equip ourselves with the armor freely given to us by our Commander in Chief. Only a foolish soldier would try to go into the heat of the battle with no weapon.

Our Lord has amply supplied us with all we need to defeat our enemy. However, if we delay our preparation until the time of combat, we will be easily defeated. If we neglect prayer, the study of God's Word, worship, accountability, and so forth, we can expect a frustrated fight. James tells us in James 4:7 that spiritual victory requires submitting to God and pursuing His will. Jesus Christ guarantees our ultimate victory as believers, but we must also "fight the good fight" (1 Timothy 6:12), standing firm to the end. That is the blessed balance. God supplies the resources; we supply the effort. Satan's attacks are subtle, deceitful, and daily! However, as we submit to God's will and put on His armor, victory is inevitable! We need to take regular spiritual inventory to see if there is an area in our life in which our footing isn't as firm as it should be. Submit this area to God; then put on the armor of God, and trust that He will give you the victory in this area in His time.

There is no winning without warfare; there is no opportunity without opposition; there is no victory without vigilance.

Alan Redpath

The Fragrance of Christ

There is a story about a press correspondent in Europe who went to eat once in a small restaurant. While he was there, a group of men entered for their lunch break. Immediately, the room was permeated with the smell of perfume. When the men left, the correspondent asked the restaurant owner who those men were. The owner replied, "They are the workmen from the perfume factory, and they bring the scent of perfume in with them every time they come to eat."

In 2 Corinthians 2:15, Paul says: "For we are to God the fragrance of Christ among those who are being saved and among those who are perishing." In other words, we are to permeate the world by bringing the fragrance of light and life to men. Every time we leave a room, we should leave the scent of Christ. Every time we leave a family gathering, we should be leaving the scent of Christ. Every time we leave a conversation, we should be leaving the scent of Christ.

May we be continually alert to the Holy Spirit working in and through us so that we will exude the godly, influential fragrance of Christ! Let that fragrance linger and permeate the lives of those we've touched.

To love someone more dearly every day,
To help a wandering child to find his way,
To ponder o'er a noble thought and pray,
And smile when evening falls,
And smile when evening falls,
This is my task.

To follow truth as blind men long for light,
To do my best from dawn of day till night,
To keep my heart fit for His holy sight,
And answer when He calls,
And answer when He calls,
This is my task.

Maude Louise Ray

Take up Your Cross

What did Jesus mean when He told His disciples to "take up your cross"? We often associate that statement with the idea of suffering. It is true that Jesus was telling His disciples that they would suffer, yet Christians will often misinterpret His words saying, "My cross to bear in this life is my job," or, "My cross is my next-door neighbor," or "My cross is my in-laws," or, "My cross is my spouse."

We need to recognize that those kinds of things in our lives are situations that God has brought about for our spiritual growth. However, they are not the cross that Jesus was talking about. The first thing that would have popped into the minds of disciples when Jesus said, "Take up your cross," would have been, "Guys, be willing to take up the instrument of death and follow me." In other words, Jesus was telling His disciples, Be willing to be persecuted, be willing to suffer, and be willing to take that suffering all the way to death. In 2 Timothy 3:12 we read, "Yes, and all who desire to live godly in Christ Jesus will suffer persecution."

Let us praise the Lord for taking up His cross, and let us be ready to take up ours.

I walked one day along a country road,
And there a stranger journeyed too,
Bent low beneath the burden of His load;
It was a cross, a cross I knew.
I cried, "Lord Jesus," and He spoke my name;
I saw His hands all bruised and torn;
I stooped to kiss away the marks of shame,
The shame for me that He had borne.
"Take up thy cross and follow Me,"
I heard the blessed Savior call;
How can I make a lesser sacrifice,
When Jesus gave His all?

Rev. A. H. Ackley

December 11

A Heart Set on God

Psalm 63:1 reads, "O God, you are my God; Early will I seek You; My soul thirsts for You; My flesh longs for You In a dry and thirsty land Where there is no water." This Psalm is a beautiful expression of the heart set in pursuit of God. The psalmist is verbalizing how much his soul hungers and thirsts for a heavenly satisfaction.

How is our spiritual appetite? Do we find it to be healthy and growing, or is it deficient? It is important to understand that God desires not only to satisfy our hunger but to increase it with each passing day! True hungering for righteousness begins with a love for Jesus Christ. Just the word hunger speaks of an intense desire or craving.

How can we know if our spiritual appetite is healthy? Our spiritual wellness can be measured in part by our satisfaction with our present spiritual condition. A hungering soul has a holy discontentment. It is not complacent but is always asking, seeking, and knocking for more! If we are hungry, we won't need someone to tell us to eat. There will be a spiritual craving that will drive us to feast on God's Word. Just as we have a consistent physical hunger, so we should have a consistent spiritual hunger; and the only way to satisfy that is with God's Word. Do we put a condition on the feeding of this spiritual hunger? Is the satisfaction of these spiritual desires predicated on God's doing it our way?

Often, our heavenly Father will allow circumstances to arise to teach us more about Himself and His righteousness. A hunger for righteousness based on good circumstances and outward happiness is not a healthy appetite. We need to understand that our pursuit of God is not determined by how we feel but by a willful determination to keep on the course God has directed. May we consciously draw near to God, seeking that fulfillment that only He can provide!

They who do not thirst for righteousness shall be in perpetual hunger and thirst.

Thomas Watson

349

Overturning Sin

In Matthew 21:12, we learn how Jesus went into the temple and over-turned the moneychangers' tables and drove out those who sold temple sacrifices. He purged the temple of all that did not bring glory to the Father. Likewise, God would have us run the things out of our hearts that do not bring Him glory. If we don't run them out, He will.

When we allow sin to roam freely in our lives, God may let it remain for a season. However, if we don't heed the promptings of the Holy Spirit and deal with our sin, the Lord in His love will come in and start overturning things in our lives to get us back on track.

It is imperative that we keep ourselves in spiritual check by reading God's Word and maintaining our accountability to God's people. If we get off track and stop dealing with sin, God will have to come in and deal more severely with us. But remember that if He does have to take drastic action to purge our sin, He does so because He loves us as His children (Hebrews 12:6).

May the Lord grant us the tenacity to overturn the tables of sin in our hearts so God won't have to.

Search me, O God, and know my heart today;
Try me, O Savior, know my thoughts, I pray;
See if there be some wicked way in me;
Cleanse me from every sin, and set me free.

I praise Thee, Lord, for cleansing me from sin;
Fulfill Thy Word, and make me pure within;
Fill me with fire, where once I burned with shame;
Grant my desire to magnify Thy name.

Lord, take my life, and make it wholly Thine;
Fill my poor heart with Thy great love divine;
Take all my will, my passion, self and pride;
I now surrender: Lord, in me abide.

Edwin Orr

Spiritual Life

People place great emphasis on extending the longevity of their lives. There are pills, potions, lotions, methods, and machines ad nauseam to try to make us live longer. The truth is, all of us are going to die.

Moreover, the Bible tells us that a person not born again is already dead—spiritually dead. The Bible tells us that we are born in sin (Psalm 51:5); therefore, we are spiritually dead (Ephesians 2:1). We are born into this world without a heartbeat toward God. We are as spiritually dead as a physical corpse that has no senses with which to respond. Likewise, an unregenerate person has no spiritual senses and, thus, no capacity to respond to God.

The only way man could be redeemed was if God came to man. So that is exactly what Jesus did! He said in John 10:10, "I have come that they may have life, and that they may have it more abundantly." Because men are spiritually dead, Christ came to give life. He said in John 6:35, "I am the bread of life;" then in verse 47, "He who believes in Me has everlasting life." He further states in John 11:25, "I am the resurrection and the life."

Jesus came on a search and rescue mission to bring life to those who were dead in trespasses and sin. The apostle Paul states in Colossians 2:13, "And you, being dead in your trespasses and the uncircumcision of your flesh, He has made alive together with Him, having forgiven you all trespasses."

A tombstone in an old British cemetery not far from Windsor Castle reads: "Pause my friend as you walk by, as you are now so once was I. As I am now, so you will be, prepare my friend to follow me." Every one of us will die physically; but through faith in Jesus, we don't have to be dead spiritually. A person who visited that tombstone was overheard to say, "To follow you is not my intent, until I know which way you went."

Seeing we are God's enemies, we must be reborn His sons.

Richard Baxter

December 14

Lamps for Christ

Jesus said of John the Baptist, "He was the burning and shining lamp" (John 5:35). Jesus is the Light of the World, and John was a lamp. In other words, John was a man who lived to reflect Christ's light. Jesus calls us to do the same. In Matthew 5:14, Jesus said: "You are the light of the world."

Four interesting facts about the physical lamps of Jesus' day give us spiritual insight.

First, they reflected borrowed light. They had no light in themselves. They had to be filled with oil and lit. As Christians, we need to be filled with the oil of the Holy Spirit every day so that we might reflect Christ's love (Ephesians 5:18). Our thoughts and actions need to be dominated and directed by the Holy Spirit so that we will bear the fruit of the Spirit (Galatians 5:22–23).

Second, they gave warmth. As we reflect the light of Christ's love, our message has the power to warm the hearts of those whose lives we touch. Because of sin, the love of many grows cold (Matthew 24:12); however, by reflecting Christ's love to a cold world, we can be a source of warming hope.

Third, they gave out light to dispel darkness. When we reflect the light of Christ's love, the Holy Spirit can use us to guide people out of darkness and into the light of Jesus Christ.

Fourth, they burned out. The nature of a lamp is to eventually burn out. John the Baptist said in John 3:30, "He must increase, but I must decrease."

Henry Martyn, that great missionary to India, said in 1805 as he set sail for the continent: "Let me burn out for God!" He lived his life burning brightly for Christ. May we do the same today.

No one is a light to himself, not even the sun.

Antonio Porchia

Blessedness through Suffering

As Christians, we often think of all of our spiritual privileges in Christ. We have been brought into a new birth, a living hope, an inheritance incorruptible and undefiled. It is a birth that doesn't fade away and was reserved in heaven for us. We are now living stones, a holy priesthood, a chosen people, and a holy nation. As such, we might have the tendency to think we should be loved, respected, honored, adored, and exalted by the world. Actually, the opposite is true.

There is a strange duality in the life of the believer: running parallel with the track of blessings is the track of suffering. In 1 Peter 2:21, we read, "For to this you were called, because Christ also suffered for us, leaving us an example, that you should follow His steps."

It is shallow theology that teaches that Christians will not have to suffer. In actuality, blessedness is usually distributed through God's appointed times of suffering!

When upon life's billows you are tempest tossed,
When you are discouraged, thinking all is lost,
Count your many blessings, name them one by one,
And it will surprise you what the Lord has done.

Are you ever burdened with a load of care?
Does the cross seem heavy you were called to bear?
Count your many blessings, every doubt will fly,
And you will be singing as the days go by.

So, amid the conflict, whether great or small,
Do not be discouraged, God is over all;
Count your many blessings, angels will attend,
Help and comfort give you to your journey's end.

Count your blessings, name them one by one;
Count your blessings, see what God has done;
Count your blessings, name them one by one;
Count your many blessings, see what God has done.

Johnson Oatman, Jr.

Jesus Healed Them

In Matthew 4:24, we read, "They brought to Him all sick people who were afflicted with various diseases and torments, and those who were demon-possessed, epileptics, and paralytics; and He healed them." Throughout the life of Jesus, we see a ministry of healing. Why did Jesus heal people, and what did it point to?

Jesus' ministry of healing pointed to three things:

1) Jesus' healings showed His compassion for men. We have a compassionate Savior who wants all men to be healed spiritually through salvation.

2) Jesus' healing power pointed to His deity. Only the Christ could do these things. Jesus did all of these things in fulfillment of messianic prophecy.

3) Jesus' healings pointed to the fact that a time is coming in His kingdom where there will be no more sorrow, no more sickness, and no more pain.

Jesus, Your name is power. Jesus, Your name is might.
Jesus, Your name will break every stronghold;
Jesus, Your name is life.

Jesus, Your name is healing. Jesus, Your name gives sight.
Jesus, Your name will free every captive;
Jesus, Your name is life.

Jesus, Your name is holy. Jesus, Your name brings light.
Jesus, Your name above every other;
Jesus, Your name is life.

Morris Chapman and Claire Cloninger

The Light of Heaven

In John 14:1–3, Jesus said to his disciples: "Let not your heart be troubled; you believe in God, believe also in Me. In My Father's house are many mansions; if it were not so, I would have told you. I go to prepare a place for you. And if I go and prepare a place for you, I will come again and receive you to Myself; that where I am, there you may be also." The defining hope of every believer is eternity in the Father's house through faith in Jesus Christ!

There is a story about a fierce storm that hit the Great Lakes many years ago. A tugboat towing a barge was caught in the middle of the storm. When hopes of saving the tugboat were lost, the captain and his crew took to a small lifeboat. All night long they were tossed back and forth in the raging waters, their lives in constant jeopardy. Finally, around the break of day, they were spotted and rescued. Once on deck, the men testified to the captain of the vessel that they had been beaten and tossed by this great tempest all night long and at any time could have lost their lives. They said that the one thing that helped them remain calm and keep their hearts from sinking into despair was the fact that, shining through the darkness of the storm, they could see the lights of home. The sight gave them hope.

All of us will go through storms of varying intensity during our lifetimes. However, as believers, we have a hope that keeps us going: the hope that Christ is preparing an eternal home for us in heaven.

I was drifting 'mid the wreckage
on the storm-tossed sea of life;
I was weary of the watching of the labor and the strife;
When I heard a sweet voice whisper
and repeat it o'er and o'er,
For your rescue, Christ the Savior
set a lighthouse on the shore.

John A. Jones

Don't Sound a Trumpet

One pastor tells of a woman who had told him that she was called to a certain ministry and to trust God in faith for all that was to be provided. She said there would be no collection or appeals for funds. Later, she stood before the congregation to make announcements. The pastor noted that this good lady took ten minutes to tell everyone that this work was to be entirely on faith lines—that no collection was to be taken, that she didn't believe in collections or asking for money, and so on. The pastor then commented, "I thought it was the most effective appeal for funds I had ever heard!"

In Matthew 6:1–4, Jesus said:

> Take heed that you do not do your charitable deeds before men, to be seen by them. Otherwise you have no reward from your Father in heaven. Therefore, when you do a charitable deed, do not sound a trumpet before you as the hypocrites do in the synagogues and in the streets, that they may have glory from men. Assuredly, I say to you, they have their reward. But when you do a charitable deed, do not let your left hand know what your right hand is doing, that your charitable deed may be in secret; and your Father who sees in secret will Himself reward you openly.

God help us to not sound a trumpet when we give but to give liberally and secretly!

He who receives a benefit should never forget it; he who bestows should never remember it.

Pierre Charron

Who Is Jesus?

In Matthew 16:13, Jesus asked his disciples the question of all questions: "Who do men say that I, the Son of Man, am?" You might call it the disciples' final examination. Jesus had spent almost three years living with and teaching these men. Now He wanted to know where they stood. Peter eventually stood up and said, "You are the Christ, the Son of the living God" (verse 16).

This is the ultimate question every human being must face: Who is Jesus Christ? The way we answer that question will determine the ultimate destiny of each person's eternal soul. Jesus came to earth to pay the penalty for man's sin so that man might have fellowship with God for eternity.

Jesus makes every attempt to bring men to the truth of the gospel. The sad truth is that many reject His invitation. However, He is ever and always reaching out to man, so that the only way that man can reject Him is by literally walking over Him.

The ultimate question that will determine the destiny of each individual is, Who is Jesus Christ? Once that question has been answered correctly, the next question is, What will I do about it?

When you have kindled your life to Christ at His love to you,
then let it burn and spend in His service and to His praise.

Robert Traill

Living Water

Jesus said to the Samaritan woman at the well, "Whoever drinks of this water will thirst again, but whoever drinks of the water that I shall give him will never thirst" (John 4:13-14).

What is it in the world that you believe will bring you happiness? What is it in the world that you are pressing for? What goals in the world are you hoping to achieve? What possessions in the world are you desiring to acquire, believing that if you gain them you'll be satisfied? Whatever it is, Jesus says that you will thirst again. It won't satisfy! Nothing in the material or worldly realm can satisfy the emptiness of man's heart. Augustine said, "Our hearts are restless until they find rest in Christ."

Some people try to fill themselves with a career; they set the goal of being the best at what they do. However, when they accomplish their goal, they're still as empty as when they began. Some people try to fill themselves with knowledge and earn multiple degrees; yet they are empty. Some people try to fill themselves with busyness; yet busyness only leads to more emptiness. Some people just give up and try to fill themselves with stimulants, drugs, alcohol, or escapism. However, there is no escape from an empty heart. Still others try to fill themselves with religion. Yet even religion, after a time, becomes a heavy taskmaster of dos and don'ts.

There is no person or thing that can satisfy man's emptiness except the one who created it—Jesus Christ. God created each of us with a God-shaped void that only He can fill. Only Jesus Christ can fill our empty hearts! Only the fountainhead of living water can quench our spiritual thirst.

> *I thirsted in the barren land of sin and shame,*
> *And nothing satisfying there I found,*
> *But to the blessed cross of Christ one day I came,*
> *Where springs of living water did abound.*
>
> *John Peterson*

You Don't Know What to Say

In Mark 9, Jesus was transfigured in front of a handful of His disciples. He revealed His deity. At that time, Moses and Elijah also appeared with Him. This was almost too good to be true: here was Jesus showing Himself to be God, and two superheroes from the Old Testament show up as well!

Peter got a little excited, as we read in Mark 9:5: "Then Peter answered and said to Jesus, 'Rabbi, it is good for us to be here; and let us make three tabernacles: one for You, one for Moses, and one for Elijah.'" Peter made a foolish suggestion: Lord, let us tabernacle with You, Moses, and Elijah. Let us just stay up here and worship you three! We read what Peter "answered and said," but notice that Jesus never asked Peter for his suggestion. God's glory cannot be contained in a booth. God alone should be the sole object of our worship. Why then did Peter make such a foolish remark? Mark tells us in verse 6, "Because he did not know what to say."

At one time or another, most of us have spoken out of turn or said something simply because we did not know what to say. As the saying goes, though, "Better to be silent and be thought a fool than to open your mouth and dispel all doubts." Unfortunately, Peter opened his mouth. Often we do, too. God grant us the ability to watch what we say, lest we be hung by our tongues!

Silently now I wait for Thee,
Ready, my God, Thy will to see;
Open my heart, illumine me, Spirit divine!

Clara H. Scott

Let the Little Children Come

Jesus said in Matthew 19:14, "Let the little children come to Me, and do not forbid them; for of such is the kingdom of heaven." Jesus is teaching His disciples that those who enter His kingdom are characterized by childlikeness. Children are humble, innocent, teachable, compliant, moldable, trusting, wishing to please. A Christian possesses childlike characteristics.

What a beautiful sight it must have been to see our Lord surrounded by children—seeing Him laughing, embracing, and playing with them. I'm sure there were a few sitting on His lap and a few behind Him with their arms around His neck. Perhaps cuddled in His arm, a tiny infant was tugging on His beard. Most precious of all was that He displayed nothing but penetrating love to all of these children, and then blessed them and prayed for them. Jesus loved children, and children loved Jesus. The disciples saw these children as a bother, but Jesus saw them as a blessing.

It is so very important that a child have a father in its life. Children need a father who will lovingly support them, physically as well as emotionally. They need a supportive father who will give them direction, refuge, companionship, love, and discipline, and who will be a model for them to emulate.

As Christians, we are God's children, and He loves each one of us. He longs to touch us, to hug us, and to hold us. When we spend time with the Lord just cultivating that beautiful childlike faith, we will come to understand what He meant when He said, "For of such is the kingdom of heaven."

Jesus loves the little children,
All the children of the world;
Red and yellow, black and white,
They are precious in His sight;
Jesus loves the little children of the world.

Anonymous

More Than an Ornament

The celebration of our Lord's birth is here once again—that special time of the year when believers muse on the greatest truth in history: that God Himself came to earth. The Wonderful Counselor, the Mighty God, the Everlasting Father, the very Prince of Peace, came to make peace for us by stepping out of eternity to take on human flesh, to live a perfect life, and to die a perfect death on the cross for our sins.

Unfortunately, the world as a whole has crowded Jesus right out of this holiday. They like the music of the season but not the Messiah. They like the profits but not the true Prophet. They like the money but not the Master. They like the ornaments of the season but not the origins of the Savior. They like the atmosphere but not the Anointed One. They like the jingle but have no lasting joy. They like the pageantry but have no peace. They like the luster of the season but retain no lasting love for the Savior. They like the decorations but won't declare Christ as Lord.

The populace of Bethlehem had no idea that the Son of God was nestled in a local manger. The shepherds and the wise men who found the Baby, though, left honoring and praising God. If only we could recapture some of the awesomeness of our Savior—the infant Child—being born into this world. What an incredible gift!

May God use each of us this season to be His hands, His feet, His voice, and His light to our families and our friends. May the truth of the season fill us with His joy, and may that joy spill over to those around us.

If we look beyond the manger
To the cross of Calvary,
We will know the reason Christmas
Brings such joy to you and me.

D. J. De Haan

Who Is Christ to You?

Christmas means a lot of different things to a lot of different people. Some see it as a time to make some extra money. Some see it as a time that brings out the best in man; there is a rise in food and clothing drives, and donations to charity soar to their highest point of the year during this season. Some see Christmas as a time to give gifts to one another. Some see it as a time to immortalize a man by the name of Nicholas. Then there are those who see it simply as a time to be with those whom they love—warm sentimentalism. Others see it as a time of music and laughter.

In spite of all the effort put into each of these things, the truth is that unless a person has embraced the Christ of Christmas, there can be no lasting joy. The joy for believers during this season is in knowing that we have a personal relationship with Jesus Christ every single day of the year.

During this time of the year, each of us will come into contact with people who fall into one or more of the categories mentioned above. Pray that God will use each of us this season to be Christ to those people, whether they be family, friends, neighbors, or even the check-out clerk at the store. Ask the Holy Spirit to keep us alert to ways to display the truth of this season. Then ask Him to fill us with His joy and let that joy spill over to those around us. Ask Him to help us love the unlovable and boldly explain to them God's gift to the world.

Come with the spirit and heart of a child,
It matters not what we share.
For Christmas isn't Christmas at all
Unless the Christ-child is there.

Anonymous

The Wonder of Christ's Birth

In 1 John 3:1, the apostle John says, "Behold what manner of love the Father has bestowed on us, that we should be called children of God!"

At this time of year, we remember that Jesus Christ was born contrary to the laws of nature. He lived in poverty, and He was reared in obscurity. He only crossed the boundary of the land in which he was born once, and that was in childhood. He had no wealth or influence. He had neither training nor education in the world's school. His relatives were inconspicuous and not influential.

Yet in infancy, He startled a king; in boyhood, He puzzled the scholars of Israel; in manhood, He ruled the course of nature when He walked across the water and hushed the sea to sleep. He healed the multitudes without medicine, and He made no charge for His services. He never wrote a book, and yet all the libraries of the world could not contain the books about Him. He never wrote a song, and yet He has furnished the theme for more songs than all the songwriters put together. He never practiced medicine, yet He has healed more broken hearts than all the doctors have ever healed broken bodies. He is the Star of astronomy, the Rock of geology, the Lion and the Lamb. He is the Harmonizer of all discords and the Healer of all diseases.

Great men have come and gone throughout history, yet Jesus Christ lives on. Herod could not kill Him. Satan could not seduce Him. Death could not destroy Him. And the grave could not hold Him. Why? He is God! We celebrate this Christmas day because Jesus Christ clothed himself in humanity so that we might put on divinity. He became the Son of Man that we might become the sons of God.

Come, Thou long-expected Jesus,
Born to set Thy people free.
From our fears and sins release us;
Let us find our rest in Thee.
Israel's Strength and Consolation,
Hope of all the earth Thou art.
Dear Desire of every nation,
Joy of every longing heart.

Charles Wesley

363

If Anyone Thirst

Remember the Old Testament story about God bringing water from the rock? Paul comments on that event in 1 Corinthians 10:2–4 by saying: "All were baptized into Moses in the cloud and in the sea, all ate the same spiritual food, and all drank the same spiritual drink. For they drank of that spiritual Rock that followed them, and that Rock was Christ."

In other words, that rock in the Old Testament was a picture of the coming Christ. When the Messiah came, He would give His people living water. It is no wonder then that Jesus came into Jerusalem on the great day of the Feast of Tabernacles and said in John 7:37–38: "If anyone thirsts, let him come to Me and drink. He who believes in Me, as the Scripture has said, out of his heart will flow rivers of living water."

Jesus was saying that He was the fulfillment of that rock in the Old Testament and that He had come to give people living water! Just as those people who drank from that rock in the wilderness had their physical thirst satisfied, Jesus had come as the spiritual rock to satisfy the spiritual thirst of all men.

Tragically, the world tries to satisfy itself with other things. It tries physical things, thinking, If I just get that shiny new car, or If I just get that new house, I'll be happy. It tries entertainment: I'll take in a movie or a play; then I'll be happy. It tries religion: If I do some good things for others, I'll feel good about myself. However, in the end, all of those things leave men empty and looking for true satisfaction. Jesus says, "If anyone thirsts, let him come to Me and drink." True satisfaction comes in Christ alone.

Let us all come to Christ and drink. Let each of us pray: Lord, I want all that You have for me today. I want to walk in Your will that I might both be satisfied and bring You glory at the same time. May it be so, Lord. Amen.

Christ is a substitute for everything,
but nothing is a substitute for Christ.

Unknown

Christ the Light

It was the day after the Feast of Tabernacles, and Jesus entered the temple treasury. In this area were four large candelabras that would have been used throughout the Feast, commemorating the light by which God led the children of Israel by day in the desert.

The candles, however, had been extinguished; and as Jesus entered the room, He said in John 8:12: "I am the light of the world. He who follows Me shall not walk in darkness, but have the light of life." Jesus was saying, in effect: "Although these lights are out and cannot give any more illumination, I am the light of the world that gives light forever! I am the light that pierces the darkness of men's hearts and brings them into a right relationship with God! Your fathers saw the shekinah glory of God in the wilderness; I am the Shekinah. I am the glory. I am God!

May we come into His presence with gratitude and prayer because He has illuminated our hearts and given us eternal life.

Christ, whose glory fills the skies,
Christ the true and only light;
Son of righteousness arise, triumph o'er the shades of night;
Dayspring from on high be near, Daystar, in my heart appear.

Dark and cheerless is the morn, unaccompanied by Thee;
Joyless is the day's return, till Thy mercies' beams I see;
Till Thy inward life impart, glad my eyes,
and warm my heart.

Visit then this soul of mine, pierce the gloom of sin and grief;
Fill me, radiance divine, scatter all my unbelief;
More and more Thyself display, shining to the perfect day.

John Wesley

Purity, Prayer, Power, Praise

In Matthew 21:12, we read, "Then Jesus went into the temple of God and drove out all those who bought and sold in the temple, and overturned the tables of the money changers and the seats of those who sold doves." The first thing Jesus did upon entering Jerusalem for the first time was to purify God's temple.

Then, in verse 13, He said, "It is written, 'My house shall be called a house of prayer.'" The second thing that Jesus did was make God's temple a place of prayer.

We read in verse 14, "Then the blind and the lame came to Him in the temple, and He healed them." The third thing Jesus did was make God's temple a place of power.

We read that the children cried out hosannas to Jesus. So He said in verse 16, "Have you never read, 'Out of the mouth of babes and nursing infants You have perfected praise'?" The fourth thing that Jesus did was make God's temple a place of praise.

In 1 Corinthians 6:19, the apostle Paul tells us that believers are the temple of God. God wants us to be people of purity, prayer, power, and praise! Having those qualities is possible only as we yield ourselves to the power of the Spirit.

> *Holy Spirit, breathe on me, until my heart is clean;*
> *Let sunshine fill its inmost part, with not a cloud between.*
> *Holy Spirit, breathe on me, my stubborn will subdue;*
> *Teach me in words of living flame what Christ would*
> *have me do.*
> *Holy Spirit, breathe on me, fill me with power divine;*
> *Kindle a flame of love and zeal within this heart of mine.*
> *Holy Spirit, breathe on me, till I am all Thine own,*
> *Until my will is lost in Thine, to live for Thee alone.*
>
> *Breathe on me, breathe on me, Holy Spirit, breathe on me;*
> *Take Thou my heart, cleanse every part,*
> *Holy Spirit, breathe on me. Amen.*
>
> *Edwin Hatch and B. B. McKinney*

Dealing with Rubbish

In Nehemiah 4:10, we read that the tribe of Judah didn't want to work on the walls of Jerusalem anymore. They said there was too much rubbish, and they didn't want to remove it. What they needed to understand physically is what we need to understand spiritually: rubbish removal never stops in the life of the believer!

When we are first saved, we repent of our sins and say, "Lord, I never want to sin again." Not too much time goes by before we realize that we still sin. We do things that we thought we were past doing. Consequently, what do we do? We confess our sins, and the Lord forgives us (1 John 1:9). The fact that we are justified in Christ does not mean that we won't sin; sin is a constant in our lives. Therefore, rubbish removal needs to be a constant part of our lives as well.

Alan Redpath put it this way: "The indwelling Christ is ready at the door of your heart to fill the garbage truck with all of the rubbish you are willing to get rid of."

Let us ask the Holy Spirit to shake us, if necessary, to reveal any rubbish in our lives that we haven't dumped out. As soon as He has revealed our sin to us, pray that we will be willing to toss it out once and for all. May the Holy Spirit be our rubbish revealer and our rubbish remover.

> *Lord Jesus, I long to be perfectly whole;*
> *I want Thee forever to live in my soul;*
> *Break down every idol, cast out every foe;*
> *Now wash me, and I shall be whiter than snow.*
> *Lord Jesus, for this I most humbly entreat,*
> *I wait, blessed Lord, at Thy crucified feet;*
> *By faith, for my cleansing, I see Thy blood flow;*
> *Now wash me, and I shall be whiter than snow.*
> *Lord Jesus, Thou seest I patiently wait;*
> *Come now, and within me a new heart create;*
> *To those who have sought Thee, Thou never said no.*
> *Now wash me, and I shall be whiter than snow.*
>
> *James Nicholson*

Go!

In Matthew 28:19 Jesus commissioned His disciples, as well as all of us, to "go therefore and make disciples." The point is that we have to go to the people, not wait for them to come to us. Jesus never said that the whole world should go to the church. He said that the whole church should go to the world. We should be doing all that we can to fulfill the Great Commission.

In light of that, we need to ask ourselves, What do I do with my time? Do I use my extra time in God's service, or do I sit in front of the TV set? What do I do with my talents and abilities? Do I bury them in my job or in my hobbies, or do I use them in God's house? What do I do with my money? Do I spend it needlessly on inanimate objects that just take up space in my house, or do I funnel my resources toward the ultimate mission of leading sinners to Christ?

If we really want to know where our priorities are, we will take a look at the past year's check stubs. We need to look at how we used our financial resources. Then let's take a look at the past year's calendar and see where our time and energy went. Those things are an actual gauge of where our priorities are and, in fact, where our hearts are. Jesus said in Matthew 6:21, "For where your treasure is, there your heart will be also."

Heavenly Father, please help us to continually evaluate our resources and do all we can to fulfill your Great Commission.

Lord, help us to tell of Your love for mankind . . .
A love for the sin-sick, the broken, the blind;
And help them to see by the way that we live
The wholeness of being that You long to give.

D. J. De Haan

Not Multiple Choice

Jesus said in John 14:6 that "I am the way, the truth, and the life. No one comes to the Father except through Me." That is pretty straightforward. Jesus is the only way, the only truth, and the only life. The Bible doesn't give us optional ways to be saved. Various choices as to how one can be redeemed are not given. Salvation is not an "any of the above" multiple-choice question.

For example, someone can't jump off a fifty-story building and apply the multiple-choice method. If someone jumps off a roof, it isn't possible to choose just any of the following: (a) fly, (b) transport the body's molecules from point A to point B, or (c) die. One hundred percent of the time, it's going to be (c) die.

Why? Because God's natural laws are secure from violation. The same hold true for salvation. Peter said in Acts 4:12, "Nor is there salvation in any other, for there is no other name under heaven given among men by which we must be saved." Jesus is the only way, the only truth, and the only life.

May we seek Him throughout our day, every day, as our only true and reliable source of comfort and help.

There aren't many ways into heaven;
The Bible says there's only one:
Confessing Christ Jesus as Savior,
Believing in God's only Son.

Spurgeon

Barclay, William. The Gospel of John. Edinburgh, UK: Saint Andrew, 1955.

Blanchard, John. Gathered Gold: A Treasury of Quotations for Christians. Englewood, CO: P&R, 1986.

Blanchard, John. Sifted Silver. New York: Evangelical Press, 2000.

Brumley, Albert E. A Collection of Songs. Compiled by the A. E. Brumley family. The A. E. Brumley Family, 1966.

Carter, Tom, comp. Spurgeon at His Best. Reprint. Grand Rapids, MI: Baker Book House, 1991.

Cory, Lloyd, comp. Quotable Quotations. Wheaton, IL: Victor Books, 1985.

Crawford, Ruth D. and Crawford, Percy B. Pinebrook Choruses. Grand Rapids, MI: Eerdmans, 1934.

Doan, Eleanor. The Complete Speaker's Sourcebook. Grand Rapids, MI: Zondervan, 1996.

du Plessis, Malcolm, Bonilla, Jo, and Owens, Buddy. Praise: Hymn and Choruses. San Clemente, CA: Maranatha! Music, 1987.

Ellis, V. B. (Vep), comp. Western Melodies: Gospel and Spiritual Songs. With the assistance of John T. Benson Jr. Nashville, TN: John T. Benson, 1960.

100 Hymns, 100 Choruses: The Greatest Hymns & Praise Choruses of Yesterday & Today! San Clemente, CA: Maranatha! Music, 1987.

Knight, Walter B. Knight's Master Book of New Illustrations. Grand Rapids, MI: Eerdmans, 1956.

Knight, Walter B. Knight's Treasury of Illustrations. Grand Rapids, MI: Eerdmans, 1976.

McKinney, B. B. Broadman Hymnal: A Collection of Standard Hymns That Stand the Test of Time Along with Some New Meaningful Songs. Nashville, TN: Broadman, 1940.

New Kings James Version. Nashville, TN: Thomas Nelson, 1979, 1980, 1982.

Our Daily Bread: For Personal and Family Devotions. Grand Rapids, MI: Discover House Publishers, 1997, 1998, 1999, 2000, 2001.

Putman, John. Revival Melodies; or, Songs of Zion. Boston, MA: Nazarene Publishing House, 1842.

Sime, Walter Hines, ed. Baptist Hymnal. 7th reprint. Nashville, TN: Convention Press, 1956.

Smith, Alfred B. Favorites: A Collection of Gospel Songs for Solo, Duet, Trio, Quartet and Group Singing. Vol. 1. Chicago, IL: Zondervan, 1943.

Smith, Alfred B. Favorites: A Collection of Gospel Songs for Solo, Suet, Trio, Quartet and Group Singing. Vol. 2. Chicago, IL: Zondervan, 1946.

Smith, Alfred B. Favorites: A Collection of Gospel Songs for Solo, Suet, Trio, Quartet and Group Singing. Vol. 3. Chicago, IL: Zondervan, 1946.

Verploegh, Harry. Singposts: A Collection of Sayings from A.W. Tozer. New York: HarperCollins, 1988.

Wiersbe, Warren, W. Be Free: Exchange Legalism for True Spirituality. Colorado Springs, CO: Chariot Victor, 1975.